Sacred America

The Emerging Spirit of the People

Roger Housden

Simon & Schuster

SIMON & SCHUSTER
Rockefeller Center
1230 Avenue of the Americas
New York, New York 10020

SIMON & SCHUSTER and colophon are registered
trademarks of Simon & Schuster Inc.

Designed by O'Lanso Gabbidon

10 9 8 7 6 5 4 3 2 1
Library of Congress Cataloging in Publication Data

Housden, Roger.
Sacred America : the emerging spirit of the people / Roger Housden.
p.   cm.
1. Housden, Roger. Spiritual biography—United States. 3. Spiritual life. I. Title.
BL73.H68A3 1999
200'.973—dc21   99-38646
CIP

ISBN 978-1-4516-8369-1

. . . And there was a new voice,
which you slowly recognized as your own,
that kept you company
as you strode deeper and deeper
into the world. . . .

Mary Oliver, "The Journey"

This book is for Maria and all those who, like her,
live by the knowing heart.

Acknowledgments

To every single one of you whose name appears between these covers, I am indebted, and I am grateful for the generosity of spirit that led you to open the doors of your lives and your homes to me, a wandering foreigner in your midst. This book is your book, exemplars that you are of the human spirit in America. Then, Diane Berke and Tony Zito in Manhattan, your love and support comes straight from the source; Jack and Nancy Goldstein in Seattle; Rick and Lynnaea Payne in Boulder; Doug Conwell in Santa Fe; Luis Michalski and Melanie Lee in Taos; Alvaro Cardona-Hine in Truchas, New Mexico; Kathy Dannemiller in Ann Arbor; Eddie Hauben and family in Boston; Bhanu Moon and friends in Atlanta; Adam Philips, and Corinne McCloghlin's friend, both in D.C.; Naomi Lake in Crestone; John Lerner, Gay Luce, and Dale Borglum in Marin County; and the Fetzer Institute in Michigan—without your welcome I would never have made it through. Florence Falk and Mark Matousek, dear Manhattan friends, the warmth of our conversations kept me going for weeks, while Mark, your critical readings and editing of the text were invaluable. Jane Hirshfield, gratitude for your friendship and also your editor's eagle eye—it contributed greatly to the final version. Vijali in Utah, Father Tom Keating in Snowmass Monastery, Duane Elgin, Gangaji, Paul Ray—thank you for your willing conversations, which, even though they did not reach the final version, contributed to it via an underground stream. Hugh Huntington in Taos, you are a master of wilderness travel and I could not have gone through Chaco Canyon without you. Neither could I have completed my research without the generous financial support of Jack Goldstein and Rob Lehman of the Fetzer Institute. Coleman Barks, your Rumi translations have been a blessing in my life, and I am grateful to be able to include a few of them in this book; also thanks for the introduction to Abdul Aziz Said. Chloe, all and everything that we have lived and loved is intrinsically woven into this work—it could not be otherwise. Faustin, Magnus, and Kreon at Soundphotosynthesis in Sausalito, your generosity with time and equipment and your willingness to jump into the breach at the last moment allowed us to create a front cover the title deserves. Finally, commissioning editor Janice Easton, you have moved graciously with every turn of events and never let your feet leave the ground. Your support has been invaluable throughout. Copy editor Faren Bachelis, your assiduous reading smoothed out the final text, and your note at the end of the ms, that "we are everywhere," was heartening indeed. Then, my family in England, for being there.

Contents

Introduction

The America of my (English) imagination was born when I first came to breathe the big open spaces in 1965 on a $99-for-ninety-nine-day Greyhound bus ticket. I was twenty. Somewhere in Texas, a woman sitting next to me, learning that I was from Britain, asked whether we spoke English there. She was hardly typical, of course; yet in that moment I had realized my foreignness; and how, indeed, I spoke a different language to the locals. And as clearly as the plains I could see through my window, that woman's question showed me how large America was; as large as the world in the minds of some of its inhabitants. I traveled all over the country on that ticket, and many subsequent visits have deepened the colors and complexity of the America in me. For more than any other place in the world, America is a country of the imagination. It has lodged itself in the minds of people everywhere as a living symbol of the best, and also the worst, of civilization at the start of the new millennium.

This, my most recent journey in the United States of America, really began in India—if anything begins anywhere. I had been in that wonderful, terrible country for several months in 1995, researching a book on the survival of the sacred in India. As I sat by the Ganges in the holy city of Benares on my last day, the thought suddenly struck me—one of those thoughts that come from behind, or from beyond the periphery of vision: India, for all its living spiritual wisdom, is not the land that holds the seal of the sacred for the next millennium. That country is America. From that moment on, the desire to explore that intuition for myself would not let me rest until I came here.

My traveling instinct is partly due to an inherent caste of character, but also to my having lived a life on that tight-lipped, cultured, crowded, little island called Britain. Its civilized, decent air has always impelled me to explore the wildness of the untamed earth—in the Sahara, in India, in Africa, and in the American Southwest. Its reserve, its gray light, its intelligent self-consciousness, has led me to seek wilder company; people who would turn their lives, not on the axis of a sensible plan, but on some love song heard in the bones.

There is much about England that Americans appreciate—its roots, of course; its gentility and civic dignity, which still exist even now; its architecture (if you go to the right places); its theater and music; the ancient tenor of the land. Yet England is not, for all its qualities, a praising country. It rarely praises itself, and others even less. Least of all does it celebrate what is beyond the daily round; the wonder and awe of being human. The air is thick with centuries of caution, with vested interests; with jaded symbols and customs, all of which together conspire to foster a vein of cynicism which is skeptical of visions more open to the unseen than the seen; to the future than to the past.

America, on the other hand, is still the country of irrepressible and—for most Englishmen—infuriating enthusiasm. And its enthusiasm (meaning, literally, filled with the breath of a god) extends not only to making the fastest buck with the least possible effort, but to visions of a deeper, as well as brighter, possible future. Yet what the world sees of America on cable television is only a flicker of the original dream. Those pioneers who were both naive and reckless enough got high on the promise of cheap land and a vote at the ballot box. Freedom for them meant the right to smash and grab, and American capitalism now propagates that same creed across the world, sanctioned by the power brokers in Washington. The glamorization of crime and violence and their sale by Hollywood into the global marketplace is what you'd expect from a culture that prizes getting what you want above all else.

This is the American dream that much of the world has bought with so many tragic consequences. The result is a global disdain for the environment, moral relativism, the denial of any reality and value other than the material, a frenzied consumerism, and the dreary standardization of technological civilization. Faced with such a dismal picture for the future of Western civilization, English caution, even its cynicism, is invaluable.

"If democracy is to have a universal resonance," said Vaclav Havel in a speech at Stanford University, "it must discover and renew its own transcendental origins. It must renew its respect for that non-material order which is not only above but also in us and among us, and which is the only possible and reliable source of man's respect for himself, for others, for the order of nature, for the order of humanity, and for the secular order as well."

This, however, is the other America that I discovered on leaving India, barely acknowledged in the rest of the world—yet it has always existed. While some pioneers dreamed of external conquest, others dreamed of a life founded on new values, free of the tired symbols and myths of the Old World. While the wagon trains rolled west in the nineteenth century, others stayed East and traveled farther in their minds than any horse could take them. The aspiration to a better life had an inner as well as an outer direction, and this deeper impulse, founded on the urge for the good and the true, has always been at the heart of what America stands for.

America is still one of the most religious countries in the world, with over ninety percent believing in a god of some kind, and this religiosity has always colored the nation's own view of itself. The flag that represents God's Country, and even the symbols on the dollar bill are sacred images of possibility, pointers to the next step toward being more fully human. This is why Americans, even if they do not articulate it in so many words, and in spite of everything that points to the whole experiment going horribly wrong, feel in their bones that there is something sacred about the United States of America.

Emerson, Thoreau, and Whitman all sang the glory of a beautiful America yet to come. Their dreams are still in the making, but if they were here at the dawn of the twenty-first century they would be as inspired as they would be horrified. They'd be horrified, of course, by the state parks turned theme parks, a lame government, the media mediocrity, the stultifying sameness of Main Street, the dearth of imagination in the arts establishment and in civic life. Yet I believe they would be truly inspired by all the ways that the human spirit of grassroots America is pushing itself up through layers of institutional concrete like so many irrepressible sunflowers.

After traveling the length and breadth of the country during one of the last years of the twentieth century, I genuinely believe that People's America is not only alive and well, but despite, or even because of the moral turpitude of Wall Street, Capitol Hill, and city hall, it is taking vigorous steps to redefine what it means to be human, what democracy means, and how a democratic humanity is itself a natural expression of the sacred.

When you put the two words *Sacred* and *America* together, most people think of the land. And they are right. The land here, its wild reaches, great scale, vast contrasts, still, in many places, restores humanity to its proper, humble scale. Its majesty, beauty, unpredictability, its sheer otherness can strike awe and wonder, even dread, into the receptive heart. Throughout my journeys in what I have called Sacred America, the sheer presence of the land has stalked me everywhere. Yet my emphasis in this book is rather the people who live here: the aspirations, genius, actions, wisdom, and compassion being woven into the social and cultural fabric in such a way as to reinvent what a sense of the sacred means for the contemporary individual.

For while almost every American will admit to having some form of belief or even experience of the numinous, neither that nor what might be called sacred is necessarily defined by a religious framework. Rather, in an immigrant's land of experiment, synthesis, and the forging of personal meaning from subjective experience, individuals and groups of individuals are finding for themselves new layers and subtleties of meaning to the term. Retreat centers—especially Buddhist ones—are flourishing in America; many churches are thriving, and not just the evangelical or fundamentalist denominations. The old traditions are increasingly willing to learn from each other in the democratic American climate, as well as to rearticulate their wisdom for a contemporary secular culture; I have met monks who have been behind monastery walls for thirty years who are studying to be Reiki masters.

Yet this is the world's first unapologetically secular culture, and the sacred, if it is to mean anything, must also be understood within the context of everyday life and activity. If the human spirit is everywhere, so are its deepest values and insights. And being America, it is not surprising that the spirit blows in a highly individual way. I have found it in Hollywood; in Washington; in corporations; in people whose business is money; in a cave in the New Mexico hills; in a one-horse town in Montana; in an educational program; among ex-convicts; in a bus driver as well as behind monastery walls; in churches; and in Native American ceremonies. Countless people who have never been near a retreat center are finding their own deeper meaning spontaneously, through their own revelations, as well as by responding in new and imaginative ways to the social zeitgeist, its opportunities and sufferings.

Practicality is central to the American genius. The capacity to apply good ideas (as well as bad ones) and materialize them in a workable way has marked American culture from the start. Like every gift, this one has its shadow, in this case the propensity for turning absolutely everything into a marketable commodity. Spiritual materialism prospers here to a degree that would stagger any European mind. Transformation, or spiritual rebirth itself, through any number of unique methods, has become a major product line, which points to how unhappy people must be with who they are already. Yet among all the marketing ploys, the need to make a buck, the personal aggrandizement, the desperate craving for anything to fill the gap in an empty life, I have found that the practical genius of America is, even so, expressing the deepest aspirations and insights of the human spirit in any number of tangible forms. These forms are determined, not so much by an organization, religious or otherwise, but by the genius of the individual for the common good.

What is significant is that no one is in charge. I mean that no one is *doing* it. This other America is not a cause that you fight for, it is something at work, like a new configuration, in the collective psyche. It is something we participate in, rather than direct or control. As when the Berlin Wall came down by itself, a broader intelligence is at work—not as some external force acting on us, but from within us as a collective. In that sense, the old ideal of personal spiritual salvation through individual effort no longer holds up in the same way. It never was, anyhow, a full representation of the Christian ideal. It is deeply Christian to recognize that we are all in this together somehow, and the effort of one can only be for the whole; the transformation of the whole, in the end, is what will see us through. It is the soul of the world, the *anima mundi,* that is being transformed, as much as any one individual soul; and yet that transformation is happening, paradoxically, through us as individuals.

"We are preparing the way for a global democracy," said Vaclav Havel, in that same Stanford speech, "but that democracy cannot emerge until there has been a full restoration and recognition of the moral authority of the universe." The moral authority of the universe is what is beginning to make its presence known in countless individual and collective initiatives around this country. There is no manifesto other than the small voice of conscience that the universe—the soul we all share in—uses to speak in and through us.

This book, then, is an exploration and celebration of this other America as seen through the eyes of a foreigner; the America of the human spirit as it is emerging in its many guises throughout the country today. That spirit can rightfully be called sacred when it is in the service of something greater than itself. Just think, as you are reading these lines now, there is a group of women in Boise, Idaho, unknown to anybody, who are busy at work making their peace quilts. When they are done they send one to a senator. Over fifty senators have slept under one so far. As Brother Lawrence said, "It is not necessary to have great things to do. I turn my little omelet in the pan for God."

Chapter One

High Plains Sun Dance

In the plane high above the Midwest I look at my watch and see it to be August 15 already. On this very day, the Greek and Russian peoples will be praising warmly the Mother of the World, for today is the Feast of Her Assumption. I remember the same day many years ago in Greece when I watched celebrants processing round the monastery of Iveron with a huge cake adorned with the blue figure of Mary, swinging censers and chanting those glorious antiphons. It was a global cake, to be eaten in communion with the Mother of all Mothers—that original Isis who is wobbling the plane at this very moment and obliging the mothers to console their screaming babies.

The plane is full of vacationers on their way to Yellowstone, while I am on my way to Billings, Montana, and I'm not sure why when I look at the map on my knee, for there seems to be a great deal of nothing in Montana and Wyoming. Sacred America, I remember: surely that must include the great American spaces of which an Englishman can only dream, the spirit of the continent still unsullied, country people who have never heard of cappuccino, life led by an earlier, steadier rhythm.

There is also the possibility, down in that emptiness, that I may have the privilege of attending a Sun Dance. I want to start this exploration of the sacred in America with the original spirit of the land, the spirit of the native peoples. Yet I don't know a soul in Montana and have heard that the dance season is about over already. Even so, it will be a retreat of sorts, a mobile contemplation of big sky and rolling land. The road retreat, known, loved, and hated by all traveling salesmen, missionaries, bums, and loose cannons. Right now, though, I'm not sure, the clouds are thick and heavy and my northern pallor, fresh out of England, is calling for sun.

The plane lands through sheets of rain and Billings looks grim, a bedraggled sprawl of brown and gray and I'm already wondering if there are any flights to Seattle, or Portland, maybe, anywhere they've heard of good coffee. But no, this is it, I remind myself: face the great spaces, the great space inside you that nothing will cover for long, so it might as well be now, and here. I head for a hotel and soup and water, no ice. On the desk is a directory of stores in Billings, and on the second page a bookshop is advertised, one that specializes in spirituality and religion. Who would have thought it, in Billings? Traveling whittles away all preconceptions.

On the bookstore bulletin board a publicity sheet describes a new retreat center a few miles out of town, one that has a sweat lodge and runs healing weekends. I jot down the number and browse through the store, picking up a national retreat guide that lists just one monastery in Montana and one retreat center in Cody, Wyoming. Cody, I remember from the map, is on the way to Powell, the hometown of a couple who are friends of friends. I call the first number and ask the woman with the sweat lodge if I could visit. "You would be welcome," said the owner of the healing retreat, "but not this weekend because we'll all be at Crow Fair."

"What is Crow Fair?" I asked.

"You don't know Crow Fair? It's the biggest powwow through all the high plains. It starts tonight on the reservation and goes on till Sunday evening."

The door opens just like that. I phone the couple in Powell and they say they would be glad to host me for the night, so I begin the drive south to Wyoming along county roads through the great ranges. Cody is the first town I reach of any size. Its famous son was Buffalo Bill, and tonight there's a rodeo show as a loudspeaker proclaims from an old Chevy with a wide spread of longhorns fixed to the hood. Cody is for the tourists, all Wild West stores and saloons, though there is an unlikely addition just out of town, as I saw in the retreat guide, one St. Thomas the Apostle Retreat Center.

Up on a low rise were two fine wooden buildings and a teepee. The two elderly ladies who came out of the garage to meet me were puzzled that I hadn't come in a van: they were expecting the plumber. They had been in an order in England for several years, and had recently joined the founder of the Cody center who had previously been living in India. She had named the center after the apostle who is said to have evangelized southern India before there were churches anywhere in Europe. We sat and had tea—which I'm sure no one else in Cody was doing—and discussed the merits of a retreat house in Wyoming. They said they had some relationship with the local Indians, which accounted for the presence of the teepee; that they had held sweat lodges on their land, and that people came from far beyond the state for a retreat at St. Thomas's. I could not for the life of me imagine these two charming old ladies who were pouring me tea sitting in a sweat lodge, passing the pipe and being smudged with sweet sage. It seems native ways can slip even under monastery doors.

With tea over, I thanked them for their hospitality and started out for Powell, barely an hour to the east, in the direction of the Big Horn Mountains. The sign said that Powell had just five thousand people, and as I drove through the town it struck me it must be a God-fearing place; on every corner there seemed to be a church, enough churches for all five thousand and many more. My friends, I discovered, didn't attend any of them. Steve Smith was a lecturer at the local college, and Janell Hanson looked after their two children and carried on her own private studies in spiritual traditions.

"We have chosen not to join a church here," Steve said, "because the only choice is Christianity. There seems to be very little room for other faiths or beliefs."

During the course of the evening they began to fill in the picture. Powell, it seems, is a fairly reactionary place, like most places in rural America, or rural anywhere, for that matter. Janell explained that the community was so invested in being in the right that they had developed a forceful current of denial. There is, for example, a serious alcohol problem in the town, and recently one student brutally murdered another. Until that happened, they thought only someone outside could have committed a crime like that.

Janell and Steve were both natives of Wyoming, and there were things they liked about the community, of course. In particular was the fact that it still gave their children a relatively protected environment to grow up in, and above all, the land, the great mountain reaches that they could roam for hours just a few minutes from their own back door. Later that evening I came to learn why Janell, in particular, was not unduly bothered by her social environment.

"I guess my inner life began in earnest after the death of my father," she began. "Things would always happen around him. He threw up his hands one day and said, 'Surely nothing else can go wrong!' As soon as he said that the eye in his ceramic owl popped out and rolled across the desk towards him. He put it back and it hasn't moved since. He was the only one in the family who would come down in the morning and say, 'What a wonderful dream I had.' For both him and me, our dream life and our daily life were always intermingled."

When he died, she went on, she felt like her head had exploded. She had already recognized that they thought the same thoughts, and she worried about what was going to happen to her own mind now that he was gone. It felt for a time as if it were being sucked up into something. That was the only way she could begin to describe it, she murmured, looking off into the middle distance, pausing for a moment. Then she said something that brought my attention up sharp. She said that since that time she had come to realize—not as a theory but as a felt experience—that all minds were connected, though families were especially linked.

"After he died, she said, "I would catch his smell and hear his voice everywhere. I had dreams of him that were so vivid and real I had to shift my concept of reality. I would be awake in the dreams and I'd often say, 'you're not supposed to be here.' Some days it felt as if I had spent hours with him, such a sense of his presence with me."

Janell had barely begun to tell me her story. From time to time I had to remind myself that this was not California, this was Wyoming. She went on to describe how events and flashes of insight kept challenging her ordinary perceptions. How one night they were driving back from Yellowstone when they all suddenly saw a flash of something coming through the air that bounced off the hood on the passenger side of the car. Steve got out, thinking it was a box, or an animal maybe, but there was no sign of anything, and no mark on the car. Janell was sure it was a warning of some kind about a car accident. The following weekend they were driving near Thermopolis when the car in front of them was hit by an oncoming car and knocked into the ravine. She had felt all week that they wouldn't be hurt personally, since the invisible flying object had caused no damage to their vehicle. But as with the flying object, the accident struck them emotionally.

A year to the day of her father's death, Janell continued, her two-year-old daughter, Kirsten, tugged at Steve's sleeve. "Daddy, Daddy, read this," she kept saying. She showed him a sheet of paper with squiggles on one side—"those are flying pigs," said Kirsten; on the other side was scrawled the word *Grandpa.*

"I couldn't understand it," said Steve. "It was before she had the motor control to form letters. I tried for weeks to get her to repeat the letters, but she couldn't. She couldn't even draw a triangle. That was the event that really began to change my own outlook on life. Until then, I could only listen to Janell and respect her experience without having any reference points to it of my own."

"There were many messages," said Janell, "but that was the one that finally got through to us. The message was saying I am still here. It changed our perception of life forever. I began to realize that life is giving us messages all the time, if only we can pay attention and decipher the meaning. The flying pigs referred to a line from Lewis Carroll that my father would quote often. It was after that experience that I started reading all I could about life after death and out-of-body experiences. I read Robert Munro, Swedenborg, and others, though the Tibetan literature gave the clearest explanation of what I was experiencing, the existence of parallel worlds. I became cautious about mentioning the 'Grandpa' experience to just anybody. I was told more than once it was the work of the devil."

All evening she poured out remarkable tales of prescient dreams and knowings, having thoughts and witnessing them played back in this dimension almost immediately. How natural it was, hearing her speak, to sense that nothing in this world goes unnoticed, not a blade of grass turns but that God, Life, Intelligence, knows it; that if only we would notice, we are cared for at every instant. Whoever would have imagined that a life such as this was being lived out in Powell, Wyoming? This is not exactly New Age country.

And yet why not? Why not Powell, or anywhere else? Janell's insights come from the inside; they have not been acquired from any cultural milieu. For every public figure who writes books with titles like *Conversations with God,* there must be thousands of ordinary people in anonymous places who have similar experiences daily, and don't write about it, or even tell the person they live with, perhaps for fear of ridicule or simple disbelief. For years Janelle had no external frame of reference for her experiences, and kept them to herself.

Now she is more confident, though she still has no need of external validation. Janell has developed a certainty, she says, that we are all part of God's body; yet she was never able to arrive at this through the more usual way of simple faith, or a love of God. "Seems like I've gotten in through the back door," she smiled.

The whole family decides to come with me the next day to Crow Fair and we head off through streams of mist over the Big Horns. Steve wants to show me the old medicine wheel on the peaks but it's too foggy to climb up there, so we drive on down the mountain to Dayton and stop for a few minutes in Wyoming's only monastery, the San Benito Contemplative Order. Five elderly sisters gather around us and when they hear we are going to the Fair they urge me to visit Brother Charles up in Crow Agency, who has been a priest on the reservation since the sixties. They would be glad, too, they say, to offer me a room in their guest quarters if I intend staying at the fair for more than a day. You can still find such kindness among a copse of old pines by a stream.

Crow Agency is a tiny settlement a mile or two beyond the hill and the stream that witnessed the Battle of the Little Big Horn. Pick-up trucks are parked along the side of the road and the crackle of loudspeakers is on the wind. A whole village of teepees surrounds the arbor, the round stadium where dancers are wheeling and stamping to the beat of a great drum. The rows of hot dog stands and trinket stalls are thronged with Indians and whites alike, everyone enjoying a day at the fair. The dancers come from all over the country, dozens of tribes represented, all in their distinctive feathers and leggings. One elderly man in a war bonnet I speak to has come from Seattle, "for the drumming and dancing," he says, "you hear good drumming here." That, I can see, is the fair's purpose, a time and place when Native American identity and tradition can be celebrated and affirmed.

After an hour or two of dance and drum I leave the family to wander off on my own in search of Brother Charles. His house is by the church on the other side of the highway, a church, I notice as I peek inside, that honors the four directions with the appropriate signs and symbols. Brother Charles is still at the fair, and Larry, a Native American, who ushers me through to the kitchen, opens the door of his house. Larry picks up his book, *Visions and Stigmata,* and continues reading. Half an hour later a stout man in a brown Franciscan habit strides in, with a more slender man at his side.

"Do you want to eat?" he asks, when we have introduced ourselves. "I'm cooking up some wild venison, a roadkill."

We are chewing on the roadkill within the hour. The other man, Fr. John Giulianni from Connecticut, tells me he is here on commission to paint a fresco for the church. During the 500th anniversary of Columbus's landing he had wanted to celebrate the native tradition in a Christian way that honored the native peoples. He began painting Christian icons with Native American symbols. "Like this," he says, and shows me a postcard of one called The Crow Trinity, with the Holy Spirit represented as a great eagle with wings encompassing a gray-haired Indian father and a son in ceremonial dress. An image to shake the mind, its universality leaps off the card. The native peoples have responded to Father John's offerings as a godsend, and his work is known and loved on reservations all over the country.

Brother Charles has been on the reservation since Vatican II, as have most of the brothers and sisters on reservations. Their calling was in the spirit of the sixties, and their work is not being taken up by the younger generation. His most common duty, he tells me, is to perform burials, people on the reservation being so prone to drugs and alcohol. At least, he observes, they are not in denial any more, as they had been for decades before. He loves the people, the land, the simplicity.

"I have learned so much from them," he says between mouthfuls. "Respect for elders, respect for the earth, patience, a deep sense of the sacredness of everyday life, an awareness of being connected to all of creation, a more tangible understanding of sacrifice. Why would I go anywhere else?"

As he is speaking another man walks in, Johnny Apple, another priest, this one visiting from the Shoshone Reservation down in Wyoming. "Our friend here was hoping to witness a Sun Dance," Charles says, by way of introduction. "I told him that the dancing season is over in Montana. Are there any more planned on the Shoshone land?" "Yes, the last dance of the year starts next Friday," John answers, "over at Fort Washakie. Anyone there will tell you where it is."

Providence responds. I thank them, and as Charles gets up to attend to a native family that is hoping to stay the night, I make my way back to Dayton and the San Benito Monastery guest house, a trailer. I am wakened in the morning by a sturdy woman mowing the lawn with a clattering machine. The monastery is a house, a chapel, and a barn where the sisters earn their living making communion wafers. I stroll over to the main house and help the sisters peel a crate of pears ready for canning, a task they perform every year in August. Never have I done such a thing in my life. There is such goodness in these women, I realize; a developed humbleness of heart and mind, an acceptance and welcome of whomever turns up at their door.

The crate of pears peeled, I make my way up the mountain to gaze on the medicine wheel. As I drive out of the gate I suddenly feel a nostalgia welling for an ordinary community of faith, content in simple activities interspersed with prayer. I remember the sweetness of Tymawr Convent in Wales, how the life of regularity, the rhythm of work and prayer, had nourished me in the same way when I used to go there in my twenties. There is something else, too, about these sisters' lives: I admire their willing submission to a rule. Once surrendered, having given one's life over to the mystery, life takes an easier turn. These people are at home, I realize.

In that moment I remember again the sensation I felt a night or two earlier of an invisible face against my cheek, just before sleep. I look up now to see a branch plunging into a naked blue sky, and I know that face to be here, too: here in the turn of silver on every leaf, in the dark earth and rock of these Big Horn Mountains, right here as well in my own heart, in the heart of the nuns and of all beings everywhere. Better in any event to stay with the small things, the little revelations there for the asking every day. There really is a community without walls that spreads out over the world; and I know myself to be part of that number, even though I miss sometimes the warmth of a solid shelter.

Up high into the hills I drive, and there on the roof of the great plains world, with a view to the far horizon in all directions, is a circle of stones, some eighty feet across, with twelve spokes converging on a central cairn. It is surrounded, like Stonehenge, by a wire fence, though this one is festooned with feathers, pouches, dreamcatchers, stones that flash in the sun, strips of colored cloth, all offerings to the spirits of this place and to the ancient ones who built it. I am, I can feel, in the presence of the living sacred. The ranger on duty tells me that native people come up daily, sometimes several in a day, to pray here and ask for blessings. No one can be sure when or by whom it was built, since there is nothing to carbon date. Certainly, it predates the existing tribes, and is possibly a couple of thousand years old.

It is one of several wheels that were made all the way from Canada down to Mexico, though this one is among the largest and certainly the most frequented. How ancient this New World is, I realize. What a travesty to crow of its discovery and settlement. There can be no sacredness in an America that does not find the humility to come into a new relationship with these old ways that whisper still over the land.

Perhaps the stirrings of such an awareness are rising now. Before 1990 there were fewer than six thousand visitors annually to the medicine wheel; at the turn of the millennium, there are more than one hundred thousand people a year making the trek up the mountains to stand in its presence. Sacred sites, it seems, are in demand, for we are a hungry people, hungry for meaning.

I sit there for an hour or so, touched by the devotions of the people today, by their wire fence offerings. Touched, too, by this mighty land, its plunging descents, soaring crests, and vast plains, barely marked by human hands; by the wildness of the wind, the scudding sky, the endless depth of blue; until back down the mountain I come, as we always must, back down to vespers in the chapel of San Benito.

Half a dozen chairs and two meditation cushions circle a wooden table with a flower spray that serves as the altar. We sit in silence for twenty minutes and then sing some warlike hymns full of the wrath of Jawheh for his enemies, those of Zion, accompanied by a sister on a miniature organ. So incompatible somehow with the sweetness of these elderly ladies. Then a reading from John Cassian who urges us to pray for Christ's help at all times.

Afterwards, at tea, the nuns tell me they sit for twenty minutes, three times daily, watching the breath, listening to the silence. The influence of Buddhism has reached even this remote corner of Christendom. Their congregation is diminishing fast, they say, with barely a trickle of novices entering the motherhouse in Missouri. "We have no idea about the lives and attitudes of twenty- or thirty-year-olds," said one. "We live in a different world. People want a different language now. There is more of a need for lay monasteries, where people can come for a few months or a year. The Buddhists cater to that very well." The five elderly sisters sense the death of their order, but they are not unduly concerned. "Everything has its time," they say.

The next morning I decide to attend the final ceremonies of Crow Fair, and see a very different scene to the festive one of a day or two before. The dance and drum competitions over, the Crow people are processing around the entire encampment stopping in each of the four directions to dance and sing their sacred blessing songs, wishing all present a healthy year until the next Crow Fair, thanking the mountains for their protecting presence with the shake of an eagle feather.

Cameras are forbidden now, and the onlookers maintain a respectful silence as the men circle the drummers and the women dance tightly round the men, the rows of elk teeth on their dresses gleaming like ivory across their backs. An elderly white woman with a limp is dancing with them, a sister who has been adopted by the tribe. She has been here well over twenty years, I am told, and I wonder what secret longing or desire led her into this native circle.

At the final giveaway in the arbor I find myself next to a man in his thirties called Tom Yellow Tail, grandson of the great Crow medicine man who recently died, and who revived the Sun Dance among his people. Tom tells me he has been baptized three years, having never been sure whether he was baptized at birth.

"There's no conflict for me between Christianity and our native ways," he explains, sensing my perplexity. "Though many are still resentful at the terrible things the church has done to our people in this last century. Our Sun Dance teaches us the value of sacrifice, gratitude for life and Mother Earth, and gratitude for our community. At its best, Christianity does the same. Both value fasting periods, too. My grandfather was Christian, along with all his family, so it has become a part of us. The early oppression is a thing of the past, and the priests here honor our ways as much as we do theirs."

We stood watching the solemn procession of warriors file into the middle of the arbor, the four men at the front then offering blankets and other gifts to their clan uncles, who stood before them.

"Gratitude is the heart of our religion," Tom Yellow Tail murmurs, as we watch the proceedings. "We pray on rising in the morning for a new day, for the beauty of the gift of life. We have regular prayer meetings, sweat lodges—we call them the little brother—and Sun Dances, the big brother. The whole adds up to a cycle of praise. What else should human beings be if not praising beings?"

What else indeed. I stand there immersed in the sound of these singing people, plaintive, insistent, hypnotic, beseeching. Like no other sound I have ever heard it sends up waves of longing into the ethers, music to the ears of the greater powers.

Before turning in at the sisters' gate that night I stop for a drink in a Dayton bar. The only other customer insists on buying me a beer. Minutes later he gets up to leave, saying, "I should be getting home, if only I knew where home was." Those Crow people, for all the alcohol and drug abuse, they know where home is.

The next morning I am awakened by a horse's whinny, and before I leave on the circuitous route I have decided on to reach Fort Washakie and the Sun Dance ceremony, the sisters tell me a strange thing. "There is a woman in Chicago," they say, "who sings in the streets to keep the drug dealers away. You should meet her. She is part of Sacred America."

There must be so many invisible people singing their hearts out in different ways, I think to myself as I wave them good-bye, these sisters hidden behind their trees in Dayton, their lifesong cascading straight from the source just like the woman in Chicago.

Out on the road I go, past Dead Horse Creek, Crazy Woman Pass, Wild Horse Creek, to Sundance, a one-street town far out in the back of Montana, then on over the Belle Fourche River through Rapid City to what would in the fifties have been one of the great sacred sites of America, Mount Rushmore. But no more. No more, because the era of American triumphalism is passing, I like to think, though I don't know for sure.

They cut a monumental figure, those presidents with their profiles etched against the Dakota sky. Conservationists today see them to be a crime against nature—all that human deformation of a cliff millions of years old that was never asked whether it was willing to be host to such grandiosity. The original people of this land had more respect. They would never turn a leaf without asking permission of the tree; what traces they left of their presence on the land were subtle. Sometimes a sacred place would be marked with just the bending of a few stalks of grass.

Mount Rushmore is the mark of a different people, one filled with pride for their conquest of nature, for their version of democracy and government, for their role as bearers of enlightenment to the rest of the world. It is the mark, too, of an immigrant people thankful for the new land of promise that gave them safe haven from the tribulations of the Old World. The most recent immigrants are always the most fervent nationalists, and sculptor Gutzon Borglum, whose vision stands here for perpetuity carved in rock, was a first-generation American. America was and still is an experiment, and like every experiment it proceeds by a process of trial and error. Mount Rushmore would surely not be carved now, the era of great presidents being apparently over, the frailties of national figures being painfully visible in the glare of the media. Imagine Bill Clinton's profile up there with Jefferson's.

A few miles along the road the tribal councils are planning to dwarf Mount Rushmore with a figure of Chief Crazy Horse cut from another ridge. When it is finished it will be the largest rock carving in the world. This, too, was initiated by Borglum, and over the years it has become a symbol of Indian pride—the centerpiece for an education and cultural center that will give the world a very different picture of the Indian peoples than the insulting cliché most of the world has been fed by Hollywood. Even so, it is a strange thing that people who used to make sacred art with a bent stalk of grass have resorted to the monumentalism of their oppressors. The monument is here because Crazy Horse was born in the Black Hills. Never having submitted to a life on the reservation, he still represents the original spirit of the Indian peoples.

The road takes me on to the town of Custer where I stop to catch the evening sun outside a cafe with a talking parrot. In the shop next door I find a woman making a bead war bonnet who tells me she left Pine Ridge Reservation the year before to get work and to find her own roots. On the reservation, she says, the role models for the kids are all from MTV, black and Hispanic, all bandannas and baggy pants. The kids do a lot of dope. Most of the men are alcoholics. Her own mother was alcoholic.

"There are spiritual leaders on the reservation," she says, continuing to work with the beads, "and great artists, too. But if they were to teach the kids, the parents would want them to feed and clothe them as well."

She went to museums, photographed the old beadwork, and taught herself to reproduce it. Her healing has begun, she says, though it is a long path. She told me of the pain she felt when she was sent to boarding school and forbidden to speak Lakota.

At that moment a towering Indian walks in, the same one I noticed making dove calls to the parrot next door. He overhears the woman's words, and joins in the conversation. "I wish I had been sent to boarding school," he says. "I was sent to a white school, the only Indian among all those white kids. I'm Cheyenne, from Oklahoma. I had long hair, and they would pull me through the mud by my hair nearly every morning. That was just for starters. When I got older I learned karate and judo. One kid broke my finger by slamming the door on it. I jumped on him and got him in a neck hold, heard his neck start to crack as they pulled me off him. I've had a lot of therapy to get through my resentment, but I've still got some rage to work through. My parents were both alcoholic, of course."

"It still goes on," he continues, rolling himself a cigarette. "I work up on the Crazy Horse Mountain. A white kid up there was always making innuendoes and snide remarks, and I just finally did some quick moves on him and laid him out. "Hey, just joking, man," he said. "I don't want to hear no more of your jokes," I said.

Such pain hidden in these beautiful hills, the Black Hills, and everywhere human beings disguise their own anguish by inflicting the same on others. The brave, hurt, big man turns to engage a couple of women tourists in conversation, and I leave to drive on into the descending dark with the evening star ahead of me all the way and big lightning crackling away to the south.

A night in a room in the coal-mining town of Wright, and breakfast in the Blue Heron Bookstore, Casper, Wyoming. Half the town seems boarded up, and the Blue Heron lady tells me it's never been the same since the oil business collapsed in the eighties. The population went from eighty thousand to forty thousand in two years, and has never recovered. Outside in faded white letters on a high stone wall next to the Christian Science Reading Room a notice hints of the old Wyoming and a way of life that was here long before oil:

KISTLER TENT AWNING CO.

SHEEP WAGON COVERS

HERDERS TEEPEES

LAMBING TENTS

BED TARPS

For another few hours I sail over the great swells of land with not a fence to be seen through tiny places like Muddy Gap and Sweetwater Station. At last I am on the Wind River Reservation, where I come to a crossroads and there etched in the hill in chalk letters as big as Hollywood it says FORT WASHAKIE. A surprisingly elegant native arts center, the odd house out on the plains, and that is Fort Washakie, population 300, elevation 5,570.

Behind a few houses I find the land where some men are building the Sun Dance arbor, the gold and blue ranges of the Continental Divide on one side, the eastern horizon on the other. I watch them tie a buffalo head to the central tree while a man of gigantic bulk stands by, a stuffed eagle in his hand with a wingspan of at least a yard. A truck pulls up laden with greenery, which they begin to stack against the twelve supports that circle and lean in to the central pole. The world tree at the center soars out of the foliage, crowned already with flags, one blue and one white that flap loudly in the wind.

By the time I have found a room in Lander, a token to middle America on the edge of the reservation, and returned to the arbor, a dozen or more teepees are silhouetted against the evening glow smoldering in the clouds now over the mountains. Many more camps have also been erected, with windbreaks of foliage around the dining areas. A big wind is coming out of the east across the plains, the eastern sky pale now, between blue and white with ribbons of gray.

There are no more than four or five other white people here, all appearing to know everyone well. Most of the Indians are women, some of them beautiful in the way of hair falling loosely to the waist and a grace of movement that stretches back down the centuries. Elderly men with big bellies, tight jeans, and pigtails cluster in groups; pick-up trucks stand in long lines. "Jesus is my best friend," says a bumper sticker on the car in front of mine. A gaggle of swaggering ten-year-olds walk by dressed like they were in the inner city, with jagged haircuts to match. I draw my car up to join the ring of vehicles gathered at the open east end of the arbor, the word being out that the ceremony is about to begin.

In the darkness we hear the beat of the drum, four beats, then three, two, one. "They're coming, they're coming!" whispers the girl next to me and as she speaks the onlookers press forward to the eastern gate. "Be sure to leave the entrance free, folks," calls a lean man with high fine bones, two braids, and a big hat.

An eerie whistling rises up in the dark and suddenly two rows of dancers appear around the arbor from different directions, all of them blowing their eagle bone whistles, made from the left wing, the one nearest the heart. Twice the dancers circle the arbor, then file in to find their places. There are perhaps fifty of them in all, accompanied by singers who fill the air with a softness to stir old longings. The men, ranging in age from twelve to sixty, grin sheepishly at each other while the women crane forward to catch a glimpse. They wear only a wrap around the waist that falls to the ankles.

After the women have lined up to give the menfolk their bedroll, little suitcases, pillows, and doubtless other little comforts, the dancing finally begins with a prayer from the chief, James Trosper, to the central pole. The drums start up, the singers break the darkness with their rolling rhythms, the sundancers prance backward and forward shaking their eagle feathers at the pole: the axis of the world, where heaven and earth meet. For a couple of hours they dance on in the dark, taking it in turns to lie down for a few moments, until James Trosper, only thirty-three but a warm strong presence already, declares the first night over, and the dancers collapse in their places.

I am there for the sunrise the next morning at 5:30. It is dark still, just a low glimmer to the east, the growing moon still high, the morning star gleaming. No one stirs in the arbor, just some snores in a corner, though in a few minutes the emcee is beating on a drum and exhorting them to rise. A couple stir, but no more. Again the emcee bangs the drum. "The sun is coming," he cries, "there is dancing to do. Prepare yourselves." Another twenty minutes and a long file of men are waiting shrouded in blankets for their turn in the outhouse. The night has peeled back already, a blaze of orange and yellow on the horizon.

The chief and his aides take their places facing the doorway and the sun, the dancers sitting behind them in a cluster round the pole. The whistles start up, the drum is pounded with a dozen sticks, the women sing their unearthly chorus, everyone fixes their gaze on the daily miracle. The sun afloat at last in the sky, the dancers form a circle, the chiefs say their prayers (in English) over a fire, sprinkling it with cedar. They ask for the help of the Almighty One, declaring that their faith in him is strong, and that they will follow the traditions they have been handed down.

James Trosper, who is of the same family as Chief Washakee, the great Shoshone warrior and spiritual leader, addresses the dancers, reminding them of their sacred purpose in making this sacrifice: their wish for blessings for themselves, for their families, and for all Indian peoples. Then he asks Eddie Box, a revered chief of the Ute tribe in Colorado, to give the circle his blessings.

A stooped old man with a pacemaker, a hearing aid, and a baseball cap shuffles up to the axis of the world, placing his hat and his glasses down on the way. Eddie faces each man in turn, looks directly at him, shakes his eagle wing, and moves on. Then he blesses James Trosper and the other chiefs, holds them each in a brief embrace, and walks slowly back to his place. Utter simplicity. Nobody doing anything, just Grandfather Spirit moving that wing through a little old man you would not look at twice in a grocery store.

Each dancer steps up to the fire, stoops to draw in its energy, and holds out the soles of his feet, for extra protection. The drums start up, the voices rise, and the dancers take it in turns to skip out to the tree and back again, whistles keening the air. On and on they dance, though one man, the only white boy, is already lying down. Non-Indians are rarely permitted to dance the Shoshone Sun Dance, and I had been told that an exception had been made for this young man because he was a close relative of an Indian family. I remembered something I had read in the newspaper *Indian Country Today* by Andrew Iron Shell, a Lakota from the Rosebud reservation in Dakota: "Four days without food and water, piercing of the flesh under one hundred-degree heat so that their people shall live? Their people are not candidates for the endangered species list as mine have been for the last five hundred years. Do they carry the dream of Iron Shell, Crow Dog, or Crazy Horse? Or do they carry the guilt of Andrew Jackson, George Washington, Governor William Janklow and the rest of those so-called great American leaders who have desecrated the traditional thought and spirit of the American Indian way of life?"

"Our Lakota people have always felt compassion for orphans and those lost. All American Indian people must consider if it is worth the consequences of letting non-Indians partake in the ancient religious ceremonies of our originally great nations. Many of the non-Indians are lost or alone, but each of us must decide for ourselves if it is our responsibility to save them. Too many times have we found that our compassion is psychoanalyzed, dissected, and commercialized to eventually become the Sunday movie of the week or locked up in the homes of collectors or the Smithsonian."

At midday James Trosper calls for a rest and I head off for the afternoon to find Dinwoody Creek and the mysterious pictographs I have heard are preserved there. They are said to precede both the Shoshone and the Arapahoe peoples; nobody knows for sure who drew them or why. Through Crow Heart I drive, the lonely place where Chief Washakee and the Shoshone people defeated the Crow in 1866 in a battle over hunting rights, now just a Conoco gas station and a grocery store selling weak coffee.

Turning onto a dirt road I bump over ruts along the shore of Dinwoody Lake and come to rest finally where the water ends and a red butte soars out of the sagebrush. Not a sliver of life anywhere but the shrikes who flap out of the reeds as I stop in a dust cloud. I gaze up at the butte and there they are, far out in this remote valley, no different than when they were drawn there hundreds, perhaps thousands, of years ago: rows of eagles with widespread wings and figures with boxlike heads, masked perhaps, with outstretched arms and a tree of life drawn on the body. I am reminded of the etchings I have seen in the middle of the Sahara, almost identical, and feel the bequest of our ancestors stretching down to us now from back through the ages, one people.

It is a slow drive I take back to the Sun Dance, which has already started up again when I take my place at the eastern door. I am there only moments when I feel the observer drop away and the drums begin beating in my heart. The tree is a column of light now spiraling up and down from earth to sky, the arbor an oven where souls are being cooked, made good, the eagle whistles shrill through the cavities in my head, the earth is singing and the native peoples across the land are being lifted up in joy, for this is a joyful dance born out of a conscious self-giving, a Good Friday and Resurrection all in one. The joy is the joy of the tight skin loosening, the heart fallen open like a ripe nut, the stars pouring in, and all for the love of you. Which community can not be healed in coming together in such a way for such a purpose, joining with the greater body of life?

That night I went softly to my bed and slept a sleep of deep dreams. When I arrive in the morning they are putting in the "stalls," tall branches of fir that will shade the dancers from the fierce summer sun. Others are outside painting friends, brothers, fathers, sons, in warpaint, the better to fight the good fight. Some have dark lightning flashes up their arms, others a red paste in a ring around their wrists. A few have daubed their whole bodies in red.

I sit down next to Mike, an Indian of mixed ancestry, who tells me he was up in Alaska earning top dollar and going alcoholic when he woke up one morning, looked in the mirror, and said out loud, "My life has a hole in it. I'm going to do a Sun Dance." Since then he has participated in twelve, and it is the only reason, he tells me, he is still alive. He knows now that he has to live the sacred way, but it is a struggle finding out how to do that in contemporary America.

"There are nearly four thousand Shoshone and there are maybe a hundred who come to the Sun Dance," Mike continues. "The Tribal Council is seeking mining rights for gold and silver in the mountains. They want our people to be comfortable, they say, live the good life in those nice little houses you see over there. But gold and silver won't do my people any good. It will only make them more lazy and greedy. We all know there is no happiness in consumerism, but it's like there's some terrible momentum to mainstream America that won't be stopped till we hit a brick wall. And I think that time is coming."

Our attention is brought back to the arbor by an old chief, who is encouraging the dancers gathered round him now at the foot of the world tree. "Barry Old Coyote," murmurs Mike as we strain to hear.

Another elder with a pacemaker, a poignant blend of old and new medicine. He is telling them that this was the most difficult day of all; but that by this evening they would be on the home stretch.

"See these three black stripes round the tree?" he says. "Those signify the three nights you stay in the Sun Dance. You have done two already, so take heart. This will be a good day, the day you may have a vision, when your prayers may be answered. This is a good day," he repeated passionately, "and with the right spirit and the right intention you will dance well and feel joy."

"These people outside, they support you, we all support you. We shall bring you sweet sage and cattails to lie in, peppermint and spearmint leaves to soothe your brow. Everyone here is praying for your success in the Sun Dance. Now have a good dance. We shall begin with the Prayer Song, and then the Flag Song. Maybe after that we shall sing the Bear Song. So dance well. Your warpaint will help you now in the inner war, just as it helped our forefathers in their outer wars. This is a good day, and tonight you will be thankful that you persevered."

As Barry Old Coyote walks off to the side, we all stand, caps off in the sweltering sun, and the singers begin. Then the flag song, someone hoisting a Stars and Stripes at the arbor door, in honor, they say, of the Indian vets who died at war for the United States. I am bemused for a moment by the Indian loyalty to a flag that has broken their ways asunder. But then the songs pour through me and I know that the tree at the center plunges deep through the earth to before the beginning of time, to before treaties were there to be broken.

Many of the dancers are lying now in their stalls, their heads lolling back, their second day now, without food or water; yet some come forward still, eager as ever, prancing young colts, waving their soft down feathers at the heart of the world. The women come up in turn to give their men gifts of sweet sage and bundles of cattails, and in the moment of exchange I can sense the current of feeling that passes with giving and receiving, the support of an individual by the community. That current is the sacred thread that spins out from the heart of the world, passes through the human community, and round again, binding us all back into creation. That is the current, I realize, that contemporary America is in such danger of losing.

Having offered their gifts the people line up to receive blessings from the medicine men and from the accumulating energy of the dance and the sacrifice. Old women shuffle forward, an old man limping, babes in arms, entire families of some of the dancers. James Trosper, Eddie Box, John Washakee, flick their eagle wings at the people's hearts and heads, leaving the wing on an afflicted place sometimes for a minute or more. An aged man who can hardly walk is led up by his wife. A young dancer comes and stands by his side, his grandson, perhaps, and I see that the real dance is in this giving and receiving, the eternal weaving that can bring the stars to earth.

As the dancers struggle to their feet again, in the late afternoon of this the hardest day, I make my own prayer toward the central tree, the axis of the world from which all blessings come and to which all return. I pray for my own family back in England, and for a love there I may have left forever; only time will tell. I am already bound by my own life story to head east now, yet I know that as I land in Cleveland, they will be laughing and singing and crying in Fort Washakie, for their day of resurrection will have come. On my way back to Billings I pass a biker with two little bears strapped to his pillion. Standing in line at the airport once again I marvel to think that just a short time ago I was here busy looking for escape routes from the Great Plains emptiness. Such a fullness have I known in this great stretch of land, and I thank life for the way its gifts come unexpected.

Chapter Two

Midwest Meditators and Monks

Out of the airport, through the gray air of Cleveland I drove, on into the Ohio afternoon and the New York evening. I found myself a room for the night in a Super 8, I don't know where. Except when I start out again in the morning, the first exit on the freeway is to Bath, and of course I have to take it, having had no idea I was so close to home, even the same street names, Pulteney Square. The small town of Bath, New York, was founded in the 1790s, and it still has a couple of fine Georgian facades remaining, though for the rest, it is the usual Kmart and Main Street drabness, with more than its fair share of boarded up store fronts. I stop for breakfast in the Cybercafe—an unlikely feature of life in Bath, I would have thought—and there the owner speaks to me in a familiar gruff Northern English, tells me he has been there ten years or more, as good a place as any to live. He made great eggs, had got the local idea of over easy down pat.

We parted with a shake of the hand and a very British look down at the floor, then I was on my way and in no time at all it seemed I was driving through Springwater, three houses, a stoplight, and a closed-down bookstore, looking for Springwater Center for Meditative Inquiry.

I find it at the end of a long track off a side road, which is what you would expect. The year before I had attended a retreat in Holland with the founder, Toni Packer, and had felt so at home with her unconventional style that I determined to visit her center. Toni is an advocate of the "no guru, no method" approach. Philip Kapleau, the abbot of Rochester Zen Center, had groomed her to become his successor. But the more she took office the less comfortable she felt with the traditional formalities and rituals: the bowing and prostrating, the use of a striking stick during meditation, the bells, the chanting, the unbending and obligatory schedule of a formal retreat, and above all, the traditional postures of student and teacher.

She finally left to start her own center at Springwater, here in a sloping meadow left uncut with flowers and grasses at their zenith now, all goldenrods and Queen Anne's lace, humming birds whirring, white butterflies on the wind gathering the last of the pollen. The hills spread out in wooded ripples to a low horizon, the light falls softly even so early in the afternoon. A long, low house sits easily in a fold of the hill, home to eight people who manage the center, with Toni and her husband living just a mile away.

Only one person in sight as I come in the door, and she shows me my room, one of a row for the guests of whom there are several. The largest room in the house, the only one of any size, is the meditation hall, with rows of cushions and one wall of big windows that give on to the meadow. No religious objects or symbols are anywhere to be seen, and the house seems no more of a Zen center than any other house, except for the cushions.

That is because, as I quickly remember, it isn't a Zen center. It isn't a center for any spiritual tradition as such. Toni left all that behind in Rochester, and has remained with the simple wish for meditative inquiry into existence, into life as it is here and now, hardly the prerogative of any creed or religion. To step out of tradition and face the bare bones of life as it is is a courageous step, fitting for the dawn of a post modern age.

Later in the afternoon, I speak to a couple, David and Heidi, who have been living at Springwater for two years or so. They tell me it is like being married to eight people, always sharing the minutiae of life, the running of the household, as well as the silence of the meditation hall. What makes it worthwhile—besides the sheer beauty of the place—is the common willingness to investigate, to wake up to one's own reactions and responses. When I press them further on what this actually means, they say it is about waking up to our storylines. It finally comes down, Heidi tells me, to a question of identity, the notion of who we imagine ourselves to be. If we are angry, for example, we are usually completely identified with our anger. We take our anger to be a rightful and righteous response to the situation, a direct expression of who we are. Yet if we inquire into it deeply enough, we might discover that the anger arises out of a spaciousness and openness that is not clinging to any notion of right or wrong. Inquiry points us to that spaciousness as our true identity.

I don't know, though, I respond. I wonder if who we are might not include all of it. We in the West live in linear time, while the traditional East lives in a circular eternity. We are obsessed with improving our lot and the social good. Old India knows that it will all pass anyway, and there will always be another bite of the cherry in the next incarnation.

What has always been so startling to me about the image of the cross is that it suggests the two—the temporal and the eternal, the personal and the impersonal—intersect at a common point, and I suspect that point is the heart of hearts that every great teaching ultimately directs us to. We are the great spaciousness, and we are also the anger of the moment. To be willing and able to hold the two at the same time is what is so unique about being human.

David goes on to say that Springwater's gift is to point them to the final truth, which is the essence of the given moment. From the ultimate perspective, there is nowhere to go and nothing to do, but that doesn't mean we don't go anywhere or do anything, for it is our nature as beings in this world to act. Toni Packer acts like the rest of us, he laughs. She also feels sad and angry sometimes. The difference is in the degree she becomes absorbed in what is ultimately passing. Just then the bell goes for the evening meditation, and we head off to join the others in the hall.

For half an hour we sit there, more or less still, I with my thoughts wandering this way and that, until eventually, just before the bell goes to signal the end of the sitting, I settle into a quiet that thins down my breathing to a slender thread. In that peace a phrase emerges inside me without commentary. "Come unto me all you that labor, and I shall give you rest," it said. My body softens further. Then out of the silence a woman's voice travels the air.

Toni Packer sits on her cushion along with everyone else and speaks with her eyes closed of the whir of the insects, the rustling breeze, the silence all-pervading, and can we know that in the midst of our conditioned life. I look around and see an erect, live presence with a fringe of gray hair, seventy now, though you wouldn't guess it. In a few minutes she has finished, and she invites others to speak as they are moved, as at a Quaker meeting. Someone talks of a hurt they had felt, how they had entered it and found that in its center a silence emerged, defense and argument falling away. A businessman says that his earlier interests—money, success, excitement, achievement—no longer draw him, leaving him sometimes depressed and at other times with the realization that there is nothing to do but tend one's garden.

Someone asks her about the lineage from master to pupil that has always supported the tradition down through the ages; whether it is possible to continue the teachings into the future without such a chain of transmission.

She pauses for a moment, lets the question hang in the air, then replies finally that truth needs no lineage; that she isn't in the least concerned for the future, that the process of inquiry in silence has always taken care of itself, and would doubtless continue to do so. As to the future of Springwater, and who might take her place after she goes, that would take care of itself too. Whether Springwater continues or not is secondary, she adds after another pause. Truth does not need a midwife or a center to come into being. Truth is not caused by a path, she laughs suddenly; and who knows why there is waking up? It's the miracle of humanity, she says.

Toni Packer is radical, and her teaching style reflects her wish to cut to the quick. Sitting on her cushion, wearing ordinary clothes, she is indistinguishable from the rest of us. Her evening talk is the only indication that there is a teacher present at all. When she runs a meditation retreat, participants are free to attend as few or as many sittings as they wish. If you prefer to do yoga in the morning instead of sitting, well and good; you can start later in the morning; or perhaps you prefer to walk in the gardens. You can literally create your own retreat within the program offered. Yet far from falling apart at the seams, everyone going off and doing his own thing, people gravitate naturally to the communal sittings in their own rhythm. An interior discipline, rather than an imposed one, has the room to emerge within the context of a shared intentionality.

At Springwater the context of alternate sitting and walking, and the community of meditators itself, is available for people to use and draw support from according to their needs. No method, then, but an open looking and listening, which is human, rather than Buddhist or Christian or anything else.

"How can it be otherwise," she laughs—she laughs a lot, and easily—"if there is in truth no guru, no method, and no disciple, but only truth, as it reveals itself to us moment by moment?"

Packer's is a very feminine way, based on trust; all very new in a culture that has valued patriarchal authority and its forms for millennia. Just at this moment, Toni is saying that no one can know what is best for another.

The next morning, as I am preparing to go, one of the community mentions that Diana, Princess of Wales, has died that night in a car crash. Stunned, I go and sit in the meditation hall for a few minutes, light a candle for her, and find myself weeping. Weeping for a young life striving for good, but weeping also for a country whose stiffness she had been helping to unfreeze. Weeping for myself, too; a sudden feeling of exile, of my life having moved on from a land at once constricting, loved, and familiar. I sit there for longer than I know, my humanity revealed to me in the truth of the moment, as Toni Packer had put it.

It was in somber mood that I left the Springwater meadow and continued north toward Rochester, turning west after some miles toward Genesee Abbey, the strictest Cistercian house in the country. I wanted to know how a traditional monastery—at the opposite end of the scale to communities like Springwater—was faring in times that would seem to have moved far beyond it. The abbey sits in the midst of its own farm-land, and Father George, who was on duty in the bookshop, assured me life there was a picnic compared to what it was.

"They used to sleep in common dormitories and be hungry all day long," he laughed. "No breakfast and a few ounces of bread at lunch. What we do may look difficult, in the chapel for offices seven times a day starting at 2:30 in the morning, but it's a rhythm you get used to."

An office was about to begin, and I hurried into the chapel to join it. It was a large, low tent of a building, a warm light filtering in through slits of colored glass, a round stone altar in the center. The reverend abbot processed in with a retinue of attendants, came to a spot near the altar, and with arms spread wide, read from a large bible held out for him by a young monk. When he had finished the monks began a long Gregorian refrain, and my spirits were lifted away from the morning sadness to a sense that all was well, that all shall be well, for Diana, for me, for all of us here on this fragile planet, even though our tears run rivers and the pain of a human life is so often difficult to bear.

After the service I managed to take a few minutes walk with the abbot, Reverend Father John Bamberger, who had spent fifty of his seventy-three years as a monk. He had started out in Gethsemane Abbey, in Kentucky, where Thomas Merton had been his tutor and mentor. Then, twenty-five years ago, he was asked to begin this sister house, since there was at the time a strong interest in vocations, unlike today.

"When people ask me what it is like to be a monk," he said, as we strolled through the fields, "I think of Suzuki, the Zen master, who said it consisted of eight to twelve hours a day staring at a blank wall wishing he could kill the abbot. The difference is for us, it's eight to twelve hours singing the office in Latin. But if you wonder what it is we learn living like this, it is quite simply that you learn to love people, and then you discover that things work out. My way of learning to love is to see the transcendent Person behind the persona, though I don't want to diminish the personality—that too has the potential to be raised up into the greater Presence. Eventually, the whole person is subsumed in Christ."

"I was often miserable in the early years," he went on, "though not, I would say, unhappy. I think I can say I have never had an unhappy day in my monastic life, because I have always known this is exactly where I need to be. The difficulty always lies in facing oneself. In Gethsemane in the early days, it was just too intense, all those offices, no communication at all. Now we have replaced absolute silence with conscious talking. I used to worry that I wasn't normal, then I would think, "What's so great about being normal?"

Such a warmth in this man's eyes, he in his old green mac and walking boots. It was their monthly "hermit day," when they were free to do as they wished, and he was off for a hike across the hills. I returned to the bookshop to continue my conversation with Father George, who had told me earlier he had joined the order eleven years ago at the age of fifty-seven, after divorcing his wife of twenty-seven years.

They had eleven children together, so he certainly played his part in the baby boom, he quips. His mother, of course, was Irish. He tells me he had several different careers, though mostly he was a federal government investigator. When he got out of the army at the end of World War II he picked up a copy of Merton's autobiography and that fired him up to go on a retreat in a Trappist monastery in Rhode Island. He arrived at two in the morning and he couldn't believe it, the place was a beehive. At the time floods of men were applying to the monasteries, and they could afford to pick and choose.

So although George loved the idea of being a monk, he never dreamed he could do it. He got married in college. When they divorced he thought about it again, and discussed it with an analyst friend. He never expected anyone to accept credentials like his, but he met John Bamberger down at the guest house, they talked for a couple of hours, and agreed on a starting date.

"I couldn't believe it, I was ecstatic," laughed George.

He found the novitiate grueling, however, the total silence and the hard physical labor, sawing logs with a two-man saw in summer heat and no time to blow your nose. The novice master had said they give everyone a guardian angel on their arrival, someone to look out for them. His angel was a twenty-five-year-old who would come down on him like his own father, and George was fifty-seven. The angel was later asked to leave.

I wondered how George's family responded to the idea of their father becoming a monk, and he said they all thought he was nuts. One of his sisters, a devout Catholic, wouldn't talk to him for the first nine years. But he knew he was in the right place; what he still loves about it is that it simply makes sense to him.

George thought I should meet the novice master, and went off for a few moments to find him. He returned with Brother Anthony, a tall man with fine, ascetic features and cropped gray hair, and left us alone to talk.

Anthony said he had no novices in his charge at the moment, though when they did appear the typical applicant was somewhere between forty and sixty, successful in business or a profession, and was having some kind of spiritual awakening. Often, they would confuse an awakening with a vocation, and would need to see that their real challenge was to develop their Christian life more fully in the world. Sometimes it was a genuine vocation, Anthony added, but you would have to have the intuition that this was really the case.

"What I look for," he said, "is a strong ego; someone who has succeeded in something. Monks need strong egos. They need to stand on their own feet, and have a high level of tolerance. I ask how his relationships are, because you can't escape relationships in a monastery. And I try to sense if they would fit into a stable life. It's not easy for people today to stay in one place. We rarely stray from our own land, and that is unusual in a restless, mobile society. Healthy self-love is important, as is pliability—after all, you are entering a formation program. The conformity and the discipline are designed to crack the individual will."

"It's a long way from twenty-five years ago," he smiled. "Then, you were told how to walk, not to cross your legs, and so on. Any faults were publicly announced in the chapter meetings. You don't have to water dead sticks any more, but you are still tested. Older people, I think, are more able to take the knocks. The younger ones have more difficulty with final commitment."

"Perhaps you are not surprised there is a shortage of novices after hearing all that," he laughed. "But these are different times. The role of the laity is much stronger now. We have lay contemplative associations connected with the abbey. They are an extended community who undertake to keep certain private practices, and to living the Rule as their life allows them. It's all quite new, really, just the last three or four years. But it's what's being called for now. Some houses have opened their doors to temporary monastics, people who come for a few months or a year, though we don't do that yet. So many people now are looking for spiritual direction, we have to respond as we can."

I asked him before leaving whether he thought the days of the monastery were numbered. He looked down for a moment, visibly saddened. He hoped not, he said, because the monastery was no longer a flight from an evil world. The monks didn't see it that way. Monasticism was a countercultural movement.

"Penance is countercultural," he explained, "in the sense we understand it now, as an interior renunciation of self-centeredness. Obedience is countercultural. If we need a new pair of shoes, we must still ask the abbot's permission. Immobility is countercultural. And those kinds of alternative currents are essential for any healthy society. For me, at least, it's a life that hangs together," he said as we shook hands. "Here, I can live unabashedly what is important and central to me, an undivided life centered on God."

Hard to argue with that, I thought, as I left Father Anthony standing in front of the church and made my way to the car. How comforting it must feel to be in a community like his and know exactly where you stand. I remembered when, twenty-five years earlier, I longed to have the simplicity and faith to join the Russian Orthodox Church in London. The Archbishop Anthony Bloom (he is still there) was a true sage; the services—the music, the icons, the incense, the devotion—would lift me unfailingly into an exalted sense of deep and sacred mystery. Yet for all that, as much as I longed to, I could not belong. Something in me deeper than the wish for a spiritual home knew that I could never rest in such a traditional form; that I was here to absorb and also to move on from the legacy of the past; to have the courage to help new forms emerge.

One Sunday the archbishop gave me a postcard. It was of the Buddha. I hadn't spoken to him, but he knew; he knew that traditional Christianity of any denomination was not what I was here for. The message on the postcard was clear: not that I should become a Buddhist, but that I should follow my love and the Buddha's spirit of inquiry in my own way. I thanked him, profoundly moved. We clasped hands, and I never returned.

Before me now, I have a long ride ahead, through Buffalo and Niagara down through Canada all the way to Motown. Couples strolling in the spray of the falls; the reserve of the northern neighbor seeming to seep out of the land, Detroit on the horizon breaking my daydreams finally.

I am in Detroit not only to take a plane back east but to meet a woman at the airport who, like the monks of Gethsemane, also lives an undivided life centered on God; yet not in a monastery, but in the midst of the everyday world. I don't quite know how I first heard of Marina Gamble; but I had her number and I knew that she lived and breathed for Rumi, the Sufi mystical poet who founded the Order of the Whirling Dervishes in thirteenth-century Turkey. I have kept Rumi's words by me for decades, and sometimes I give recitals of his work. For years now I have slept beneath a large portrait of him that hangs over my bed.

Rumi, a man who wrote in Persian some seven hundred years ago, is currently one of the most popular poets in the United States. His success is certainly due in part to the recent flurry of translators, especially Coleman Barks, who have rendered his ineffable lines into a plain and colloquial English that still manages to convey the profundity of the original. Yet Rumi speaks directly to the spirit of our times; he speaks the language of love, of lover to his beloved, to Shams, his flesh-and-blood teacher. Romantic love is one of the grand myths of our culture, and Rumi takes the passion of that love and subsumes it into a love of the divine. In his ecstatic verses, earthly and divine love merge so seamlessly that the contemporary reader's own experience of love is given expression in a way that elevates it without either 'spiritualizing' it or making an abstraction of it. In Rumi, the personal and the divine come together as one. That is the joy I find in his words.

My meeting with Marina was a last-minute arrangement, and the only time she could manage was right before my flight to Boston. We were due to meet in my departure bay, and she was already there when I arrived; a gloriously large, Latin-looking presence in her early thirties, with a shock of long frizzled black hair and wearing a coat of rose pink. Little did I know what I was about to hear.

We had barely sat down and introduced ourselves when her story began pouring out with an energy and rapidity that had me gasping to keep up. She told me her parents, who were Filipino and Portuguese, had always wanted a boy, and she was deeply rejected when she was a child.

"I was even born on Father's Day," she laughs. "Like, no pressure! I knew I wasn't wanted right from the beginning. My father dropped my mother off quickly at the hospital because he needed to get to the football game. I did everything a son would do. I even played football when all I really wanted was to play with my Barbie doll. But the strange thing was, I knew from very early on with complete certainty that I was absolutely loved; not by people, but by whatever it was the nuns at my convent school called God. And I knew that this force, or intelligence, that loved me wasn't at all like their description of God—the one who was jealous, and would punish you for sins. They were mean to me because of the way I looked, and I used to pray to God every day not to be hard on them, because they truly didn't know what they were doing; they couldn't help it."

This woman is for real, I thought in the first minute. This is no show; it's an unstoppable flow. She can't help herself. She knew the world was false, she was saying, and that there was something else that was not supernatural, but supremely natural; that there was an unseen force that she knew how to love because she also knew from the beginning how to love what she could see. It always puzzled her, she said, that the nuns would talk so much about loving their God when they plainly didn't know how to love what was in front of them.

"I knew right from the gate," she explained. "You're gonna hear all this stuff, but you're gonna know the difference. I don't know why no one else seems to know this, but they don't, so just lie or they'll think you're crazy. So that's what I did. I lay low, especially when the spirit world started visiting me. The spirit of my cousin's mother came to me when I was twelve, but I didn't say anything. All through my teens people's spirits would come to me, usually someone's mother. When I asked them why they came to me and not to their own kids, they would say that their children couldn't hear them, that they didn't know the language. I knew I knew this language, even as a child."

I asked her what that language was, and she said it was the language of love. She didn't hear it, so much as feel it or know it. It was a kinesthetic thing; an absolute knowing, an utter certainty.

"There's my usual chaotic mind," she laughed, "and then there's this knowing. There are no words for it really; a wordless language. The closest I can come to describing it is that it feels like being honored in a beautiful way. If I go there, I start to cry, so I feel I have to pull back in social situations, like now."

When she was approaching twenty, Marina said, her night dreams started coming true, and she would instantly know when someone was lying to her. She had still only ever told her mother about her experiences when a man, a complete stranger, stopped her in the street one day and said, "You speak the language, don't you—in dream and in the waking state? That is what lets you discern the voices of spirits. You are safe. All is well."

The voices were coming in thick and fast at the time, and Marina was grateful for this confirmation from a stranger out of the blue. She would be in the middle of a conversation and hear the person's spirits all around her. "It's just like the movie *Ghost*," she said. "Everyone has their entourage, and they go crazy when someone can hear them. 'Tell them about me, about me.' I had to learn to manage it all, and understand more of the realms I had access to, so I took some classes at a psychic institute, and that was helpful."

As for the stranger, she never saw him again. We hadn't even got to Rumi yet, and before we did, Marina told me how for a decade she had been a beautician, selling the Borghese line in a mall.

"I had always been fascinated by beauty, because I was told from the start that I didn't have it. Yet I had always been honored, held high, by this loving presence, the God thing. What then, was beauty, I wondered, if I'm not beautiful? I'm gonna figure this beauty thing out. I knew that beauty was far deeper than what people thought. But I still used to get all the magazines, and I always knew what the hip thing was. I had this absolute certainty that I was going to be very successful in this business. I was hired by a woman who said, 'You are going to be my best seller.' She knew I had zero experience, but I just knew, so I didn't care, and she could see that. And I knew she was lucky to have me." Marina paused for a moment, though not long enough for me to come up with a question.

"See, that kind of attitude is all part of it," she went on. "I absolutely knew that about the God force from the beginning. It can be Dirty Harry one minute and Jesus the next, as long as it's true. I've seen myself go from one to the other and I know I can only love myself no matter what. I made a promise to myself a long time ago about that—I'm loving myself. I love me; I'm married to me. Any questions? Catch the bouquet! If I didn't know that I'd be in the gutter right now."

The point was, she explained, she knew that if she could see beauty within herself when no one else could, she could see and bring out the same beauty in anyone. And sometimes she needed to be outrageous to do that, to leap in where others would fear to tread.

"That's the Dirty Harry part again. I knew from the start that God met Satan, fell in love, got married, and I'm the child. I knew it. We are *all* that child. Maybe that's why as a kid I was sorry for Satan. I'd say, 'I love you, even if God won't. I'm going to love, no matter what, even if it seems to violate God's rules. I know you're bad and all that, but I don't know what to do but love.' I just had to step out like that—'love is reckless,' says Rumi, 'not reason. Reason seeks a profit, love comes on strong.' That's the disco Rumi version."

Marina quickly became the top salesperson in the entire chain because of her repeat business. She used to love to do makeovers. "Get in my chair, I'll show you!" It wasn't the make-up that people came back for over and over. It was the fact that they were being touched by someone who saw their beauty and recognized them. Not only that, she could also bring it out with the makeover. Many of her customers were unhappy housewives. They couldn't see their own beauty, but as they sat in her chair they would find themselves telling Marina their story, releasing it all to someone they felt they could trust. Marina could see who they really were, and would chip away at the self-doubt and other negative programming that they hid behind.

"You *are* beautiful. If others don't see it, too bad," she would tell them.

Behind her counter she would have a shrine with the St. Francis prayer, words of the Buddha, and other inspirational sayings. Messages, lines of poetry, intuitions, would come to her any time of the day or night, and she would always keep a notebook by her bed.

One morning, standing at the counter, she heard a voice that said, "Ralph, that's not the Sufi way." Who's Ralph? She wondered. The voice was loud and insistent, and there was no Ralph that she knew of to ask, so she asked those around her what the Sufi way was. No one knew. "Gotta go, be right back," she cried, running out into the mall. "Excuse me, anyone know what a Sufi is?" she called out. "I need to know."

Two students standing in the bakery line said they knew that a Sufi was a truth seeker, and that if she needed to know more she could go check out the Nimetallahi Sufi Order that was around the corner on 19th Street.

"Thanks! I got on the phone, and said I wanted to know more about Sufis. They said sure, come around the next day. So I did, knock knock, it's me, and I told him about the voice in my head. He sat down, we talked, and it was good, but you know, not life-changing, like I'd met God or anything. It was like, okay, thanks, truth seeker, thanks for the tea. Then he said they had a library downstairs, and I jumped—me and a roomful of books, I love that. But none of the titles really drew me—I know when my heart falls out of itself. Then I see this thing on the wall, some poem. I went over to it, read the first few lines, and fell on the floor. I was weak, *weak*! Who is this that knows me? Who knows my heart? Who is shamelessly putting this on the wall?"

> *Who gets up early to discover the moment light begins . . .*
> *Who lets down a bucket and brings up a flowing prophet . . .*
>
> *Jesus slips into a house to escape enemies*
> *and opens a door to the other world.*
> *Solomon cuts open a fish, and there's a gold ring.*
> *Omar storms in to kill the Prophet and leaves with blessings.*

She stopped for a moment. *"But don't be satisfied with stories,"* I continued, remembering the last verse suddenly,

> *. . . how things have gone with others.*
> *Unfold your own myth, without complicated explanations*
> *So everyone will understand the passage*
> *"We have opened you."*
> *Start walking towards Shams.*
> *Your legs will get heavy and tired*
> *Then comes the moment of feeling the wings you've grown lifting.*

I had not recited that poem for a couple of years, and here it was now fresh as a new creation. It had been Marina's first meeting with Rumi.

Now someone knew her, she murmured, her voice low and tender suddenly, when she had worked so hard to hide. The love she had known all her life, Rumi had put words to. That was all she needed, and she was out of that library and into the street.

Over the next few years she clung to Rumi like a barnacle. He was her secret confidant, and he began to take over her life. She stopped working as a beautician and became an administrative assistant for a recording company that sold Rumi tapes, just so that she could listen to them all day. Yet no one knew how deep Rumi went for her. She would collect Rumi books, but more often than not she would just hold them rather than read them. She would know the whole book that way, as if it were already somehow stored in her heart.

One night a year later, just before Christmas, she heard a voice telling her to expect a gift in gold wrapping. Marina knew it would be a gift from the deceased mother of her friend Lola, even though it would come through Lola. "It was from The Realm," she explained. "I knew it was a direct communication from them. I still thought I was crazy, though, so I wrote it down, sealed it in an envelope, and gave it to Kathy, another friend, to open after Christmas. It came, of course, and inside was a string of pink pearls."

Here the story takes off, and you will believe what you can. As Marina was telling it to me there in the middle of that airport lounge, with announcements of delays and departures cutting in every few moments, I had absolutely no doubt that this woman before me was not only telling the truth, she was being the truth. I could feel it, a palpable sensation of aliveness that comes in the presence of authenticity.

Shortly after Christmas, she began to have recurring dreams of being by the ocean, and of spirits pouring water over her as she lay down. Then she would become the water, merged with the ocean. A few months later she was in a bookstore and a book fell out on her by the Rumi section. It was one of a series called *Mercy Oceans, Pink Pearls,* imported from Turkey.

"Click click, ding dong! Rocket scientist! Did I need anything else to tell me to pay attention? I opened the book up in the middle and there I found my life laid bare. It said there is plenty of sand on the beach, and quite a few shells. But if you are really seeking, you'll want to go into the ocean. One of the things you will find if you dive deep enough are pearls. The rarest pearls are pink. If you are willing to swim deep enough in shark-infested waters, and can hold your breath long enough, then you may find the treasure. But how many people are willing to do that? My God, I thought, I am known completely; but not by someone in a body.

I could never get anyone to explain the thirst I felt for God, or the things that were happening to me; but here it was."

Years went by; Marina became filled with her love till there was nothing else left, though its source was still a secret lived underneath her working day. A full ten years later, she heard a voice out of nowhere telling her to sleep with the *Mercy Oceans* book by her pillow. At 2:00 A.M. she awoke to a command telling her to open to page fifty-three and phone the number there. On that page was the stamp of Jamil's Oriental Carpets, with the number. She had never noticed it before. Not one to wait around, Marina phoned immediately, knowing she'd have the right words when someone answered. Not surprisingly, nobody did. The next day she phoned and asked if the store had any more *Mercy Ocean* books. It turned out that weekly Sufi gatherings were held above the store, and the sheikh, the man who answered the phone, invited her to come.

"The sheikh knew exactly what was happening to me," Marina said, quietly now. "He was the first person I ever met who could see me. That very first evening he said he had a message for me from Rumi. I was to continue doing exactly what I was doing in life at present, but it was time to remove the last veil. The next week, you phoned. I don't know what it all means. I am just responding to what comes, so here I am."

The Boston flight was boarding now, and we parted warmly. Marina's secret was out in the open. What a wonderful intelligence shapes our lives, I thought, even as we think we are calling the tune! Turning to watch her walk away through the crowds, I remembered Fr. John Bamberger's comment, that the whole point of spending your life in a monastery is in learning to love people, which leads you to realize that things work out. How many people like Marina are out there, behind beauty counters, working in bars, in the lawyer's office, even in Wall Street, discovering the same thing, I wondered. Everyone has his or her own myth, as Rumi's poem says. What matters is that we live it, in a monastery, in a mall, anywhere. Marina is living hers; and this journey, I can feel it, is my own myth unfolding.

Chapter Three

A Very New England

For much of American history, colleges and universities included in their mission the shaping of an undergraduate's
moral character. Many private institutions, beginning with
Harvard in 1636, were founded by religious men and
women who expected that chapel attendance and religious
instruction would be woven into the fabric of student life.
As these schools became secularized, such requirements fell
by the wayside. But now, in a time of outward tension and
inner searching, when many Americans worry about social
decay and also show a growing interest in spirituality, students, teachers, and administrators on campuses are asking
whether colleges ought to try once again to build moral and
spiritual character as well as the intellect.

"Educators Go From Mind to Soul,"
The New York Times, August 4, 1996

Driving west out of the Boston suburbs you are not long in reaching the small town of Wellesley, and there, in acres of undulating
land on the edge of a lake, you will find one of the most prestigious women's colleges in America. For me, with my English heritage,
prestigious means exclusive, stuffy, and conservative; "old school" we
would say. Here, I am to discover that my preconceptions do not apply.
The dean of religious life at Wellesley—his predecessor was called the
chaplain, but those times are long gone—has invited me to the Flower
Festival, the multifaith celebration that launches the beginning of Wellesley's academic year.

I arrive from Detroit the evening before the festival. On the way to

my room at the College Club I can see that the bulk of Wellesley, like so
many American colleges, is a nineteenth-century Gothic fantasia, constructed, it seems, on the image of old Oxford.

Drawn by the waves of organ scales tumbling out of the chapel, which
is set on a mound among a grove of trees, I stop for a moment to peek in.
A Korean woman is playing, every sinew of her body engaged in the music. The chords lift my gaze to the long west window and the willowy
feminine figures in stained glass, glorious testimonies to Victorian yearning. At the chapel entrance a table gives notice of the spiritual groups active in the college: the Wellesley Buddhist Community, the Hillel
Community, Al Muslimat, Catholic, Protestant, and Unitarian gatherings.

The Office of Religious and Spiritual Life was formed to respond to
the diversity of religious beliefs at Wellesley, and the college celebrates the
major festivals of all world religions—including the African Heritage
Kwanza, the Jain, Bahai, Sikh, Native American, and many others.
Wellesley goes further still, for the Religious Life Team organizes multifaith events like the Flower Festival to encourage students at Wellesley to
discover the common spiritual threads that bind us all together as one
people. The team itself, representing the various traditions and headed up
by Victor Kazanjian, the dean, meets weekly for prayer, meditation, and
program planning. So they themselves model a way of working toward
common goals while respecting diversity.

The next morning when I get to the chapel, the three doors in three
directions are flung open already and even the aisles are packed with
waves of laughing, expectant faces. We are given a spray of white flowers
as we go in, a thousand young women, and half a dozen men. At first as
I sit down, the only man in a row of girls, I think I must be in the wrong
place, then I look round and see that all the rows right back to the doors
are filled with young women, Asians in flowing dresses, black women, Indians, and ranks of golden hair.

A team of African drummers starts up and the whole place crackles
with excitement. Then the dean stands up, a vital, passionate presence,
and welcomes us all by saying we are in for a feast of the senses, for are
not the senses the bridge between the inner and the outer? What we are
here for, he says, is to make this place sacred by our shared presence in the
truth and beauty of all religions.

"For you are sacred, you are special," he cries, his voice rising. "You are
the ones who shine with the beauty of the world." And I made a note to myself to think the same of the next grouchy woman I encounter at the end of
a checkout line, and the beggars I will see next week in Manhattan.

As he ended, a Zoroastrian lit a candle before the altar and told us this was the symbol for the fires within—the fire of inquiry, the fire of compassion, the fiery longing for God. I must be a Zoroastrian, I thought. Then a radiant Jewish girl took us through the ceremony her people perform to carry the atmosphere of the Sabbath over into the rest of the week. She lit some spice, put it in a box, waved it before us, then passed it round so we could savor the sweetness of the Sabbath for ourselves. A woman priest followed her by suggesting we savor the empty space that was brought to life by Mary's immaculate conception, that in the empty darkness, creation and life are born; that we too should nurture the spaces in our minds and our lives. Never had I heard the Christian message quite that way before. As she says her last word a Buddhist nun strikes a gong and for a moment the place stirs only to the faint rustle of leaves on the beeches outside.

The dean ends the silence by asking us to imagine a place that means peace for us, where we can be fully at rest. "See yourself there," he suggests, "breathe that peace in, feel your heartbeat. Now take the hand of the person next to you, sense their heartbeat." The African drummers start up their rhythm, and the whole assembly resounds to a single beat.

As we thronged out of the church finally, heart and senses overflowing, it struck me how this incredible celebration had served to shift the tectonic plates that hold fast our perceptions. A ritual in the truest sense, it had conspired to rearrange how we viewed each other and the world. All those costumes, races, and cultures, all touching a chord that anyone can hear because we are human and the spirit in us speaks a universal language.

Then off I went to the dean's place for lunch, a party right on the lake and everyone there. He took me to one side and said, "It's not as easy as it looks, you know. I mean, this college is going through an identity crisis right now because of all this stuff. There was nothing like it when I started in ninety-three, though they knew they couldn't carry on with the same old Presbyterian line for everyone with such a diverse body of students. So they hired me, a priest from the South Bronx and the hard end of Boston, though here I don't represent any tradition in particular. I coordinate programs on ethical and spiritual issues, along with multifaith celebrations like this one. Anyway, now that I have organized this conference next year on Spirituality in Higher Education—this is for the Ivy League colleges—the cracks are beginning to show."

Victor Kazanjian, I am coming to see, is something of a Trojan Horse. Ivy League colleges such as Wellesley are bastions of a traditional worldview that places ultimate value on objective academic study. Their whole reputation is dependent on it. As soon as you attempt to validate other forms of knowing, such as the knowledge of feelings and subjective experience, you are calling into question the superior status of the whole Western canon. That is exactly what is normally kept out of the equation. Now here he is bringing it in through the back door with celebrations like the Flower Festival and weekly groups where students sit in meditation and then discuss their spiritual journeys.

"Harvard is the same," Victor went on. "They are all the same. That is why this conference is causing shockwaves. The word *spiritual* is subjective, and therefore dangerous. Harvard has agreed to come if it is a conference on pluralism. That's safe, you see. You can have theories and discussions about that. They don't want any mention of spirituality. But that's okay, we're opening the door even so."

"It's no accident that this is all beginning in a women's college," said Victor as I was leaving. "The president here is a great example of someone who is truly wishing to embrace the intellectual and the spiritual, without needing to reject the one or the other. It is hard for her, though; there is a lot of opposition. What do you expect after centuries of domination by a worldview that values only reason and objectivity. Whatever that is," he laughed.

"Whatever that is": Victor's words ring on in my mind as I continue on to Barre, Massachusetts, to meet others who are encouraging the spirit in young people, though in a setting very different to Wellesley. Through Northampton and Amherst I pass in the autumn glow, then up a long dirt track to some inarticulate paths traced in long grass, ending in a cluster of low buildings in the middle of a wood.

Here then is the Insight Meditation Society (IMS), the one place more than any other in America responsible for the popularization of Vipassana, meditation on the breath shorn of all ritual and foreign accouterments, without religion, without even the necessity for belief, since everything is in the practice. A very American Buddhism, with echoes of Thomas Paine, who as long ago as the eighteenth century proclaimed that "my mind is my church." IMS was formed from a confluence of people in the early seventies returning from monasteries in Thailand and Burma and from devotional teachings in India. Now they have a public retreat program throughout the year, offering everything from introductory weekends to three-month sessions with meditation up to sixteen hours a day. Silence is in big demand; you have to book way ahead if you want to get a place on a cushion.

Steve and Michelle Smith live in a cabin in the woods there, and the door is open when I arrive, catching in a pool the light falling from trees.

The Smiths are part of a team of meditation teachers here, which includes writers on Buddhism like Joseph Goldstein and Sharon Salzburg. Such an idyll it is, the cabin in the woods, pine floor and simple wooden furniture, a laptop by the window, meditation hall over the way. The kind of radical self-reliance that Emerson or Thoreau would have approved of, made not at the expense of, but for the benefit of the public good.

Steve and Michelle are drinking tea as I come in, and I join them. A relaxed presence between them, words spilling easily between us and plenty of silence. They have been teaching meditation for many years, though their more recent initiatives are taking them into new territory. Steve is running meditation retreats for corporations like Monsanto, but what they really want to tell me about is their Youth Meditation Program, which they and their team run with some sixty teenagers over five days every summer.

"They come from all over the country," Steve began, "though most are from the inner cities. We get kids with chains and black leather, middle-class kids, African Americans, Puerto Ricans, all between fourteen and twenty-one years old. There are twenty-four people on staff, offering music, journalling, mime classes, chanting, and two or three discussion groups a day where we raise everything from drugs through death and peer pressure to dharma. Then we have six meditation sittings and four walking meditations a day, and personal interviews with the meditation teacher. You can imagine that at the start almost all of them do anything to avoid the meditation, but I tell you by the end they are all there waiting for the bell to go. One fourteen-year-old has got into it so seriously he now joins the nine-day adult retreats. Many of the parents are so inspired by what they see in their kids they come here to experience meditation for themselves."

"You know what they seem to get a lot from?" added Michelle. "Being made to feel welcome in a spiritual home. One that is a safe context for them to be exposed to; nondogmatic, yet spiritual, ideas like awareness and loving-kindness. The loving-kindness meditation allows them to feel that everything is okay just as it is, and that gives them a certain self-esteem, especially since the language they use comes out of their own personal experience. No one's doing a trip on him or her, so they can relax with us and with each other. In fact, the intimacy they discover with each other in the discussion groups is often something they have never experienced before, all that sharing of personal stories across boundaries of color and privilege. Teenagers just don't do that normally, especially these kind of teenagers."

What they were telling me made me wonder whether the current young generation was being attracted to Buddhism in the same way people were in the sixties and seventies. I read somewhere that Buddhism is the fastest-growing Eastern religion in America, with an estimated 750,000 adherents.

When I voiced my thoughts, Steve said it wasn't Buddhism as such that they were responding to, but to the practice of being human. When you practice awareness, it just makes sense to respond in a more open way to life as it presents itself.

"It's also about wanting to participate in the world," he added. "Many of them go away intending to start some service project. One sixteen-year-old has started his own soup kitchen. Several are going to Burma to help out on some project there, as well as to do some more meditation."

I wonder if a college like Wellesley will ever take the bold step of teaching meditation as part of its curriculum, I thought, an hour later, as I made my way back along the path through the grass to my car. Surely the wise use of the mind is an educational priority? Surely it is, but it will need a wise culture to make such a move. We are not there yet, but I was beginning to suspect that such a leap was not unimaginable.

I headed back east and before long there was a sign saying Walden. Though a national shrine of sorts, Walden Pond was quiet that afternoon, shaded as ever by the tall forest surrounding its dark waters. I ambled round the sandy shore, watching the way the sky shifted clouds against the beaches and in the ripples lapping below me. Thoreau had known these waters with an intimacy that stirs people now as it ever did: "In warm evenings, I frequently sat in the boat playing the flute and saw the perch, which I seem to have charmed, hovering around me, and the moon traveling over the ribbed bottom which was strewn with the wrecks of the forest."

The water and the forest are the same as when he lived here in his cabin; and if much of America would be unrecognizable to him today, yet his engagement with nature and practice of a radical individuality persist as ever in the American imagination. The world knows mainstream America for the self seeking individualism that has become its trademark; Thoreau's individualism was different. It was a freedom of mind he was seeking, liberation from the stultifying conformity of Concord, not to proclaim his superiority, but to be able to serve the larger community with the fruits of his dreaming. I am about to discover in Boston that this freedom of mind is thriving still; not just on the edges of mainstream society, but also where we might least expect it, in the very heart of corporate culture.

Chapter Four

Boston: A Different Kind of Bottom Line

I first met Kristen Ragusin in, of all places, the Sahara desert. Occasionally I take small groups there to walk in silence for a week, a kind of ambulatory retreat. Kristen, who lives in Boston, had come on one of these madcap journeys earlier in the year, and it wasn't long before I noticed something unusual about her. Whatever the conditions—walking into a big wind, an especially cold night, the same soup every day for a week—Kristen would always respond with a smile. Not one of those smiles that hides something different, but an obvious acceptance of whatever life threw at her. She was twenty-nine then—a lot younger than many of the other participants—but it was often to her that people would talk when they were finding the going tough.

I learned that she was a financial consultant with Merrill Lynch, and that her joy and acceptance of life had grown not in spite of but because of her daily work with her clients and their hopes and anxieties over money. Her story intrigued me, and I wanted to hear more, but a silent retreat in the desert was not the right setting; so we agreed to meet when I next came to Boston.

I left Walden Pond in time to meet her at a restaurant the same evening. Kristen was at the table already, a slight figure with a shock of black hair tumbling down to her shoulders. When we had settled in I suggested that some might consider her kind of work—with an eye on the bottom line all day—to be at odds with a life lived in the spirit.

"Oh, but I don't see life to be divided like that," she laughs. "To begin with, my work is a continual voyage of self-discovery. For all the information we have, there are still no maps or strategies that will guarantee what the market will do today. I find it truly liberating to see that there is no way I can control or know the answer. When I really got that, I saw that there never could be any closure. Yet problem-solving and the desire to make people happy is so hard to let go of! I worked and worked, studied and studied. When I finally saw that it was impossible—how like a great ocean the market is—it was a huge release. That was one of the greatest spiritual lessons I ever learned. I had the freedom then to wake up in joy and know I can only do the best I can. The strange thing is, my performance has increased the more I have let go."

She paused for a moment, then resumed her flow of thought. "There's nothing like money to reveal people's values and their sense of meaning. My engagement with clients brings up the deepest questions. Who am I? Who are these people? Often they come in scared, excited, happy, guilty, all at once. Then, financial planning is itself a process of self-discovery—where are your priorities, what do you want to do in retirement? People are generally uncomfortable with knowing who they are other than as consumers of the American capitalist myth. I know that consumerism is filling a black hole inside, so I listen for the signs of that in their story. In them, I see the richness of who we all are, how our core issues are all the same."

I wondered how that might affect her, to see herself in the stories she listens to. "What it does is to awaken compassion in me—for them, for myself, for all of us," Kristen answered. "It's as if I sit there with them aware of two levels at once—the need to get the job done, and the beauty of who they are. I hear their financial concerns, but in essence I hear their wish to love and be loved. It's both a serious business and all so silly, and the two sides each need to be honored." She laughs again, a young woman's giggle. "Every day my work shows me how tied to the earth we are, and how free we are at the same time."

My desert intuition was right, I thought. This woman is unusually free of the reactive mind. She must have learned this somewhere; steeped herself in some spiritual teaching that helps her be impeccable in the process of life, yet free of it at the same time. But no, Kristen is another natural, like Marina in Detroit. She remembers crying out at the age of nine that she didn't want to be here. A white light appeared, moved toward her, and then faded away. She would have precognitive intuitions. Among her earliest memories is the experience of feeling our intrinsic oneness, and her work has returned her to this through a long and painful process of wearing away her resistance to playing the game. Earlier on—she has been a financial consultant for several years now—she would be so physically exhausted that her body would cry out; her mind would shrink from all she had to do in a day. It was a tough arena to play in and at the end of the day a voice would wail, Why? Why?

Then, when she was twenty-two, she had a dream that changed her life. At the time she was feeling profoundly displaced, forsaken; even though, on the outside, she was already highly successful. She prayed for guidance that night, and cried for the first time in years. "If this is what life's about, it's not for me," she wept. Kristen had—and still has—no particular Christian affiliation, but that night she dreamt she was in a classroom, and Jesus walked in. He walked straight up to her, his eyes full of love. His energy filled every ounce of her being. The attention made her feel guilty and shy, and she moved away, but he moved with her.

Three times she moved away, she felt so unworthy, but each time, he followed her. The third time, she could finally accept his love. She was filled with bliss, and knew beyond all doubt that everything would be all right just as it was. He looked deep into her, eye to eye, and spoke about her later life. She felt so equal, so profoundly worthy, and she knew that to be his message for each one of us.

"When I recall the dream now," she added, "I still have the physical sensation that every tiny cell is loved and accepted; and that everything is exactly as it needs to be, no matter what. I have the sensation of a totally free and unconditional loving that is my ultimate security."

With the popularization of depth psychology, dreams have once again come to be seen as a sacred language of the soul—a direct communication from worlds that are parallel to, though not separate from, the concrete one we live in. In a time of increasing spiritual autonomy, the authority of dreams has a significant role to play in the individual journey. I remembered my own awakening one night, just before leaving England and the woman I loved, by a single image that filled me with joy for days. It was the smiling face of a radiant woman, ensconced in a scallop shell. It filled me with warmth, and I knew that although my loved one and I were parting, perhaps forever, the feminine presence was alive inside me, and would nourish me through any dark days to come if only I would remember.

"From the time of that dream," Kristen was saying, "the tension around my work relaxed. The pain and fear of building my own business has again made me put my life into God's hands. The pressures are the same, but I sit with them now in a different way."

How would that show up in her daily relationships with clients, and with the market itself, I wondered? It's one thing to say that everything is in God's hands, and another to translate that into a concrete daily experience that is something more than fatalism.

"For one thing," Kristen responded, "I no longer want my clients to change. I used to want them to get my perspective more quickly, not to have their eye only on the numbers rather than the bigger questions the

numbers pointed to. I have let go of that now, which means I can really
be with them as they are. When a new client comes in, I simply hold the
questions: Who is this soul? What does he or she cherish? That's where I
go now, and the plan is simple then. At the same time, I do all I can to
act impeccably within my role. We can never violate the play we are in.
The two levels go hand in hand; they are different, but not antagonistic
to each other. Again, my client list has risen dramatically since my own
understanding changed."

When I asked her about her personal life, how it had been touched by
the knowledge of love, she responded that she is aware in every part of her
life of the intrinsically abundant nature of existence. Whenever she buys
something new, she always gives something away. She always donates to
her clients' charities, and encourages them to invest in their own businesses, to have faith in their own enterprise. The point is, Kristen has discovered, the more she gives out, the more comes back in some other way.

"How do you see our financial situation collectively?" I asked. "Even
George Soros, one of the biggest speculators out there, is saying the game
can't go on."

"What I am seeing in our financial culture is a collective opportunity
for spiritual awakening," Kristen answered. "And that will not be painless.
The whole picture points to a showdown some time around 2012, when
the baby boomers will be in retirement. People are living longer, while
medical costs are increasing exponentially and more and more people will
be drawing social security. College costs are increasing exponentially, currently around 7 percent annually, while inflation is running at 3 percent.
So we have these accumulating costs combined with the consumer's desire
to feed the bottomless black hole, compounded with deflation and dropping returns on savings. The average fifty-year-old has just $2,500 in sav-
ings. It will be impossible to sustain the consumer's hunger with a
pittance like this, and that will inevitably fuel both a deeper questioning
and a deeper despair. We shall have to start looking at self and community in a new way, because we just won't be able to satisfy our habitual
feeding desires. We will need to see collectively that we are not in control,
and I believe the pain and sense of betrayal in that will bring about renewal."

I thought of the maverick philosopher Terence McKenna, how he has
predicted that there will be a radical change in global consciousness
around the year 2012. Kristen had not heard of him. She has simply
drawn on her intuition and her knowledge of the statistics. The time had
flown, and the restaurant had almost emptied. Before we parted I asked if
her dream of Jesus was the only one to have marked her journey in such

a significant way. She smiled and looked at me warmly. There was one other dream, she said; and she had had it in the Sahara desert.

"The main reason I came on your Sahara journey was to ask for guidance, for a reaffirmation that I was still on the right track," she explained. "It was several years since I had had that first dream, and I was beginning to wonder whether, after all, I would be better put to use in a working environment that more directly reflected my inner life. On the second night in the desert I dreamt that I was sitting at a table, when Jesus came in and pushed two oddly shaped stones toward me. I grimaced, hardly content with the message. He grimaced back at me, and said, 'Work with your stones.' 'Be more specific,' I thought; and he pushed the stones closer still. I looked at them, and knew the message was that I had been given the materials to work with; I had all I needed. I already have the raw working material to create what I'm here for, both inwardly and outwardly."

The next day, she wondered if she had misinterpreted the dream. As she walked into camp in the early evening, there in front of her were the exact stones of her dream. She almost didn't pick them up, seeing them simply as a blessing, a reconfirmation of her interpretation. Then she changed her mind, picked them up after all, and saw that they fitted perfectly into each other. She hadn't realized that in the dream—now she could see beyond all doubt that her material and spiritual life were one and the same thing.

"That is how I want to live my life," Kristen said as we parted. "I want to live in this world and use the tools I have been given: the realization that we are all one being; the release of expectation; the acceptance of people just as they are; an appreciation that our natural state is the abundance that flows from the creative and divine power that we are. Then I can see God, not in any outer spiritual practice, but in those stones, in the man who bags my groceries, in the person who just calls. In this lives the Great Peace, in this daily place of miracles."

I know that peace, I thought, as I made my way to my hotel. Yet how easily it can be broken; how easily, rather, I fall from its grace into a state of forgetting. Then life is a struggle, and the way is hard. One way to remember, though, is to pour one's love and attention into life around us, instead of being lost in self-absorption. The more we do that, as Kristen has discovered, the more life seems to return in abundance. Yet attending to others can itself be a foil that helps us avoid looking at ourselves. Self-inquiry, or examination of conscience, is not the same as self-absorption. The one leans into the process as a witness with a compassionate eye; the other is identified with a personal drama to the extent that nothing else shows up on the screen. Our inherited Christian ethic of "Love your neighbor" has all too often been used as an escape from the work of ac-knowledging one's own needs. Even so, the dictum can still apply: serve others, and free yourself.

Nowhere in Europe that I know of is this spirit expressed in the pub-lic domain to the degree that it is in the United States. An almost quasi-religious fervor for volunteerism has long been ingrained in the mythos of this country. It has drawn its force not only from the religious zeal of the early founders, but from a more secular, humanist concern for the good of the community, and of the country in general. Another reason I had come to Boston was to witness this spirit in action at the Mass Summit, which was taking place the following day.

The Mass Summit grew out of the President's Summit for America's Future, which in 1997 launched a nationwide plan for children and youth. That first summit generated some unprecedented partnerships be-tween corporations, foundations, nonprofits, faith organizations, public and private agencies, groups, and individuals. Gen. Colin Powell, who was coordinating the various initiatives, called on state delegations to hold their own summits, and in the long tradition of that state, Massa-chusetts responded first.

So in the cold clear morning of the next day I met Maryellen Vis-conti, a woman in her sixties, half my height and with the energy of a power battery, who had arranged for me to attend the summit. A broad-caster and business consultant, Maryellen had herself worked as a volun-teer in the president's office in Washington. We set off for the campus of Northeastern University, to find a choir of children singing *America the Beautiful*. There must be a few thousand people in the hall, a giant video screen on stage showing Bill Cosby welcoming us all, saying that the worst enemy of youth is boredom, so we'll get them to volunteer and they won't be bored no more.

All the regional luminaries are up there, eager to associate themselves with such a good cause: Senators Ted Kennedy and John Kerry, Governor Paul Celluci, the presidents of Bank Boston and Fleet Finance, the spon-sors, and the mayor of Boston, Thomas Menino. The mayor tells us how proud he is of the Massachusetts volunteer record, why only yesterday 10,000 people were in the streets cleaning up under the driving rain.

The president of Northeastern tells us that the two great virtues of American life are freedom of the individual and community conscience. They have long sustained each other, he says, though now volunteerism is declining, and individuals are feeling too pressured and self absorbed to look up. "This is why we need this summit," he calls out. "To encourage the young to want to give back. Volunteerism ennobles; it opens the heart, allows you to make a difference, feel part of the larger whole. America needs these qualities."

The tone of the speeches, the star turns, the song-and-dance routines—as the morning unfolds I realize I am witness to a great rallying cry of in-your-face-American-will to the good by the combined forces of state, government, and grass-roots organizations. "Say after me," cries out the CEO of the local United Way, "these are our five goals: mentor, protect, nurture, teach, serve." As one voice the entire assembly calls back the response.

"Shame on us, shame on us," declares Senator Kerry, "if thousands of kids go home after school to an empty house for hours. Shame on us as a community, not them as a pressured family." The whole place erupts in cheers and claps and a standing ovation, the senator visibly moved by his own words and the response.

With barely a moment for breath we all pick up a lunch box and head off to our chosen group for the afternoon, to have a discussion on each of the five goals. Our group focuses on the mentor action plan, which aims to establish an additional fifty thousand mentors in the state by the year 2000. (At the time, Massachusetts had just 10,000 mentors, just 3 percent of the perceived need. Over 227,000 young people under eighteen were in poverty, with over eighty-five thousand in extreme poverty.) I had already heard how positive adult role models can make a difference in young people's lives through the example of Eugene Rivers, a black pastor in Boston. Through his church, he has established mentor programs throughout the black community. When asked recently what had led to the significant drop in juvenile crime in the city, the Boston Police Department pointed to the mentor program initiated by Rivers as the single most important factor. Before the afternoon was out, our group had secured commitments from a whole variety of sectors in the community to provide mentor volunteers.

So high were the aspirations of these New Englanders, so intent were they on achieving their goals, so fired up on the fuel of American can-do, that I left convinced that the year 2000 would see their dreams realized. If heaven is ever to be made on earth, it struck me as I left, then this kind of vision, hard work, and generosity of spirit can only help it on its way.

"You're not kidding," exclaimed Maryellen. "You should have been here at the weekend, you would have seen all three in abundance. Do you know about the AIDS rides? They happen all over the country, and last Saturday more than three thousand cyclists left Boston for New York to raise money for the treatment of AIDS patients. My son took part, I was so proud of him. It was one of the most spiritual moments in my life watching them all take off. The music from *Riverdance* was playing, they were all heroes on their own quest to make a difference for the good of others. There was a minute's silence to reflect on the courage you were rousing to do the ride, then everyone took the hand of the person next to them to acknowledge that they were all in this together. It was an incredible example of how the will of the individual is heightened through a sense of community, of a shared endeavor."

"All kinds of people were there," she went on, reliving the occasion, "straight people, gays, fifteen-year-olds, seventy-year-olds. One eighteen-year-old rode his dad's bike, having lost him to AIDS already, and a seventy-three-year-old rode his son's bike in his memory. Then there was the riderless bike to represent all the people who had died of AIDS. The riders have to raise $1,500 sponsorship to take part, so it's quite a commitment. People were organized to cheer along the way, they spent two nights in camp, and finished up in Manhattan to the sound of Enya pouring into the street. I tell you, it beats church."

I guess it does. I remembered a saying of an author and dancer friend of mine, Gabrielle Roth: Sweat your prayers, the title of her book. The AIDS riders are doing that all right. Maryellen dropped me off that evening at the house of Eddie Hauben and his family, friends of Steve and Michelle Smith at IMS. I was about to have a glimpse of a whole other America. After we had settled in and I had told them about the day at the Massachusetts Summit, I happened to ask them if they practiced their inherited Jewish faith. They answered in a way that reminded me, once again, that I was in the country, par excellence, of creative synthesis, or multicultural soup, depending on your view.

"We are Jewbues," Eddie explained. "We are Jews who practice Buddhism and observe all the Jewish holy days. There's a group of us who meet every month. What we appreciate about Buddhism is its emphasis on the personal experience of truth through the practice of meditation. The Western traditions have largely lost contact with the contemplative dimension, so we use Vipassana meditation (watching the breath) to deepen our understanding of our own tradition. Our rabbi, Moshe Waldocks, is dropping by this evening so you can talk to him."

Once you start looking for the spirit, it arrives in every imaginable guise and at any time. Another glass of wine and I am delighted to meet Moshe Waldocks, who was one of the Jewish delegation that went to India a few years ago to discuss Buddhism and Judaism with the Dalai Lama.

"I see my work to be part of the Jewish renewal movement," he says as soon as he sits down, no time to waste. "Renewal has always been open to other paths, and in recent years Buddhism has been especially helpful to us. My services always start with twenty-minute meditation sittings, and in our group at Eddie's we have meditation followed by Torah discussion. It's not so strange, really. You see, the secret of Jewish longevity is that we have always been able to adapt to cultural paradigm shifts."

The great paradigm shift of the twentieth century, Moshe continues, was the holocaust. With a third of their people killed, the Zionists responded by saying the Jews should have a state of their own. Others, something like 70 percent in Europe, Moshe says, decided to assimilate, but in America at that time, in the fifties, you had to belong to something to be a good American. So here, there was the tendency to become a sort of Protestant Jew, going to synagogue on the Sabbath without religion having anything to do with your daily life.

I remind myself that what we are leading up to is the emerging presence of the renewal movement and offshoots like the Jewbues. When I ask him if there have been any more recent shifts that have helped to usher in renewal, he tells me about a major demographic study in 1990 that showed that 50 percent of Jews were intermarrying. That meant, in effect, that the Jews were disappearing.

"The strongest response to that," Moshe says, "has been a rebirth of spirituality, which also mirrors the growing interest in the culture generally in spiritual, as distinct to religious, life. The renewal of spirituality has meant that non-Jewish marriage partners have become interested in converting, because so many people today are looking for inner substance and meaning. The Protestant, white-bread kind of Judaism of the fifties just doesn't work any more. The reason so many Jews were marrying out was that there was a loss of faith. Renewal has meant that Jews can return to the tradition not as some empty form but as a means to find out who they are in a personal, psychological way as well as spiritually. Judaism is not a museum, we're interactive. Renewal allows our life experience to impact on the tradition."

One of my own resistances to the Old Testament has always been its patriarchal, authoritarian tone, and I wanted to know from Moshe how the experience of democracy had impacted Judaism.

"It has revolutionized it by the inclusion of women," said Moshe almost before the words were out of my mouth. "I am sure that in a thousand years time this will be seen as the greatest contribution made to Judaism in the twentieth century. Jewish renewal is a kind of feminist Hassidism. It's not a movement so much as an approach that anyone interested in living Judaism can adopt. For the last twenty-five years modern orthodoxy has been educating more women than men, and I can predict that in twenty years we shall see women rabbis in orthodox circles. To be honest, I think that what prevented women from being made rabbis and priests in the past were the deep-rooted psychosexual conflicts in the culture and in the male power structure. Those conflicts have far less hold on us now."

The thought crossed my mind as to whether Moshe and his friends had brought up the question of the inclusion of women with the Dalai Lama, whose own religion is overwhelmingly patriarchal and dismissive of women, but I let the thought go as he was still in full swing. He had moved on to tell me how seriously the renewal people take ritual, because symbols and the reality of the imagination were living elements for them. There was an upsurge of interest in the sanctity of the Sabbath, he said, and a return to the traditions of not working and not using the car or the phone.

"But these are not laws you have to follow because you've been told to," he explained. "That would be to miss the point. The point is the practice of awareness. In doing something different on that day, by not turning the lights on, for example, it changes your awareness. We are wanting to avoid a purely automatic, Pavlovian way of life."

Awareness: a word brought back into current coinage by the Buddhists more than anyone. The Buddhist influence among a small but significant section of Jews, I realized, should not really be surprising: practically every teacher of Vipassana meditation in Buddhist centers around America is Jewish. I can see how the clarity of mind sought in Buddhist practice is naturally attractive to a people who have lived by the lights of the mind for centuries.

"If renewal is anything," Moshe said finally as he got up to go, "it is to get to see God as a verb and not as a noun. We need a living God, one who is active in every speck of creation; one who is accessible wherever and whoever we are. To see God as a noun, some inactive being presiding over everything from above, is idolatry. In the original Hebrew God said to Moses, "I will be what I will be." That is, he will be anywhere and everywhere, in whatever form pleases him. So we are pluralists. How could we be anything else?"

A far cry from the notion of the chosen people with the one direct line to God, then. That was a relief, since the specialness of the Jews had always been something of an obstacle to my appreciation of their tradition. Moshe had opened a door in my mind onto a whole new way of appreciating the Jewish faith. Which was fortunate, because when I left Boston the next day it was for the Catskills, to take part in a renewal retreat for Rosh Hashanah, the Jewish New Year.

Chapter Five

Rosh Hashanah in the Catskills

I remember crossing a bridge over a lake on the edge of New London, Connecticut. I remember a red sign saying Mystic Harbor and a dozen ducks on a floating white board, low wooden buildings, mostly white, gliding by, woods, and more lakes. Then I remember the train moaning its way through the backcountry of New York and as in a dream I am lifted by my intentions into a short-line bus. This bus hurries me into the woods of the Catskills to an old vacation camp with a new name and identity, Elat Chayyim, the renewal people have called it.

The woman in registration tells me the Catskills are a graveyard for Hasidic vacation camps, relics of the fifties; this is the only one that has found a new purpose. I walk over to my room in a wooden chalet, sit on the iron bed, on the edge of tears suddenly. Where do they come from, these fountains of sadness? From a lost love far away, her name is beloved; from a wave of exile in the home of the exiles, from the yellowing leaves of the tall trees outside. I don't know the source of sadness, its roots somewhere deep in the warp of being human.

That evening some fifty of us gather in the big house. Jeff Roth and his wife, Joanna Katz, both rabbis and founders of Elat Chayyim, start by telling us that Rosh Hashanah, the new year, is when everyone is seen in the light of the divine. It is the time of the great turning, the turning to God.

"But Jewish renewal doesn't see this turning in the traditional way," Jeff explains. "The old way was to try to get as close to God as possible. Our model is inclusive, one in which everything is interconnected. God isn't anywhere else, outside of where we are now. God is the one flowing web in which we all partake. With this view, our task is not to get anywhere, but to wake up to where and who we already are. See, Jewish renewal is a truly holistic Judaism. It engages the whole person. It is shaped by the whole people, not just by Torah scholars; and it is concerned for the whole planet, along with everything and everyone on it. How could it be otherwise if we see life to be one interconnected whole, which is what unified field theory makes clear beyond a doubt?"

"Sounds pretty Buddhist to me," retorts one man in his seventies. "Why do you call this a Jewish retreat?"

"It's as Jewish as it is Buddhist," replies Jeff. "You will find the same understandings in the mystical traditions of all religions. The Bal Shem Tov had a unified view. He said that since there was only one God, then God was not exclusive to any religion. The Talmud says that there are many mountains and they all touch the sky. And Buber said that the holy is what connects us. What's new is not the perspective, but the fact that it is coming into the foreground now, supported by the science of quantum field theory."

Jeff and Joanna take it in turns to tell a few stories of the Bal Shem Tov, accompanying each other on the guitar, and then Jeff goes on to explain something of the name of Jawheh. *Y,* the first letter, he tells us is the smallest one in the Hebrew alphabet. It is a point of emptiness, meaning I am holy, and designates spirit. *H* means all is clear, and represents the domain of mind. *V* signifies you are loved, and points to the emotional level. The last *H,* meaning it is perfect, signifies the body. So the name of God encompasses everything we are.

"It was forbidden to say the name," Jeff continues, "so traditionally the word *Adonai* was used, meaning lord, or king. But now that we have an integrated, biological model of life, we in Jewish renewal say Ruach Alaam, spirit of the universe. That spirit is breath, so when we say praise his name or remember him, we are calling attention to our own breath. Seen in this way *YHVH* looks so":

> *Y is the empty point before the inbreath*
> *H is the inbreath*
> *V, the longest letter, means fullness*
> *H is the outbreath.*

"So let us praise that spirit with our breath," he ends, picking up his guitar. "Blessed are you, Shekinah, guiding compassion of the universe, who kindling this light, fills us with the holiness of the Day of Remembrance. Blessed are you, Yah, spirit guide of the planet. You have kept us alive, you have sustained us, you have brought us to this moment. Let us bless the source of all blessings! The One. Every single One. Each One joined and united to the One."

As the prayers ebb away candles are passed round and we all light one in honor of the new year. People bring in food, and we dip challa (bread) and apples into bowls of honey to carry sweetness along with us into this new era. Finally, before going off in the dark to our chalets, we break into small circles and share with each other the gifts the old year brought us.

"We call that dialogical davening," says Arthur Waskow when I mention the sharing circles the next day. Arthur is a large, jovial man with a lush growth of beard who is the director of the Shalom Center, a Jewish renewal center in Philadelphia. He is also one of the intellectual leaders of the movement, and Jeff had invited him and his wife, Phyllis Berman, to help run the retreat. He tells me that dialogical davening is a way of experiencing the I-thou relationship that Buber spoke of. In sharing themselves with each other, they create a circuit through which the electricity of God can pass from heart to heart. Renewal, he adds, sees our relationship with God to be a horizontal as well as vertical exchange. That's also why they emphasize the equal right of both men and women to have a say in shaping what Judaism is.

"I suppose from a conventional point of view we are quite radical," he continues. "In our willingness to learn from other traditions, but even more, in our conviction that God intends for both families of Abraham, not just one, to live freely in Israel. And also in our wish for Judaism to go beyond itself and contribute to the healing of the earth and of the non-Jewish societies in which we live."

Arthur leaned back in his chair. We were eating breakfast, bagels and scrambled eggs, and he paused to chew on a mouthful.

"There's something else, too," he said finally. "We need to encourage a new ethic about how much time we spend at work and how much in rest and re-creation. The sabbath is making a comeback as far as we are concerned. We need to take time to let in the next great wave of I–thou-ing, of love and restful *be*-ing, of deeper, broader, more meaningful community into the world."

What a simple thing, to take a day off a week from secular life, I reflect. Yet how difficult to step off the wheel, to go against the cultural norm. For the first time, I could see the sense of not even using electricity, the phone, or the car. As Moshe Waldocks in Boston had said, it is a question of awareness, of shifting ourselves out of the general hypnosis.

When I asked Arthur what had led him to become a rabbi, he surprised me by saying he was a political activist till he was thirty-five, and not interested in religion at all.

"Then Martin Luther King was shot, there was an uprising in D.C., which is where I was living at the time. It was Passover, and I went home, as I had done every year of my life, to begin the Seder, a ritual meal with intense retelling of the story of the Exodus from slavery. This time, however, something entirely new happened. Suddenly, I had a kind of vision, where I saw the U.S. Army, who were enforcing a curfew against all Black people being on the streets, as Pharoah's army. My whole life changed. I devoted myself to the study of the Torah, became a rabbi, and developed my own form of Jewish renewal. Rabbi Zalman Schachter was a great inspiration in those years. He was in Philadelphia, sowing the seeds for what Jewish renewal has become."

Arthur finished his eggs and went off to begin the morning session of Torah analysis. Jonah, he tells us, was cast upon the waters. Ishmael was cast under a bush when his mother had no means of feeding him. We have all felt like this at one time or another, cast out and left to fend for ourselves. But what we need to understand is that Ishmael and Jonah were not discarded, they were made open to transformation through the power of Providence. Wandering this great country on my own, I have already had more than a sense of what it must have felt like for Jonah. In any event, Arthur warmed me with his rendering of the text, and that afternoon, in our sharing group, I, the only non-Jew at the retreat, felt at home.

When the seventy-year-old next to me tells us how he longs in this New Year to be free of his anger toward his long dead father, my judging mind is washed away by a sense of comradeship for this man I don't even know. Others—there are men and women from twenty to the late seventies—tell how they combine their Judaism with Buddhist or yoga practices, while almost all of them are returning to their original faith after exploring elsewhere.

Later in the afternoon, Joanna Roth explains to me that there was a sharing group for gays, a twelve-step sharing group, and a group for sexual abuse victims. It is very Jewish, she says, to believe that the voice of revelation is to be found among marginalized people. What they have done at Elat Chayyim is to extend and adapt that belief to contemporary circumstances. Then she adds that one of the most important ramifications of women exploring religion was the issue of inclusivity. As a woman she couldn't assume that the established categories necessarily address reality as she experiences it. That had to change now, with so many women entering the seminaries. The first woman became rabbi in 1979, and now 50 percent of the intake for reform and reconstructed rabbinical schools are women.

Joanna is a chaplain at a local college in the Catskills, a mother and a rabbi. A busy lady, though you wouldn't know it from the way she holds a conversation, as if she is there with you for as long as you need her. An hour or two later I was privy to another conversation on the short line back into Manhattan, a man and a woman behind me.

"You know, all it takes is for someone to say I believe in you. A little faith in yourself, and you're on your way, I'm telling you."

"Yeah, well, ten years ago me talk to you about God, you gotta be nuts, man. Now, I tell you, every day is a fresh start."

God talk is everywhere in America, it seems. I went that evening to B'nai Jeshrun, a synagogue always full to overflowing on West 89th. How different this was to the Catskills renewal, the solemnity, the dignity, the beauty, too, of an hour of song in Hebrew, the great longing wafting around the cavernous space in minor key. Rolando Matalan, the young, charismatic rabbi, heads a conservative community on highly liberal lines. He shares many of the views of the renewal people, but conveys them in a more traditional form. Here, the guitars and tambourines of Eilat Chayim are replaced with a full choir and professional soloists. It is obviously the right mix for the upper West side, his congregation being one of the largest in the city.

These days are hard, Rolando is telling the people. The days of Roshashannah are spent in hours of prayer, day after day, culminating finally in the feast of Yom Kippur. But our hearts need softening, he says, in a quiet voice lifted to the back only by the quality of the microphone. And this is the way, beating, beating at the door. Turn us, as we turn to you—let this be our prayer. He tells the assembly how privileged he feels to be in their company, that they are willing to return here to pray daily. Then the lament begins again, and me not understanding a word, though it didn't matter, the key said it all: give me a rock to strike against the rock of my heart, so that the waters of a new life might flow. Only when we cry out, empty and at the end of our resources, shall we be filled. God is merciful. Let him come to me, let him come to us all in this New Year, we who suffer and are found wanting.

Chapter Six

New York Visions

The following Sunday I arrive at Lincoln Center to find several hundred people already there, with more pouring in all the time. At the front of the sloping auditorium is a podium decked with flowers. A body builder in gold lamé and bare midriff swings down the aisle and plants himself in the front row next to an elderly black lady with a yellow rose in her straw bonnet. A large man strides to the mike, belts out a song at the top of his tenor voice, and then ushers in a tall woman in hugging long dress with a slit, high heels and a blond bouffant that was probably set for all time in the sixties. This is Olga Butterworth, who must be in her seventies; and this is the Butterworth's service at the Lincoln Center Unity Church.

I lose the first few minutes of her talk because as she starts a tall black woman with half a breast bulging from a tight black waistcoat, bronze curls, and legs that go on forever, sways down the aisle followed by an Indian woman in a body suit that threatens to divert my attention for the rest of the service. Then there is the man next to me, who must have flown in from Malibu, blond locks cascading over his black surfing gear.

Olga has welcomed Eric, her husband, onto the stage by now, and they stand there erect together, hand in hand to begin with, as Eric begins to speak about the need to reconstruct our concept of God. Forget anthropomorphism, he says, and also the idea that God is inside us like a raisin in a bun. There is nowhere where God is not, nothing in which he cannot be found. Time to replace the notion of worship with worthship, he goes on at a pace that has me straining to hear him. We are worth our place here, and we are called to play our part as co-creators. We are here to celebrate the spirit in our own unique way as it moves through our lives, just as the ocean moves through the wave.

This tall, frail man has been a Unity minister for over fifty years, and for more than thirty-five years he has led the Unity Center of Practical Christianity. He speaks with no trace of charismatic theatricality, no bombast, no apparent wish to play on the emotions of the audience. He almost mumbles, speaking so fast that it is difficult to catch the whole of his meaning. Yet there is a quality of being in the two of them, an unapologetic presence that finds no need to play to the crowd, which holds the room's attention undivided. They stand there as one, gazing straight ahead out over the audience. Be still and know, is what they are saying.

Eric tells us how a woman phoned in to his radio show and said she had never heard any response to her prayers. "What are you waiting for?" I asked her. "Some voice to tell you the answer, that it's all okay? Prayer is not to someone sitting in the clouds. Prayer is you, yourself abiding as spirit, letting that source be there as you. Emerson said it a century or more ago. 'Why should we not have a firsthand direct experience of God?' he said. He also said that to be a contemporary influence, religion must be redefined for every generation in the light of that day's thought. That is what we are doing here. We are no longer in the time of great gurus and masters. We are the ones who can be that for ourselves."

Eric went on for a good forty-five minutes, the same thought being delivered in a dozen ways, every minute of it arresting because you knew this man meant what he said, lived what he said, and knew you could live what he said. The whole service had a kind of no-nonsense air to it, the big tenor and other music lifting the heart now and again, but the message was the thing, more than any community feeling; and also the silence that the Butterworths drew us into as Eric finished speaking.

As I joined the streams of people on the way out, it occurred to me that the individual signature and flair so evident here and there among the audience was endorsed by Eric's view of life as a unique and individual expression of spirit. After all, why not gold lamé? Why not a celebration of the body in a skintight dress, all the more when you are in your seventies? Where is the spirit if not in the senses? Where would we be without the body, and anyway, this is New York, if you can't flout the staidness of conformity here then where can you?

I know that show is the mark of Narcissus, who wants to be looked at, adored, and admired, but I would like to think that every now and then it can also be the mark of an inner radiance that is willing to reflect itself in the material world. The notion of the spiritual as sackcloth and ashes and pious humility doesn't go with the tone of the age. We have to work with what we've got, start where we are. What we've got is a large dose of ego, sanctioned, even demanded, by the culture we live in; and it's no good pretending we don't. What we've also got, according to Eric Butterworth—what we are—is the radiance of spirit waiting to be recognized and claimed. If it comes in gold lamé, then so much the better.

Something about Eric's message prompted me to take a trip all the way downtown to the Staten Island ferry. Not to go to Staten Island, but to get an open, unencumbered view of one of the world's greatest symbols of human aspiration. Gazing over the water toward the Statue of Liberty, I remembered how deeply the history of America was entwined with the story of our developing understanding of freedom; and how fitting it was that the torch of freedom was conceived and fashioned in Europe and then offered as a gift so that the new world could light its flame.

I know Lady Liberty is up there in plastic, with the best of kitsch, on mantelpieces all over the world. I know her name has been taken in vain by market forces, brutal repressions, greed, hatred, and envy; that Philip Morris ads once carried a picture of Lech Walesa and a quote on freedom and the Bill of Rights, implying we all have the freedom to poison ourselves with cigarettes. Yet I believe that what she has to say is even more poignant now because of all the mud in her eye.

Freedom in the Magna Carta was limited to the rights of white English noble males. The American Declaration of Independence extended that to all white landowning males. Nearly a century later, the abolition of slavery cut across a behavioral pattern that had been worldwide for millennia. Universal suffrage in the early twentieth century marked a quantum leap in our understanding of what it meant to be human: suddenly, the other half of the species was acknowledged to be worthy of a say in human affairs. Then in 1964 the Civil Rights Act recognized the inherent equality of the races, and most recently, in 1974, the Endangered Species Act has extended the concept of rights to include nonhumans. We have now come to the point of declaring that Homo sapiens is a part of the web of life. If Jefferson were with us today he would be calling for a Declaration of Interdependence.

Now here was Eric Butterworth and others like him all over the land proclaiming that there is nowhere where God is not; nowhere and nothing that does not also partake in the value and worth conferred by the recognition of being divine. Butterworth is democratizing God, not by devaluing the divine but by raising life up to its own ultimate value.

All our previous declarations of freedom continue to suffer outrage and abuses. Yet once stated they are like the genie that has flown out of the bottle and cannot be put back. This last, most audacious idea—that of our inherent inner freedom—has also taken wing, the harbinger perhaps of a truly democratic individuality of the spirit that will eventually replace the waning star of rugged frontier individualism.

As the ferry drew level with the goddess I envisioned myself climbing the spiral stairs to the window in her crown, and gazing out across the whole land of America. I imagined the struggles that the country had been born out of: the continuing tragedy of the native peoples whose land had been usurped in the name of freedom; the hordes of impoverished Mexicans stealing at night over the border; the street people filling the doorways of all the great cities; the devastation of the forests of Alaska and the Northwest, far more extensive than the damage done to the rain forest in Brazil; the ghostly crowds with empty eyes in the shopping malls and casinos; cities like Miami or New Orleans, with more homicides in a month than the whole of England has in a year.

I thought of all this, the fallout from the grand idea of freedom, and then I thought of all the people I had met and had still to meet on my journey who were turning another way. America, I saw, truly is the first universal nation; it is facing challenges of integration that no other nation has ever contemplated. Its destiny is to discover for humanity the deeper meaning of individual, community, and their interdependence. There is a freedom, I realized, encoded in the inscription on its dollar bill, E Pluribus Unum, Out of The Many, One—a riddle the country has still to unravel. The old polarity of self and other is beginning to be more and more difficult to sustain in a world of increasing interdependence. A world where an action or event in one part of the world sends ripples everywhere else, and where you can be on top of the heap one moment and in the gutter the next.

One mark of true individuality and freedom of spirit is precisely the recognition that we are all in this together. Of all the groups that I have met in America, the one that uses the notion of one for all and all for one most successfully is undoubtedly the twelve-step program in its many guises. When I got back to Manhattan that afternoon I decided to follow the advice of my friend Tony. Tony, a psychiatrist, describes himself as a recovering alcoholic, and knowing I was writing a book to be called *Sacred America* he had urged me to accompany him to one of his AA meetings.

He took me that evening down into the basement of the YMCA on Central Park West, into a room with panels of blue Turkish tiles on cream walls. It felt like the vestibule to a sauna. A large circle of people, mostly women, is sitting in the middle of the room. One woman is reading aloud from the twelve steps. "Let's use step number ten as our theme today," she said. "Love everybody."

Nothing like starting at the top, I thought.

"For me," the woman went on, "sobriety is coming to be as much about holding the door open for someone as it is about not having a drink. It's about the daily encounter with the cabdriver, the store attendant, the person on the street corner. If I can't share some warmth with them, then I have no business talking spiritual."

"Well, for me," said the young black man next to her, "it's about giving up the voice that wants to scream out, "Don't you know who I am?" I was looking for an apartment to buy near here and walked into a building wearing a baseball cap.

"Can I help you?" the guy said.

"I'm looking for an apartment."

"Yeah, are you sure this is the kind of building you need?"

"I only just managed that time not to blow it. Then later, when I had bought one in that block, I came in the door with some bags and the doorman thought I was a deliveryman. 'No, I live here,' I said. He was profusely apologetic, saying he'd only just started. 'That's okay, no problem,' I said. It was such a relief for me not to get off on my indignation. It saved me so much energy, and let the doorman feel okay."

We went round the circle, everybody introducing themselves by name as a recovering alcoholic. Most people have been dry for years, yet still call themselves alcoholic. Someone says they have been dry for thirty days and everyone claps. We clap two anniversaries, too. I feel a fraud because I am not alcoholic, though when my turn comes I tell them I am a recovering romance-aholic. One addiction is like another after all; they are all futile attempts to fill an emptiness we may not know we have.

An old guy named Jack quoted various books he had read on love, and finished by saying how much harder he found it to receive love than to give it. "I pray for people I have a hard time with," continues Thelma. "I don't even know that I believe in God, let alone believe in prayer. But I do it anyway. It seems the only thing to do when I don't know what else to do."

"When I first came to AA," said Joan, "there was this loudmouthed woman I couldn't stand. She would start gabbing and I would stomp out of the room. Then I noticed that for some reason other people seemed to like her. One day, I couldn't believe it; she called me up and asked me if I'd like to go for coffee. From that day on we've been the best of friends. Her act of kindness opened a door in me. She showed me how limited my perceptions are by snap judgments and prejudice."

On our way out Tony suggested that more people now come to a sense of the spiritual life through twelve-step programs than any other medium. There are well over a hundred different types of recovery programs now, with a combined attendance in excess of 15 million. There is even a program for the children of unreformed hippies! Tony explained that, whatever the particular addictive circumstance you are recovering from, the program is always based on the premise that life is unmanageable, and that our only recourse is to turn our life over to a higher power.

"I would say that this is true for everyone," Tony went on. "But if you are an alcoholic or drug user it sort of stares you in the face, if only you are willing to look. Access to that power is found through prayer and also through the common willingness of the individuals in the group to share their vulnerabilities and to act as a support for each other. God, in other words, is in human relationships as much as anywhere. He is in the small victories, the tiny word of encouragement, the shift from anger to compassion. He is in the daily particularities, and that is what we try and work with, one step at a time."

He's right, I think: my life is totally unmanageable, blown as I am like a straw in the wind from one preoccupation to the next, hesitant as I am to fall into the one love that has been at my shoulder since the day I was born. Lord have mercy on us, we of little faith and big talk. I know that what Eric Butterworth says is true. I know, and not just with the mind alone, that there is nowhere to go and nowhere to look other than where we already are. But sometimes the clouds come by and I lose my bearings and am ready to clutch at the nearest life raft, only to find of course that it is sinking along with everything else.

And yet still I hold on sometimes to memories, to pleasures and pains, still I suffer the pain of it, still I try and make concrete what cannot be captured, sunlight in a tree. And I shall do so as long as I myself need to feel solid inside, need to fill the gap in the belly with substance. Not just the alcoholic, but anyone engaged in the interior journey must pass through that vale of fear and emptiness to reach the other side. All our cultural addictions hide a deeper, simpler joy. "The sacred attitude," said Thomas Merton, "is one which does not recoil from our own interior emptiness, but rather penetrates into it with awe and reverence, and with the awareness of mystery."

We are sitting now at the polished black table in Tony's apartment on the fourteenth floor. I gaze out over the dark stretch of Central Park to the glitter of the south side spires and in the distance to an endless column of lights pouring down 60th Street on the East Side, all those people hoping for fun tonight. A few blocks north the trees are draped in lights, ice blue ones, to announce the presence of the park restaurant. All those dinners waiting to be eaten, bottles to be emptied. Meanwhile, the world goes on. Meanwhile, the woman pushing her cart down Broadway is still aching with cold. Earlier this evening I had pressed some money into her hand. She turned to thank me, beamed from ear to ear, and opened her coat to reveal a bulging womb.

"I want better for this little one," she said, eyes gleaming with a dream she hardly dared speak. "I'm gonna get a house soon as I can and look after him well. If I can do that my life will have been worthwhile."

Tony went off to make coffee, and I picked up *The New York Times* from the polished black table. A piece caught my eye about a mother who had been bitter and angry for years at her daughter's murderer, and who prayed one night not to have to live the rest of her life like that. In that instant, the article said, she felt an overwhelming descent of love and was compelled there and then to write to the murderer in San Quentin, California. She told him how she had felt all those years, and how she no longer wanted to feel that way. When she mailed the letter she felt a surge of forgiveness. Three days later the prisoner wrote back saying her letter had been a gift from God. Then she went to see him, and they cried together across the visitor's table. Now she sees him regularly.

The newspaper piece was on the power of forgiveness. It went on tell the story of Kathy Becker, whose fourteen-year-old daughter, Loren, had been killed by a hit-and-run driver. The prosecutor rang to tell Kathy that Jorge, the seventeen-year-old driver, was curled up in a fetal position, rocking back and forth, unable to lift his head. The boy, he said, could speak only in whispers. He kept saying he wished he could exchange his life for Loren's.

"Suddenly," said Kathy, "I felt a mother's compassion for this emotionally devastated child. I saw no enemy, no culprit, just a heartbroken child who was frightened and alone. In my heart I became this broken child. I felt his pain to be the same as my own. In that moment his absolute innocence was revealed to me. 'Tell him I forgive him,' I wept.

And then, starting deep down in my abdomen, I felt new words, alien words, coming out through my tears. 'And tell him I love him.' I didn't think I'd ever be able to get those words out, because there was another voice in me that was saying, 'Girl, this time you are going too far. How will you ever be able to live with this?' But a kinder, inner voice overruled. 'It has been spoken. You will get used to it.' A huge burden evaporated from my shoulders. I still missed Loren. I still wanted her back. But something essential had changed. My husband and I asked the judge for leniency and Jorge was given six months. I visited him when I could, and we helped each other heal the pain of life in the aftermath of Loren's death."

The sirens are howling again, a fire or a death, maybe, and the doors of 5th Avenue are open wide to the droves of hungry ones who long to cover up the hole in the heart with a new coat. Yet wherever people are gathered in such concentration, and with such ambitions and lust for life, there is I believe an invisible countertow equally forceful that streams around the city from heart to heart. It whispers all the while in the din of the traffic that even so, even so, all shall be well, whoever we are, no matter how lonely. And all over this beating heart of a city, there are those like Kathy Becker who have changed lives forever with a single word or gesture of kindness.

The last time I had looked out over the city from this table, I remembered, I was with my love. Even with the vision of an ever-present fullness like the one I had had on leaving England; even with the knowing that all is well, the grief of a departing love only leaves the heart in its own time and measure.

Her absence made me think suddenly of the elderly couple I was going to meet the next day, their love and creative outpourings spanning more than half a century. I began to tell Tony something of their story. The lives of Frederick and Claske Franck, I explained, have all the color, diversity, and romance of questing Renaissance artists. Frederick Franck left his native Holland to study medicine and dentistry in Edinburgh, and then promptly wrote a best-selling piece of comical fiction on the trials and revelations of the dentist's chair. While Franck was at Edinburgh, Albert Schweitzer happened to give the Gifford lectures, profoundly impressing the young man with his humanity and selfless service. Shortly before the war Franck closed his practice in London's Harley Street, emigrated to the United States, and held his first one-man show of drawings in New York. Some twenty years later, he was to receive an honorary degree in fine arts from the University of Pittsburgh.

In the States, Franck continued to pursue his careers of dentist, writer, and artist, all with equal success. Then, in 1955, when he was already married with a one-year-old child, he met the love of his life. He was in Europe, en famille, and his latest manuscript was being typed up in Holland by some woman who had been recommended to him, but whom he had never met. Some alterations were needed to the manuscript, and he decided to meet her on the beach to dictate the changes to her. They were walking by the shore, when a thunderstorm blew up and Claske—for it was she—threw off her shoes and started dancing in the rain, laughing like a child. Franck followed suit. He was in ecstasy.

"My God," he thought, "she sees what I see!" ("And still does," he added, when he told me the story, almost forty-five years later). He turned to her and exclaimed, "Do you know who you are? You are my wife!"

And so it was. Their great adventure together had begun. A couple of years later, one of Franck's dental patients, a South African heiress who knew Schweitzer, told him how badly the doctor needed an oral surgeon in Africa. Franck always responds when he hears the call, and in weeks he and Claske were at Lambarene, where they were to work with Schweitzer for three years. When he wasn't working on the teeth of a local, Frederick was drawing; drawing Schweitzer, the hospital, the local people, the sick, the rows of people waiting in casualty, the river, the village, the life of traditional Africa. The natural joy and humanity of the people in Africa stirred Franck deeply, as did Schweitzer's principles of reverence for life and radical simplicity. Schweitzer would run his operation with no official aid or publicity, raising money himself by giving periodic organ recitals in Europe. It was the kind of foreign aid where you put nothing less than yourself—body, mind, and soul—on the line, and it was a principle that was to mark Franck's work for the rest of his life.

Within a year of the Francks' return to the United States, the Vatican Council of 1962 had begun. Franck heard Pope John XXIII's first speech to the council on the radio, and was so inspired by its message of hope at a time when the world was submerged in the Cuban Missile Crisis, that he dropped all he was doing, followed an irresistible impulse of the heart, and flew to Rome to draw the proceedings. He was convinced the council would be a great watershed in the spiritual life of the world, and that it had to be recorded. The only difficulty was that no observers were admitted, but that was secondary; Franck could only respond as the artist he was, and pick up his bags and go.

He contacted Graham Greene, an old friend and admirer of Franck's work, to see if he could pull any strings. Greene gave him an introduction to the English archbishop, but nothing came of it. In Rome, it transpired that Claske knew an American bishop who was staying in a convent with fifteen other bishops. The Francks began visiting the convent, Frederick losing no opportunity to draw the good bishops.

Then one morning, Franck, dressed in black hat and suit, went arm in arm with the American bishop into Vatican II. He made friends with the head of the gendarmerie of the Vatican, who was so fascinated by Franck's work that he made sure the artist would get the best view each day. The gendarme even showed him the men's room behind the altar, encouraging Franck to draw the bishops hoisting their robes. Franck went to all four sessions of Vatican II, from 1962 to 1965, and was the only unofficial observer. The whole adventure was a love story. He had never, he told me later, loved anyone except Claske as he had loved Pope John XXIII. Though he drew him often in those years, he never spoke to him.

He was for Franck a true bodhisattva, an utterly natural human being who had overcome all ego in the service of humanity.

On the very day of the pope's death, Frederick received a medal of the pontificate in appreciation of his drawings of the council. The drawings had been collected in a book, *An Outsider in the Vatican.* Again, Franck was prompted to go to Rome, this time to draw Pope John on his bier.

Before they went to Rome in 1962, the Francks had already bought a ramshackle old house near Warwick, New York, that they had begun to restore. On the other side of a stream was the ruin of an eighteenth-century water mill, which had long been used as a garbage dump. On their return from Pope John's funeral, Frederick had a vision of the garbage dump being transformed into a transreligious sanctuary, an oasis dedicated to the spirit that he had heard through the voices of Albert Schweitzer, Pope John XXIII, and also the Zen master D. T. Suzuki, whom he had met in New York in the fifties. He saw it all, a multimedia work of art with a roof that would soar like the wings of a dove, and sketched it immediately. Now, more than thirty years later, I said, getting up from the table and leaving Tony to prepare dinner for his wife, I am about to see it for myself, *Pacem in Terris,* Peace on Earth, there by the stream that runs by their house.

I stepped off the bus in the main street of Warwick the next day, and a wiry woman with a long, Modigliani face, and short gray hair, stretched out her hand to greet me. Claske Franck, in her eighties, has the vitality of a woman thirty years younger. She would need it to keep pace with her husband. She is the one who administers their affairs, produces their handwritten newsletter, *The Shoestring,* and responds to the continual flow of letters and calls from a public that seems to have more need than ever of a *Pacem in Terris.* More than a hundred people a week make the pilgrimage to the Franck's extraordinary sanctuary, and the Francks have no paid help to assist them.

"The idea is that it runs itself," Claske explains. "Although it is never quite like that. But it is free, we have no gift shop or anything for sale, not even a theory or ideology. So it is more a matter of being willing to let people wander through our garden and be responsible for themselves and the impressions they receive. We want *Pacem in Terris* to be a reminder of what cannot be bought, sold, or advertised—the fullness of life."

We drove out of the town past fruit orchards and pumpkins for sale and turned down a lane, which ended in front of a house by a stream. We passed through a wooden gate into a garden with two black metal fish with large eyes planted side by side on sticks in the grass. I could see that other sculptures were placed right down and even into the stream. The house felt like an English cottage more than a New York home—low ceilings and doors, exposed stone, narrow oak staircase. Frederick was sitting at the table, his legs on a stool. His wonderful dome of a head, a sculpture in itself, was fringed with wisps of white hair around his ears. His eyes gleamed a welcome, his face broke into a wholehearted smile as we came in the door.

A shared pot of green tea and he was up and ready to take me to *Pacem in Terris.* Down the lane a few yards we went, over the bridge and through another gate to a building by the stream with a wooden roof that soared up like the wings of a dove from low stone walls, just as he had imagined all those years ago. By the stream, near the door, a round steel moon of a face, some four feet in diameter, looked on through closed eyes.

"The Original Face interests me because it is the source of all," Frederick said. "You know what Hui Neng said, 'the meaning of life is to see.' Nicholas of Cusa said much the same thing in Latin 'in every human face is visible the Face of faces veiled as in a riddle.' "

The moon face dreaming awake: it was a theme I was to see repeated in a rhythmical way around *Pacem in Terris,* along with Frederick's other favorite motif, the fish, inherited from his Catholic heritage. He turned to the door of the building, a massive wooden sculpture in the form of the sun and its rays, and pushed it open. I saw that it turned on a central axis, so that only one-half of the door was open at any one time. To remind us, Franck murmured, that we walk into this sacred space as we walk into life, alone and silently. We stepped into a dim cave of a room with stained glass windows and an amphitheater that rises steeply away from an open arena with a pit full of water that stems not from the river but from springs in the rocks. Living water, then; a lifespring. Over the pit, where once the mill wheels had turned, now floats a fish carrying three candles.

I looked around me and marveled at this ninety-year-old man from whose hand had sprung everything I could see. He had cleared the old mill of rubble, built and designed the new structure himself, and out of stone, wood, and earth had made what was now a sculpture in its own right, one you could walk into, sit down in, and climb out of renewed. He had carved the door, made the stained-glass windows and every other object in sight. *Pacem in Terris,* I realized, was one man's act of artistic faith: a work of art outside the parameters of the art world, and also a religious statement unconfined by any religion.

Frederick suggested I climb to the top of the amphitheater and let the whole work act on me from there. I sat for a few minutes in the semidarkness, letting the *Pacem* of the place seep in. My eyes fell on a recess in the wall below me, with its dozens of flickering candles. The vault of the ancestors, Frederick explained, whom we carry with us not from the past, but as a presence that lives on in our own genes. I asked him a question and was astonished to hear the clarity of my own voice and his response. He added that the exceptional acoustics made *Pacem* the perfect place for chamber music, and that they ran a series of concerts every year.

As I joined him down by the pit of living water and followed him back out through the sun door, Frederick told me that artists had volunteered concerts there, plays, poetry readings. Lovers had married there, children had been christened; *Pacem in Terris* had been host to Catholic, Protestant, Jewish, Buddhist, and Shinto ceremonies, and to countless of the unaffiliated, but no less religious, who have found it conducive to reflection, meditation, and prayer.

He led me back out through the gate and over the road to another stretch of grass by the river to show me his sculpture known as *Hiroshima—The Unkillable Human*. Passing the *Every One Face,* another moonlike contemplation, and the carving of a white dove, we came to a human figure, larger than life size, head craning upward, hands and feet wide apart, that had been cut away from an erect sheet of black metal. Through the human aperture I could see, perhaps twenty yards further on, the same shape in black silhouette cut out of the same material. I had seen a replica of this sculpture in the Cathedral of St. John the Divine in New York, and knew there were others in Nanzan University, Japan; Washington, D.C.; and Sarajevo, Bosnia. I could feel for myself now why the Francks often referred to *Pacem* as an "oasis of inwardness." All these sculptures, icons, shrines, were pointing me back to the human condition; to the current of life that ran its course in the midst of all suffering and joy, a current that I shared with everyone.

A few minutes there in silence and we made our way back to the Franck's own front door, and round the house to the Resurgence Garden, an organic garden that, Franck explained, was a symbol of the rehabilitation of Mother Earth from all the violations we had inflicted upon her. We walked down by the waterfall to the *uroburos,* symbol of eternal life, again in metal, and on down the path to the seven-element steel-and-glass icon that Franck calls *The Seven Generations.* Seven tall rectangles of metal with the head and shoulders of a human cut out of each one, stretched away from us all in a row, so we could see and feel the echo effect of our actions on the seven generations to come.

"The idea for that came while I was on the phone," Franck explains. I had to wait in a call line, and I started doodling. Then I began talking, looked back at the doodle, and saw *The Seven Generations.* All my sculptures are like that; they come from nowhere. Paintings I can't predict. I stopped having exhibitions in 1965, I was so disillusioned by the gallery scene, the whole modern art world seemed to me to be one of self-deception. As for books, they come when I can't help it."

I looked about me at the life work of Frederick Franck, and realized that everywhere the same theme was celebrated. Schweitzer would have called it "reverence for life." It was this that impressed me, I realized: the effect of the whole, rather than the virtue of any one work. The indomitable spirit of a single individual, whose entirely self-supported, self-generated love and veneration for life gave inspiration and serenity to the constant stream of people who found their way here.

"People often ask us," laughed Franck as he led me back to the house, "what we get out of all this; why we go to such trouble, even, with the Resurgence Garden, opening our beloved backyard to strangers. They cannot believe we don't have some ulterior motive, and I tell them we do: what we really want is to demonstrate that you can do something without an ulterior motive! That is only characteristic of any artist, of course: he or she makes art the way a warbler warbles."

I found myself wondering whether the Manhattan gallery owners and their stable of artists would agree with him. They would have their doubts, I am sure, above all as to how their rent would be paid on the back of a philosophy such as Franck's. Perhaps that was part of why he didn't get on with them back in the sixties.

"Well, we do get something back, of course," Franck's voice broke in on my thoughts. "We get notes on the visitor's pad like, 'This is the dream attic of my childhood,' or 'It is like walking through a poem.' It is foolish, yes, that is why we refer to *Pacem in Terris* as a 'poor man's folly.' It has proved a wonderful gamble to let strangers walk through our backyard, to see people saunter with delighted eyes down the path, point out things, a little shrine, the three hundred-year-old cherry tree. No one has ever disturbed the quiet. Once in a while there is a knock at the door, someone stands there, holds out a hand, says, "Thank you very much." And we say, "You are very, very welcome."

All this, an hour from 5th Avenue. A few minutes later we were giving the same thanks to each other. Claske took me back to the bus and stood there as it left, waving. Back there in those woods by the stream, such a generosity of spirit that perhaps no one traveling this highway would ever suspect. I am the only passenger, and the driver, a woman in her forties, asks me what my business was in Warwick. When I tell her she says she is an artist too; that she raises sheep and Shetland collies, and that she makes it all work by following in her father's footsteps and driving this bus.

"If he could raise a family on this, I thought, then it must be okay for me. See this beadwork," she adds, pointing to a colored strap hanging from her belt. "It's Lakota Sioux, from the Pine Ridge Reservation in South Dakota. The Indian ways have helped me a lot. I usually go to a sweat lodge ceremony every month, and I have learned to use the drum. I often pray for some of my passengers in the evening with my drum. A lot of them are poor people, and I don't ask them for a ticket. One woman, Wanda, I pray for every evening. She needs it."

It's everywhere you look, once you start looking, I thought. Don't take any disguise for granted; not a bus driver's, not a street person's, not a buinessman's pinstripe down on Wall Street. The human spirit is alive and well, even in the Port Authority Bus Terminal.

Chapter Seven

Engaging the Spirit in Washington, D.C.

A house divided against itself cannot stand. I believe this government cannot endure permanently half slave and half free.

Abraham Lincoln

Seeing ourselves as separate is the central problem in our political thinking.

Al Gore

Only now, in the last moments, on pulling into D.C. from New York on the Greyhound, do I realize finally that I am entering the city of the New World sun king. There before me in the gathering dusk stands the illuminated Capitol, presiding over squares and avenues that echo Versailles and back farther still, the lofty forms and aspirations of the Greece of antiquity. People stream to Washington from all over the world—except the world is much bigger and smaller now—as once they did to the court of Louis 16th or to Athens: to find their own access to power, to bask in the presence of power, to influence power.

Washington is the seat of the most powerful government on earth. Yet to enter this Jerusalem of the new secular world is to encounter the chilling paradox of American life at the end of the twentieth century: of all places in the nation, Washington, D.C., is the most powerless. The District of Columbia has little more than the status of a colony in relation to Capitol Hill. To this day, D.C. residents (more than 606,000 people) have no voting representation in Congress, and all actions taken by the elected city government are subject to congressional veto.

The vast majority of the city's population is black. Just a few minutes away from the White House and elegant, tree-lined avenues is 14th Street NW, teeming with drugs, poverty, and violence. Here are the people, if they have a job at all, who sweep the streets, flip hamburgers, open doors. This could be Sao Paulo, Brazil, or Mexico City. Washington, D.C., the standard-bearer of freedom and opportunity, is in reality a stark image of the two-tier system that our global economy is building itself upon, with the gap between rich and poor widening daily.

I, too, have come to Washington in search of power; yet power of a different kind, one that unites and doesn't divide, that acknowledges the connection between the one face of Washington and the other and is striving to heal it. Even here, there are people who are carving a different path, who are seeking a new way beyond tired ideologies and who stand for a political vision that ennobles the human spirit. Yet the likelihood is that the guiding conscience of the future will be a grass roots, truly populist movement acting at the local level.

I am on my way, my head bent into the rain, down some empty streets through Columbia Heights, murder capital of the murder capital, they call it locally. Pigeons line the rooftops. Bits of masonry and rubble are strewn in the gutter; a burned-out car sits by the roadside. There on the left is a large detached building that looks as if it may have been the home of some white professional a hundred years ago. I knock on the door of this, the Cultural Enrichment Center of the Sojourner's Organization. Sojourners has been working for decades to express through action the intersection of faith, politics, and culture. It refuses to separate prayer from peacemaking, contemplation from action, spirituality from politics.

I am meeting Jim Wallis, the founder, in the main office a few minutes away; but first I want to stop by at this, their local neighborhood project. Rev. Jim Keys, a tall African American in his thirties, welcomes me in and leads me to a tiny office on the top floor. He tells me he had worked for Congress "on the Hill" for seven years before coming to Columbia Heights and Sojourners.

"That was theoretical," he smiles. "This is practical. We cater for kids between the ages of five and seventeen. We are here to shine 'em up. Make that brilliance shine. What we do is spiritual, leadership, and community development. We have an after-school program where they do their homework, discuss their belief systems, and how those beliefs hold them accountable. We refer to the Ten Commandments as "God's Urban Renewal Plan." We have courses on self-esteem, where we inspire them with positive images of black people, telling the life stories of leaders who have come from poor backgrounds. If we weren't here they would all be on the street and prey to the dealers. We have thirty to forty mentors come in from Howard University, which is a Mecca for the black intelligentsia. They also serve as tutors. We teach computer skills and other courses."

As for the parents, Jim adds, they are working to revive the traditional neighborhood support system that black communities used to consider normal. Even in South Central Los Angeles there were people known as the Power of Mama, women who would look out for each other's kids. There used to be a natural respect in their community for elders. Now, Jim murmurs, that has been replaced by fear.

"So our job is to explore ways of empowering people and the community again," he concludes, pointing me in the direction of the Sojourner's main office. "To help them be in touch with that sense of purpose and possibility that will take them far beyond the expectations of society."

If anything is sacred work, it must surely include this, the work of men and women like Jim Keys in sullen gray backstreets around the country. These are the people who are putting into practice the ideal of America at its best, that the individual will come to fullness not at the expense of but in service to and celebration of the community and the spirit.

Like the Cultural Enrichment Center, the offices of Sojourners are in a fine old building that has seen better days. Jim Wallis's assistant ushers me into a room bare except for an old sofa, a chair, and a coffee machine. By the coffee machine is a copy of Jim's best-selling book, *The Soul of Politics*. Reading that book is what brought me here. It calls for a political morality combining social justice with personal responsibility, and grew out of a lifetime of living and working with the underprivileged, as well as a deep understanding of the emptiness of public life in America.

Harvard professor Cornell West has called Jim Wallis the most prophetic evangelical Christian voice in the country. "He refuses," says West, "to allow the religious right to have a monopoly on morality and spirituality; he also calls for the secular left to speak to the crucial issues of personal meaning and individual values." Too easy, I think, flicking through the book by the coffee machine, to equate all evangelists with the likes of Pat Robertson; to forget that most African Americans are evangelists, as were many abolitionists. The work of Jim Wallis seems to confound all stereotypes and traditional boundaries. Your dogma or creed does not concern him: what does is the practice of faith—whatever your faith is—through action to the poor.

Jim bustles in and apologizes that he has only a few minutes. He has just returned from meetings with gang leaders in the Watts district of Los Angeles, and he has to leave soon for the Religious Persecution Summit on Capitol Hill. Not one to waste time, he throws himself into the chair and tells me that we need a change of heart and mind in the country, and that change will demand a new kind of politics—a politics with spiritual values.

For far too long, Wallis points out, conservative evangelicals have been the Republican Party at prayer, while liberal religious leaders have been hard to tell apart from the left wing of the Democratic Party. Political predictability is not what he means by spiritual politics. The function of a religious perspective on politics is not to identify with one ideology or another, but to transform the nature of politics itself by bringing independent moral values and social conscience to the public forum. For years now, the religious right has controlled the public debate on politics and morality, but the longing they have tapped into—for a new emphasis on values in public life—is for much wider and deeper alternatives than the narrow interpretations offered by the evangelical right wing.

Wallis feels that the moral vacuum is being filled by a new, prophetic spiritual movement for social change, visible now in every Christian and Jewish denomination. A new dialogue that cuts across the political spectrum is emerging between the religious and the nonreligious about the shape of social and political morality.

"And this is not a liberal plot," Wallis goes on. "Big changes are happening in the most conservative bastions of faith. I mean, it is no small step on the part of the Southern Baptists, the largest and most conservative of the American Protestant denominations, to issue a statement—as they have recently done—repenting their historic support of slavery and segregation. And I do see a deep and growing desire among many grassroots evangelical and fundamentalist Christians to address directly the problems of poverty and urban decay. Many of them now are breaking with mainstream economic conservative thought."

What is new, explained Wallis, is that this movement of prophetic conscience is political without being ideological. It draws evangelicals with a compassionate heart and social conscience, mainline Protestants seeking spiritual revival and justice, and Catholics who seek a spirituality for social change. It includes African American, Latino, Asian, and Native American faith communities who are intent on shaping a more pluralistic and just society; and it extends the dialogue and cooperation to other religious communities, like the Jews and Muslims.

I know what he is saying; that spiritually based activism is becoming visible in initiatives all over the country; that congregations are providing homes for the homeless, sanctuary to Central American refugees, care for children, active protection of the environment. The Buddhists, too, are getting involved, as I had seen at the Insight Meditation Society in Massachusetts. Yet what was the civil rights movement if not a spiritually based activism? Lincoln and the Puritans too, equally held the vision of individual righteousness expressed through social justice. The current renaissance has a long and honorable lineage. It is an intrinsic part of the American story. After so much neglect and decay, communities need to find a connection to each other across traditional sectarian lines; people want to feel a kinship not only with their neighbor but also with the street person and the kid dealing drugs on the block. Only that kind of spiritual connection will bring a creative renewal of justice.

I glance at the man across from me, wondering how he ever manages to avoid burnout. Every year for the past few years he has led town meetings in more than a hundred cities, bringing together evangelists, Catholics, Protestants, Pentecostals, liberals and conservatives, blacks, whites, Asians, social service providers, business leaders, and elected officials in the cause of justice and a more value-centered politics. He's on the road all the time, encouraging thousands of people to action, editing the *Sojourners* magazine, fronting the various neighborhood initiatives here in Columbia Heights. It sounds like a sure recipe for the classic activist's downfall—too much concern for the horizontal dimension of relationships and the problems of others, not enough regard for the inner nourishment of the spirit.

When I bring up the question, Jim Wallis tells me of a Lenten fast he undertook after having done everything in his power to prevent the outbreak of the Gulf War.

"Forty-seven days on water and juice brought on many changes in me," he explains. "Despite all that was happening in the outside world, I began to feel a growing trust in a power beyond myself in the midst of my own powerlessness. I realized that the real question was where my hope lay. Was it in the power of the world to save itself, even transform itself? Or was it in the spiritual power that lies beyond our own wills? To just hope in the power of our work is to hope in ourselves, and finally in the power of this world. So to answer your question, I give time to hear that inner stillness. And I no longer imagine that the results of our work depend on us alone. There is a greater will that has its way. Knowing that, I think, is the key to avoiding burnout."

I could see Jim was preparing to move already, but he surprised me by suggesting I might like to come with him to the Religious Persecution

Summit, which was happening downtown in a hotel near the Hill.

"Practically every human rights and religious affiliation will be there," he said. "It's another example of the power of cross-party and cross-denominational coalitions. You will see senators and congressmen from both sides of the House. This is not just about the persecution of Christians, though it is true that is what most people are there for. The Dalai Lama's representative will be present, and this version of the bill specifically covers all victims of persecution of all religious groups in all countries."

So we were up and away and off to the summit; Jim Wallis to his delegate's seat, and I to the press row. Congressman Ben Gillman was speaking as we came in to the room. He was impressing on the assembly how this bill was a defining moment for the United States; how people's lives were at stake around the world, and how, too, was the soul of the American nation. Not to sign it, he said, would be an indication of our deep spiritual malaise. Yet he believed that the grassroots coalition in the room was enough to push the awareness of persecution to the national agenda. Democracy, he declared to applause, would work its magic and the people would lead the government. The ultimate intent was to establish opposition to religious persecution as part of American foreign policy.

A few minutes later he was followed by the special envoy of His Holiness the Dalai Lama, who emphasized the bill was not limited to Christians, and that the Campaign for Tibet was as committed to its success as the Christian Coalition, the Jews, and the Catholic bishops.

Others took their turn to describe the atrocities being perpetrated on thousands of Christians around the world. Then Senator Frank Wolf of Virginia, who drafted the bill along with Senator Arlen Specter of Pennsylvania, took the stand to say that it was no use America being powerful if that power was not used for the good.

"Help us to do the right thing," he urged. "We haven't done the right thing in decades. We supported Ceausescu in Romania for years. We should be mourning when Madeleine Albright says we won't allow human rights to derail our China policy. The State Department Report on Human Rights in China has entirely beautified the situation."

In speaking of the right use of power, Senator Wolf put his finger on the paradox that has been at the heart of the American dream since its inception. The great American ideals I am seeing in action around the country and in this very room have always run parallel with the country's deep commitment to power, domination, and exploitation. This commitment, at the end of the century, has brought its citizens to an unsurpassed alienation and the culture to the brink of ecological disaster.

A few hours later, one of the last people to speak before I left was Abe Rosenthal, the *New York Times* journalist. He began by saying the whole question of personal responsibility first came to his attention in June 1964 when a woman was murdered in the street and thirty-eight people stood by and did nothing. How far away does someone need to be, he wondered, for it not to be my responsibility? He went on to say that the defining piece around this whole issue was who we are as human beings, and as citizenry.

"China has captured the CEO elite of America, and Clinton has betrayed both Tibet and China." Rosenthal continued. "Yet we are beginning to pierce the mind of America. This is a huge grassroots coalition representing millions of Americans, and we are looking here at the fundamental question of what it means to be American. We take business very seriously, but free enterprise means freedom, requires freedom. We have to respond to the higher call implied in what we take so seriously. This bill is a modest, flexible, and significant effort. It seeks to withdraw nonhumanitarian foreign aid to offending regimes. Senators Wolfe and Specter have worked long and hard over this one. They know what is feasible, and they have adjusted their aims accordingly. Let's make it work."

Abe Rosenthal's words brought to my mind the inscription in stone by the grave of J.F.K. in Arlington Cemetery across the Potomac River: "Let every nation know, whether it wishes us well or ill, that we shall pay any price, bear any burden, meet any hardship, support any friend, oppose any foe to assure the survival and success of liberty. In the long history of the world only a few generations have been granted the role of defending freedom in its hour of maximum danger. I do not shrink from this responsibility, I welcome it. The energy, the faith, the devotion, which we bring to this endeavor will light our country and all who serve it and the glow from that fire can truly light the world. . . ."

These sentiments are from another age, I reflected; before the United States met its nemesis in Vietnam. It may be true that freedom is this country's historic challenge, yet the fantasy of protecting and saving the world, with the president in the role of savior, can only obstruct what it strives to bring about. There is a genuine and naïve goodheartedness in these words. What is missing is humility, never a common American virtue. While the Religious Freedom Bill is not fueled by the same romantic hubris, it sails close to the same righteous waters.

As I left the summit to stroll down elegant Connecticut Avenue, it struck me that the bill was a development of the ideals of Lincoln and King. Both saw it to be part of America's historic role to extend the bond of moral commitments to other peoples and also to other generations. In fact, the truest version of the American ideal of freedom and justice as a goal for humanity has surely been expressed most continuously, not by Congress, nor by white liberals, but in the prophetic-messianic character of African American Christianity. Right here in Washington are some of the most inspired and active preachers for change in that tradition, and I decided to make a point of attending one of their churches.

The following Sunday, I turned up for morning service at the Metropolitan Baptist Church down on R Street. I arrived in time for the community breakfast, and joined hundreds of people in the crypt for an egg over-easy and home fries. I was the only white person in the room, and I remembered when, years before, I had gone into an uptown hotel in London with Ysaye Barnwell, of the acapella group Sweet Honey in the Rock. We were there for five minutes, when she asked if we could leave. "Everyone is aware of me," she said. "This doesn't work." I had no notion of what she was talking about. Now I did, with the difference that here the gazes made me feel welcome.

It was my good fortune to sit down next to Nawanna Miller, a woman in her forties who had left the Metropolitan some years before to start her own church in Smyrna, Georgia. She tells me the visibility of women has increased dramatically in the African American church, that the black Episcopalian and Methodist seminaries today are more full of women than men. I remembered that Joanna Katz at Eilat Chayyim had said the same of the Jewish seminaries. However, Beacher Hicks, the preacher at Metropolitan, she added, had been expelled from the Minister's Alliance for ordaining women. The Baptists are much more conservative, though even there it depended on the particular affiliation. The Metropolitan, part of the American Baptist Convention, was on the progressive wing.

Nawanna had been a pastor for ten years, and had "planted" her own Messiah's Temple in Smyrna three years earlier. It was part of a growing nondenominational movement that was working to unite the religious regardless of denomination. Walls were breaking down between different congregations, she said, because people were realizing that no one group had the whole picture and that dialogue took everyone to another level of faith and understanding.

"Part of what I do," Nawanna went on, "is to rearticulate the role and value of women. I think that God can express through us what is not possible in the same way through men. The church population is mostly women, so it makes sense that a woman can put forward God's message in a way that is more relevant to them. Women are nurturers, they raise kids, they have a particular sensitivity. When you recognize the nurturing side of women you understand more the nurturing side of God. All pastors are called to be shepherds, but I give out of a different set of experiences than a man. Perhaps it is easier for me to hear more, feel more."

Many of the women around us were holding decorated eggs, and when I asked Nawanna what this meant she said there had been a women's gathering the day before, and that the eggs were a symbol of new birth. They had spent the day freeing themselves of some of the pain of abuse, of fatherless families, of poverty, and sickness; sharing their hearts with each other and turning their pain over to God. Many had dressed the eggs up like babies to represent the renewal they were asking of God. I was intrigued to see—right here in the heart of Washington—the echo of a practice I had seen all over southern India. There, women hang egg-shaped pebbles dressed in cloth on a sacred tree as a symbol of their desire for new life in the form of a child or a husband.

People were streaming into the church now, and I followed full of interest to hear the man who for many years had been the inspiration for the vision of the Metropolitan. The church is actively engaged in beautifying R Street, in stimulating economic development in the area, helping the poor and homeless to help themselves, establishing livable rental housing in the area. The annual men's retreat brings men and boys together for mentoring and nurturing, the lamentations class encourages people to share their pain and grief while moving through Jeremiah's lamentations. The Metropolitan is no ordinary church: it addresses the psychological, social, and cultural health of its members as intrinsic elements of a spiritual mission.

There was a band on the stage already, and a full house of perhaps two thousand people. The band was playing a slow tempo of gospel/blues; Beacher Hicks, a tall, heavy-set man in red cassock and white surplice, was strolling casually up and down the stage with a microphone in his hand. Softly, almost reflectively, he began to sing, "I feel joy when I think about it, what he's done for me . . ." The band picked up, his voice grew louder, "You don't know like I know what he's done for me, *I said I feel joy when I think about it!*"

All two thousand people were singing now, a rising crescendo giving voice to spirit, then Hicks brings them back down to almost a whisper, saying almost as a casual aside, "That should be written down deep in a person's soul. What should? That I feel joy when I think about it," the crescendo rising again, people waving their arms now among all the flower bonnets and white Sunday dresses.

Down he brings them again, and says, "You ever hear those people who sit around saying things like, 'From time to high time I have a periodic experience of exaltation and elation when I use my cognitive processes to understand the activity of the eternal in my existential circumstance'? *I get joy, joy, joy, when I think about it!*"

Now he is belting it out for all he is worth. People are dancing in the pews, the band is giving a full-blown blues concert, and I am laughing my socks off at the accuracy of the parody he has just made of me and my kind, white, middle-class intellectuals with a faith but no religion like this. I jig up and down along with everyone else, I sing out my joy, hold the hand of the person next to me, and marvel at the gifts of this singing preacher.

"Anybody feel better?" he asks as the music fades away at last. "Hear me? Does anyone feel better?"

The response comes loud and clear, and everyone sits down again to hear what Beacher Hicks has to say in his sermon.

He begins quietly again, saying that at the close of the twentieth century we need a radical religion if the church is to survive. Even the word *church* is falling out of favor now, and being erased from the signboards of institutions. Denominational distinctions, he goes on, are becoming a thing of the past. If the church is to remain viable it must bring to an end its romance with the past. The bible is and must remain the same, but those who read it are far different to those who wrote it. The Gospel we preach and the Jesus we serve are the same, but we need to understand Jesus in light of our own pain, predicament, and cultural context. We need, he says, his voice rising, a radical religion. "Go on, tell us," a voice cries from the pews.

"The Jesus of history is not sufficient for contemporary faith," says Hicks, in his stride now. "We need to speak clearly to restore timeless values. We live in a corporate culture that is unconcerned with make-believe religion and an irrelevant church. We have churches on every corner, but still they have not found the will to build enough houses for the homeless. While we sit here getting filled with the Holy Ghost, the blood of our children is running in the streets because of a society that values guns more than life. What kind of a religion is it"—his whole body behind the words now, his rich voice booming—"that sits by holding concerts and chicken dinners while our schools have lost the capacity to educate our children; while generations are lost forever to drugs and alcohol? While African American men are being locked out and locked up during the most potent years of their lives? What kind of a religion is it that won't speak out in a culture where men want to marry other men, that permits women to be treated as objects? No," his voice coming down to a quiet urgency again, "I know you don't want to hear this, but we need a radical religion."

"We want to hear it, we want to hear it. Go on, tell us." Voices cry out from all over the church.

"The church itself must be saved or it will soon find itself on the shelf of some museum of religious antiquities. The world will just not respond to what we are doing in here as long as it is tired, trite, and silent. We need to speak out and act. Let's stop playing at church and *be* the church," he ended with almost a roar that was raised by the band and assembled choir to the rooftops.

I staggered out of that church my senses reeling, knowing now why *Ebony* magazine had cited Hicks as one of the top fifteen preachers in the land. I went to his office to meet him in person, and over coffee I asked him how he thought the African American church, which seemed to me so rooted in tradition and historical circumstance, could best address the cultural ground that was changing under its feet.

Flux was nothing new for the African American church, Beacher Hicks told me; they had always addressed a people in flux who lived within a culture of change. At the same time, the ministry worked to change the culture so it would accommodate more of the church's own theological underpinnings; and in that they had become far more sophisticated. Previously, he explained, churches had birthed colleges; now they founded elementary and secondary schools. They were more sophisticated as agents of economic development, too. They knew how to use governmental and philanthropic resources to establish beachheads against urban and rural decay.

Another image I had brought with me from Europe about the African American church was that it had always defined itself in relation to the exodus experience; that it was inextricably linked to the era of slavery and the cries of the Israelites in the wilderness. Is that part of what Hicks meant in his sermon, I asked, when he said that the church needed to move on from the past?

"Not at all," he said. "The story of slavery, freedom, and redemption is still as relevant today as ever, not only in America but for people of color all over the world. But the African American church is not defined by the exodus experience—our experience encompasses the whole of scripture. We identify with the experience of Ezekiel in the valley of death seeking to bring about life, with the three Hebrew boys finding themselves in the fiery furnace, with Jesus dissolving barriers, healing, and empowering individuals. We are Pauline, in his egalitarian reading of the gospel. Our experience is reflected from Genesis to Revelations and all points in between. Unless we understand that we shall have missed the genius of the black religion to be able to identify ourselves, our circumstance and our culture, throughout the Bible."

When I asked him about his response to the Promise Keepers, he paused to reflect for a moment. He said that the Promise Keepers had stepped into the void of a culture that had lost touch with anything outside of itself. People were hungry in America for a spiritually grounded life rooted in biblical integrity, and sacred values that had served generations. Two or three years earlier, he commented, *Time* magazine had run a cover before Easter that said, "The Generation That Has Forgotten God." When the most prestigious magazine in the country runs a story like that, it certainly pointed to a void in the culture waiting to be filled.

"With the Promise Keepers, however, there are cultural and racial issues lurking under the surface," Hicks went on. "We as African Americans cannot be certain that the repentance of whites is genuine when what we see in America politically and socially is the very reverse of the justice and compassion which they proclaim. It is always difficult for the oppressed to believe in the full conversion of the oppressor. We have learned through the years not to trust the protestations of regeneration that the plantation owner periodically made. We know better than that. And then, any deep reading of the New Testament will show the equality of men and women, whereas there seems to be the traditional male tendency in Promise Keepers to empower men by diminishing women."

I wondered how he would gauge the spiritual pulse of America in general, and he said he thought maybe there was evidence of an infection or some low-grade fever.

"There is a sickness in our country and all over the world," he went on. "There is a prevalence of the instruments of darkness who want to bring about that which is ultimately not productive. I do know there is only one source of healing, and that it is the balm in Gilead, available now as ever. When placed on the spectrum of the church as a whole, the African American church may be the strongest expression of religion in America. Even though it is growing and moving in new areas, it must do so more. It must be in the vanguard of social justice. It must continue to be a source of healing health and hope for our people, and it will do that not by being content with its history, but by pursuing its future."

"What then," I asked, "does the African American church have to offer to the present cultural conversation on religion and spirituality?"

"Our understanding of oppression," replied Beacher Hicks, "but also our understanding of the victory that has been the history as well as the hope of the African American church. By our presence we raise the question: How is a people in the face of injustice and economic and educational inequalities still able to forge a faith and an understanding of who God is and how he acts in the world?"

I told him I thought there was something else, too. There was the un-fettered joy I had been part of in his church a few moments earlier. The irrepressible spirit and faith of African American people despite all they have endured is a beacon for the rest of the world. Perhaps that is what he meant; it struck me later, when he spoke of his people's victory.

Chapter Eight

Salaam D.C.

A bdul Aziz Said first saw America's greatness in a watermelon. He was born into a desert Bedouin family in Syria over sixty years ago. He was approaching twenty when he dropped out of the Sahara silence into the teeming world of New York City. Yet, as spectacular as the city seemed, it was rather like seeing the movie after reading the book. It was, after all, what he had expected. His second day was more powerful. He saw two halves of a watermelon on a fruit stall, each for sale. He stood and stared in amazement. Never, in a world where everyone ate watermelons, had he seen half a watermelon for sale. That, he thought, is the true American genius.

I was sitting in his office in Georgetown University. Professor Abdul Aziz Said holds the Chair of Islamic Peace Studies there. A few minutes before, he had welcomed me in the Sufi way, with three kisses on the cheek; such a warmth in this man, the presence of something larger, more generous than the conventional formalities of duty and business. I could see he was serious about the watermelons. It has been a blessing, he explains, to live in such a practical culture that truly respects talent, creativity, imagination, and freedom. We Sufis always aspire to see the big picture, he says; to see reality from a million angles, to experience the connection between the inner and outer, the material and spiritual. Everything has meaning. Everything.

It was because he was a Sufi, a practitioner of mystical Islam, that I had come to meet Dr. Aziz Said before leaving Washington. I had met many Sufis in the Near East and in India, and had always felt an affinity for their sense of the inherent unity of spiritual paths and their love for the Beloved. For many Westerners, the name of Islam conjures an image of bearded fanatics who survive on a power base of violence and fear. Yet the word *Islam* means "surrender," or "obedience," and the common form of greeting between Muslims is *salaam,* meaning "peace." There are three million Muslims in America—more than the total membership of the Episcopalian Church; and I was looking for the other Islam—not the political variety, but the living spiritual tradition. The Sufis, I knew, were part of it.

"My responsibility, my beloved brother," Dr. Aziz Said went on, "is to live that view: that everything has meaning. And what that means for me is to recognize that the whole world is implicate in every corner of the world; that the whole world needs the whole world. Now, being in America is for me the ideal place to experience this recognition. The temptation here, though, is to sit back at the apex of the pyramid and not recognize this truth. When America does recognize its need for others we shall be completing the circle. You see, this paradigm means that nations can meet each other in a new relationship. The strong gives the best it has, and receives the best that the weak has. For me, this is democracy in its deepest sense."

He is interested in my theme of a Sacred America, he says. The Sacred America I am looking for will truly emerge, he thinks, when Americans discover for themselves the limits of materialism. He has found in his own life, as I may have done in mine, that only when we acknowledge our limits do we come into our strength. Many Americans still truly believe that scientific materialism has no limit, yet Eisenhower understood the fallacy of that a long time ago. Beware, said Dwight, of the military industrial complex. America is great because America is good. If America ceases to be good, it will cease to be great. A sentiment, it occurred to me, that goes all the way back to de Tocqueville.

Dr. Aziz Said's "cover" in the world is academic, and his particular way of expressing his deepest convictions is to develop peace and conflict-resolution programs and to work with people from around the world within the paradigm he has just described. Conflict resolution, I gathered, was the centerpiece of the Islamic Peace Studies program at the university. The Sufis have always participated fully in society, and in making his work his spiritual practice, Abdul Aziz Said was following a time-honored tradition—one that happens to fit especially well with contemporary culture.

"You know, I remember getting my B.A., then my M.A., and feeling how educated I was. Then a voice said to me, 'Do they give anything higher than the M.A.? Then get the Ph.D.' Later, it happened again. 'How are Ph.D.'s awarded?' asked the voice. By professors, I responded. 'Go and be one of them.' The voice was telling me I was still living in my head, that I had still not discovered the limitations of the mind, so I couldn't transcend it. 'Keep learning,' it said. 'Keep learning until you come to the place where you feel, What do I do now?' I was being told that as long as I try and transcend the mind without discovering its limits, I am avoiding sweating it out and making the discovery for myself. We all have to do that; we all have to sweat out our growth."

When I ask Abdul Aziz what there is left for him to do, he tells me there is nothing he wishes to have, nothing he has that he can't give up. What remains is to experience a still deeper surrender to the grace of the Beloved.

And who is it that assists him in this? No, no great master hidden in the hills; his students. With them, he says, he experiences his relationship with God. With them and also his family. His family is his teacher because they show him his limits. We ask God in our prayers what we can do for him, and that is the basis of his relationship with his students. Then he delivers an ancient yet unusual view of what a university is. Students don't come here for degrees, he says, even if they imagine they do. No, they come here because this is where seekers of truth congregate. We are all here, professors and students, in the name of truth.

"You know, my brother, my younger son called me the other day. He wanted to know if there was such a thing as absolute truth. Absolutely yes, I said, and absolutely no. In the end, everything is part of an overall ecology. The human contribution to that ecology is Love." Dr. Aziz Said had another appointment, and got up to show me out. "By the way," he added, as I was leaving. "We have an international conference beginning here tomorrow, on the contribution of Islam to Peace in the twenty-first century. I would be delighted for you to come as my guest, if it is Allah's will."

By the grace of God, then, I joined perhaps a hundred intellectuals, academics, peace activists, and political figures at the conference the next morning. Some twenty speakers, including two or three women, were seated in the half round. Most were in Western suits, one or two men from India and the Middle East wore traditional dress, a few women wore headscarves, others looked like professional women from Capitol Hill. Dr. Aziz Said, in suit and sneakers, loped unobtrusively about the proceedings, stopping occasionally to kiss an acquaintance on both cheeks.

As I came in, a speaker was saying that Ramadan in the United States was making history. People would fast during the day, then meet in community in the evening along with Jews and Christians, often four hundred or five hundred at a time. Religion has always been shaped by its context, and a distinctively American, democratic Islam was in the making. The imams in the States provide counseling services, and act as Islamic spokesmen to a community in which Islam is not yet understood. Many American mosques now secure a bank loan to build, despite the traditional Islamic ruling against usury.

Then one of the women takes the chair, a philosopher and lawyer. She speaks to the issue of women and equality in Islam, its necessity. Another young woman from Afghanistan speaks movingly about the atrocities being perpetrated in her country by the Taliban in the name of religion.

During a break I find myself in conversation with Dr. Suleyman Nyang, a slight figure from Ethiopia with an easy manner. He is a professor at the African Studies Department of Howard University. When I ask him for his thoughts on the way democracy is shaping Islam in America, he says that one of the main differences between American Islam and traditional Islam is the value given to the individual. With his rights protected by the Constitution, the Muslim in America is beginning to recognize he doesn't have to conform. He has the individual religious freedom to construct an Islam unfettered by the heavy weight of tradition. In the Middle East, on the other hand, Islam has been hijacked by factions in the name of religion or in the name of a philosophy that is in reality the opposite of Islam.

As for the Sufis, Suleyman says in response to my next question, they are emerging in America openly. Many of the schools were imported by immigrants in their traditional forms, but other teachings which do not necessarily require conversion to Islam have been developing for some time that are intended more for the white American culture.

"You see," said the doctor, animated suddenly, "Muslims are in a profound intellectual, moral, and political crisis. If they are to go into the twenty-first century with any self-esteem and bargaining power in relation to non-Muslims, they will have to deal with the intellectual and philosophical issues, including the implications for Islam of democracy. The old truths are still relevant, because the natural order is still the same. But circumstances are different. How can you expect metaphors from an agricultural society to continue to strike a chord in the culture of the cellular phone? Both Jews and Muslims have to look deeply into how they can carry the message of Abraham into the next century with a new language. The Jewish renewal movement is responding to that challenge," he says, as we join the others back in the room to hear the keynote speaker. "What we really need is an Esperanto of spirituality."

A new Esperanto. I think I am beginning to see the first signs of a grammar for that very thing on this American journey. The different groups and individuals I have met all seem to espouse a few common themes: the primacy of individual experience over dogma (the conservative Christians like Beacher Hicks or Jim Wallis would qualify this); the light of the individual put to the service of the community; respect for and dialogue with all faiths; and a sense of the global, mystical body of humanity and all creation. I am wondering if Sayed Nasr, the keynote speaker who is about to start, will speak a similar language. From the little I know of him, he might be less likely to use such radical language. Nasr, professor of Islamic Studies at George Washington University, is a traditionalist in the finest sense of the term; he relies not on dogma but on the perennial values inherent in Islam.

His subject is salaam, peace, and he begins by saying that while peace today is seen negatively as the lack of war, peace in Islam means not an absence or lack, but a presence. Peace is a word coming from God, who is its origin. Salaam, says the Koran, is the language and condition of paradise. Peace is in the nature of things as God created them. Our soul yearns for peace, he explains, because it is our primordial nature. "I was an angel, and paradise my abode . . . ," Nasr quotes Hafiz, the Persian Sufi and poet, and goes on to say that we carry something of that paradisal bliss in the depths of our souls, but since we are not fully there we are always yearning for it. I can't disagree there. Nor is it easy to refute his next proposition, that the first consequence of such a view is that no peace is possible without obedience to God. You can't say that peace is of paradise and be a secular humanist. Conversely, he is saying, you can't be a humanist and know true peace. Nasr is radical in his own way.

Even more so when he goes on to say that peace is impossible without *jihad,* which in the West is normally translated as holy war, and seen as an example of fundamentalist doctrine. But no, says Nasr, jihad literally means exertion in the path of God. Exertion implies struggle, and there is the paradox, that it is impossible to find peace without jihad. We live in an inner and outer world of tension, and peace implies a removal of tension through the establishment of equilibrium. We need to exert ourselves in order to re-establish equilibrium; the holy war is within, yes, but also without, for an exertion is required to maintain equilibrium between all the various circles of God's creation.

If traditional Islamic life is anything, declares Nasr, it is equilibrium; the whole Shariah, divine law, is there for that. We have to be constantly watchful. If we let things go, there will not be peace. If we human beings have a role on earth, it is first and foremost to be peace guardians. Just go into any traditional mosque, he says, and you will feel it there, even in the midst of a busy city. What about outside the mosque, I wondered. Nasr is painting a beautiful picture, but the reality of the world of Islam is a long way from such high ideals.

He must have heard my thoughts, because in the next breath he says that the traditional world of Islam has all but disappeared. Even so, he goes on, peace today can only mean what it always has. We can define it by a series of concentric circles that endure whatever the era or cultural context. What we are hearing, I realize, are the foundations of perennial wisdom, found in every ancient tradition East and West.

The first and supreme jihad is surrender to the divine reality of the soul. Nasr is passing quickly through the concentric circles now. Ramadan is a recurring test of this ultimate surrender to God. Then we must find peace with ourselves; with our blood relations and local community; with all Muslims and with all human beings, whether or not they share our views; and finally, peace with the rest of God's creation.

Ecological awareness is hardly a new thing, the professor tells us. Traditional Islamic society was in deep equilibrium with nature. Just look at the air-conditioning system in the great mosque in Cairo, while the irrigation systems still having Moorish names in New Mexico today echo the medieval technology of southern Spain, where Muslim culture held sway for 500 years. The Shariah prohibits the pollution of water and the felling of trees, and until the nineteenth century no government could supersede the law of God.

It was the same for the Hindus, I reflected. It was unthinkable to pollute a holy river, and even thirty years ago people would voluntarily sweep the leaves from the surface of the wells dedicated to Sura the sun god along the banks of the Ganges in the holy city of Benares (Varanasi). Now the Ganges is one of the most polluted waterways in Asia, and the wells are filthy with everyone's garbage. The divine order that Nasr is advocating was once the foundation of civilization everywhere. Those days are gone.

Yet we can still achieve this peace, Nasr is saying in his closing remarks. We achieve it first through faith, then worship, and then by adherence to the divine law. What we have now, he admits finally, are institutions in the Islamic world that are themselves part of the problem. They are there to remain in power, not to bring peace. And you can't have peace without God.

And you can't dwell in God and keep your neighbor in prison and your people without freedom. I was reminded of Suleyman Nyang's comment, that we have to find a language—metaphors and analogies—that can free the perennial truths from the shackles of both outworn tradition and secular materialism so that people can hear them again. Not only that: we need to make our language credible with action. The following day, I was heading south to meet some people who were doing just that.

The finest talk will never be enough. Even so, I left the conference in Georgetown feeling grateful; grateful to be reminded by Sayed Nasr that, whatever personal or collective difficulties we face, the first and primal truth still holds. You can't have peace without standing under some power higher than the personal ego; and the essence of Islam, along with every great religion, shines forth that truth for the world.

Chapter Nine

The Lawn at Charlottesville

I was on my way from Washington, D.C., to North Carolina, but Tony Zito back in Manhattan had urged me not to pass so near to Charlottesville, Virginia, without taking a short detour to meet William McDonaugh. McDonaugh is a leading figure in the ecological design movement; an architect dedicated to creating forms that honor the earth. Architecture for people like McDonaugh is a way of expressing the unity between humanity and nature. His practice is in this small West Virginia University town. It doesn't look far; why not follow Tony's advice, I thought.

Charlottesville is not exactly on the direct route south from Washington, but "near" in America is often far in England, so I wasn't so surprised to find the short detour took me the best part of a morning. McDonaugh was out of town, so I had arranged to meet his partner, Russell Perry, in the firm's downtown offices. Russell began by showing me some of the drawings for their current contracts, saying that corporate acceptance of their working principles has been growing rapidly. I could see from the plans for the new Gap headquarters in San Francisco, for example, that beauty, as well as function, was important to them.

"Beauty is essential for the uplifting of the human spirit," says Russell. "We don't want people saying, 'Yeah, you can have a green building if you don't mind it being ugly and expensive.' If we want to show that our environmental and social justice principles are sound, we have to be able to meet all other standards as well. You have to deal with all measures of quality—beauty, justice, economy, function, environmental responsibility."

"Don't you find it astonishing," he exclaims, "that with only minor modifications a school could be converted into a factory or a prison? Our buildings seem to teach that disconnectedness is normal. Think about it;

if we entered industrial society into an intergalactic design competition, we would be tossed out in the first round. It doesn't fit. It won't last. The scale is wrong. And even the apologists admit it isn't very pretty. You know what Frank Lloyd Wright said? He said he could design a house that would ensure a couple's divorce in one month. Well, what interests us is how design can be a statement of the opposite; how it can illustrate that we are in fact connected to the larger community of life."

That's why design is so crucial, it occurs to me as I listen to Russell: it leads to the manifestation of human intention.

"If what we make with our hands is to honor life as a whole"—Russell is in full flow now—"then it must not only rise from the ground but return to it, soil to soil, water to water. So that everything that is received from the earth can be freely given back without causing harm to any living system. That for us is good design and ecology."

These are just the principles, he says, that are active in the new Environmental Studies Faculty building at Oberlin College in Ohio. The professor there, David Orr, personally raised $5 million for the project. A team of twenty-five students and a dozen architects developed a building that purifies all its wastewater on site, generates more electricity than it uses, and includes no carcinogenic or mutagenic material. Further, this building uses only products that are grown or manufactured sustainably, is landscaped to promote biological diversity, and its full costs are factored in over the lifetime of the building.

"The way I see it," Russell continues, "colleges and universities, more than any other institution, have a moral stake in the health, beauty, and integrity of the world their students will inherit. We have an obligation to provide students with tangible models that express both our values and our capabilities. In the larger view, if we want to ensure the human tenure on earth, then we will have to cultivate a new standard to define beauty. We will need to appreciate beauty as that which causes no harm or ugliness, either human or ecological, somewhere else or at some later time. Rene Dubois said it all when he said, "the worst thing we can do to our children is to convince them that ugliness is normal."

Then he said a surprising thing, something that was to turn my day in a whole different direction. He said that if I really wanted to see one of the best examples in the country of design in the service of the human spirit, I should go just down the street and visit The Lawn. The architect? None other than Thomas Jefferson. The Lawn was the origins of the University of Virginia, which Jefferson called the hobby of his old age. He was seventy-five years old when the Commonwealth's legislature finally voted in 1819 to establish the university. Jefferson created an innovative curriculum, recruited distinguished scholars from around the world, and designed what Russell assured me was one of the world's great architectural treasures.

Those Founding Fathers, they were unstoppable. They were youngsters, in their twenties and early thirties when they forged the Constitution. They made decisions then that were to shape the earth, and they knew it. Adams, in a letter to Jefferson, for whom he felt great love in his older years (though not earlier) wrote, "no one will ever know what we had. It has gone now, but it was something very special." And then, here was Jefferson, not content with the founding of a nation, but at the close of his life designing a university on just the premise that Abdul Aziz Said had put to me in Georgetown—a place where seekers of truth may come together for the highest good. As a child of the enlightenment, the pursuit of knowledge for Jefferson was a sacred task that had no limits.

The Lawn. This is why I had come to Charlottesville. I knew as soon as Russell Perry mentioned it. I had no idea I was in Jefferson country, his house, Monticello, just outside town. Russell inspired me less for his drawings—though they were impressive—than for the love of his work that came through his eyes and his words. There, I thought as I left him, is a man content with his place in the world. He puts every ounce of himself into those plans, his beliefs, his aspirations, his knowledge, and his vision.

Soon after lunch I was in a campus of green acres with a mixture of architecture spanning the last 175 years. Up a low slope of grass I went and there before me the Rotunda rose, a half-scale version of the Parthenon that formed the north end of a long rectangle of white buildings in Georgian style. Framed by the buildings was a lawn that stretched away to the south end, now enclosed, but originally left open by Jefferson to symbolize the limitless freedom of the human mind.

I, whose mind and aesthetic sense had been shaped from childhood by the Georgian city of Bath, stood there in awe at the finest expression of enlightenment idealism I had ever witnessed. I had come this far, and to America of all places, to have Bath dislodged from its preeminent place in my imagination. As an aesthetic whole, The Lawn (the name for the whole conception) knows no blemish. This is architecture with an intimate and sensuous awareness of function, a function expressed with astonishing beauty.

The pavilions that intersperse the long terraces on the east and west sides were designed for the professors, who would live on the first floor and give classes on the ground floor. The rest of the terrace consists of student lodging, with a porticoed walkway allowing dry access in all weather to any other part of the complex. Students occupy those lodgings even today. It was a community that Jefferson was designing, not just a campus; a community in which life itself was centered round the pursuit of knowledge. He called it The Academical Village, and it finally opened as the University of Virginia in 1825 with forty students.

It seems as if he had to wait for this final accomplishment in order to die, which he did the next year, on of course, July Fourth, fifty years to the day after the signing of the Constitution. As if we might not get the message that the lives of these men and the country they had created were in the hands of a destiny far greater than any of them, fate decided to play another hand. That same day in 1826, John Adams lay dying. On his deathbed he was heard to say, "At least Jefferson is still alive." Three hours later, on the same day, Jefferson, too, was dead.

I turned to gaze up at the Rotunda, a great sphere whose top half forms the library, the cranium—literally the brain of the university. Here, in pride of place, in the center of the Rotunda, the library affirms Jefferson's belief in the preeminence of knowledge. This was his temple. "It is a pristine space," says Robert Hughes, the art critic, "a precinct of intelligence, light, clarity, and harmony—the most beautiful room in America."

The Academical Village is certainly the most beautiful set of buildings I have seen in the United States. I am not alone in my regard for it: in 1976 the American Institute of Architects proclaimed it the most significant architectural achievement of the nation's first two hundred years. We may have moved on from the fancy that intellectual knowledge is the only, or even the highest, way of knowing. We are certainly beginning to realize that Jefferson did not have it quite right when he said, "knowledge is power, safety and happiness." With all the knowledge now at our disposal, the happiness he enshrined in the Constitution as a right of every citizen seems as elusive as ever. Yet we would be blind not to acknowledge the foundation for happiness that rational thought and the Enlightenment have given us.

In the Constitution, the Founding Fathers gave to the world the architecture of freedom, dignity, and happiness—a structure that, like no other before it, allows the possibility of human fulfillment. Yet the structure does not have the power in and of itself to guarantee the freedom and happiness it stands for. The flame in the hearth has to come from elsewhere, from deeper than the most brilliant rational thought—from our relationship to something unspeakable, which transcends us.

Jefferson and the rest, I am sure they knew this. They did what they could and they moved the world. Now we are being called to catch the flicker of that flame and do what we can to internalize democracy; to create an environment (as Valclav Havel puts it) of self-examination that wants more than anything to serve the common good. That environment, rather than any fixed ideology, is the essence and true spirit of democracy. And Jefferson—how clear it is in his works, I realized, as I gazed on his Academical Village for one last time before heading on down to North Carolina—lived in and epitomized that spirit.

Chapter Ten

North Carolina Kindness

The essence of our work is simple: Everyone is Holy Company, every place is holy ground, and every act is Sacred Practice.

Bo Lozoff

Prison is like a monastery if you want to see it that way, Bo Lozoff says in his book *We're All Doing Time*—especially if you are in solitary. You're there; might as well make the best of it. Might as well, if you are so inclined, turn it into a spiritual practice. All that loneliness, all that fear and denial, that negativity, it's hard not to face in a prison, or a monastery, or on the ocean in a solo yacht. So why not look it in the eye and see if there's anything on the other side? For more than twenty years, Bo's book has been an inspiration for people in prison all over the world.

I knew a man in England who took Bo's advice. Lee Squires had been in for nearly twenty years when I met him, on an armed robbery charge that had ended in a murder, which he didn't commit. After years in solitary wishing he were dead, then working through his denial with a psychologist, and then practicing yoga and meditation, something began to happen to Lee. A light began to come into his eye, which many years later grew into a beacon not just for his fellow prisoners but for the prison staff as well. Lee is one of the most compassionate and radiant people I have ever met. He now teaches meditation to the staff of his prison, and is always on call as a counselor for other prisoners. What he found on the other side of that suffering was a big sky of open and loving awareness.

Lee had told me that it had been a saving grace early on in his prison life to be given a copy of Bo Lozoff's book; that it had been an invaluable tool for hundreds of prisoners in England for many years. And that is how I came to be rolling down the freeway to a secluded country setting some twenty minutes from Durham, to spend a day or two with Bo and Sita Lozoff at their Human Kindness Foundation.

Some twenty acres they have there of rolling grassland; a big farmhouse where up to half a dozen ex-prisoners live, work, and do spiritual practice together; an office; a small row of guest cottages; and a tiny wooden house which is the home of Bo and Sita. They have been running this spiritual community—for that is what it is—for five years now, the natural extension of two decades of work in prisons all over the country.

Sita came out of the office to greet me with the kind of welcome you give someone you love and have not seen for some time. That, I soon realized, is the warmth she has for this world. Bo and his son were working on a new building with the other community members, and I joined them all a little later for the evening meal.

For grace, Bobby, one of the ex-prisoners, read something from *A Course in Miracles,* a manual of spiritual practice, which he told me later had kept him sane for years in prison. Bruce and Tony were the two other ex-prisoners there at the time, both of them free for just a week after having served seventeen years each. The meal was simple, frugal, even, as was the conversation, the accent being on a relaxed mindfulness more than socializing.

I sat for a few moments after the meal with Tony, a large, powerful man whom I thought was Hispanic, but turned out to be half Mohawk and half Lebanese. He had just been released from San Quentin. What got him through his time there more than anything else was the weekly sweat lodge the Indian prisoners had. Cleaned out the negative vibes, he said. The pipe holder in San Quentin was on Death Row, he added. Then Bruce tells me he used to sit six or seven hours a day in meditation in his cell in Florida. His cellmates would always ask to be transferred within a year or so because he was such boring company. Everyone else in prison tries to fill the gap, if not with drugs then with sound, or both. Inmates would have televisions or radios on night and day. You could hear the music from one guy's headphones half a block away, Bruce says. Sita, overhearing him, adds that the noise level is the most difficult thing she finds about prison visits.

Over in the Lozoff's house, barely more than a cabin, Bo fills me in on the background of the men I had just met. We can have no real idea, he says, of the suffering and abuse these people go through routinely. Bruce was just nineteen when the judge sentenced him to ninety years for bank robbery. Bruce is black, he had no family, no representation, and he was being tried by a white judge in rural Florida. People are killed in prison over a pack of cigarettes. These men have lived life at the worst end of the mean-spiritedness of our times. After seventeen years of an exemplary record, Florida released him with $50 and a short-sleeved shirt. It is just a lie to hope they don't go back into prison. Fifty dollars means one night in a motel and then you have to figure out whom to rob.

"How would you or I cope, starting life with $50 and no support, nobody you know? We would find it impossible," says Bo. I had to agree.

"Being here makes it hard to be stuck in middle-class neuroses when you see someone like Tony," Bo goes on. "He has had an entire lifetime of abuse, most of it in prison. When he was seventeen he was sitting on the couch watching TV with his friend. His friend's brother came in and asked him if he had taken his ring. The friend replied that he had. The older brother went out, came back a few minutes later, and shot his brains out. These people have been through unbelievable stuff, yet here they are struggling for *dharma,* for God, at forty. I tell you, we would have quit fifty times were it not for how much these people inspire us."

Bo goes on to tell me that one day, as his workshop was about to begin, he was standing outside the Islamic chapel at San Quentin when he looked up at the crisp blue sky, felt the cool breeze on his face. He said to the guy next to him, "Beautiful day." The guy, with his eyes closed, shiny black shaven head tilted to the sky, replied softly, "Every day"—this from a rough, tough inmate of San Quentin. There's the disguise again, I thought. You just never know.

Then after the workshop, one burly guy came up to Bo and asked him if he would smuggle out a letter.

"Well, I don't know, what is it?"

"Well, I know you're going to see the Dalai Lama tomorrow, and I need you to ask him to say a blessing for my wife, Juliette. She's having a real tough time these days."

The next day, three thousand people listened in silence as the Dalai Lama gave that blessing.

As I continued to listen to them, it began to dawn on me just how much this couple was doing in prisons. In just the one month of April 1997, they visited two thousand men in eleven Texas state prisons, including Death Row. Texas had never allowed them in before, in twenty years. People in every prison had been corresponding with them for fifteen, twenty years. One guy said their book had saved his life four times when he had hit bottom. Many had a photo of Bo and Sita on their cell wall.

What struck the Lozoffs more than anything else on that trip was how the nation puts more effort into recycling cans and paper than it does human beings. They saw units specifically for older inmates, many of them in wheelchairs and walkers, soft-spoken, kind men who supported each other. With the humility and compassion they had gained, they could become valuable elders in the community. Instead, taxpayers throw away $30,000 to $40,000 yearly to keep them in prison till they die. There are nearly five hundred condemned in Texas. The Texas homicide rate is 9.1 per month per one hundred thousand, while in the states without the death penalty, the monthly rate is 4.7. These are not well meaning, ignorant liberals talking. The Lozoffs know what prisoners do to each other; they also know what they can become.

The most disturbing prison for them on that Texas trip was the Ferguson Unit for violent offenders. Of the three hundred attending their workshop, two hundred were aged fourteen to seventeen! Yet even there the Lozoffs met some staff who actually cared. One correctional officer didn't just guard the room during the workshop, as most do. He watched and listened. On the way out he said it was the best thing he'd ever seen in the prison, and would they come back and do in-service training for the chaplains.

"They really need to hear you talk about goodwill and compassion," he said. "The Protestant and the Muslim chaplains in this unit won't even speak to each other."

The Lozoffs' son, Josh, came by for a few minutes. He was spending a year as a volunteer with his parents before deciding which direction to take in his life. Josh was just twenty-seven, had been a Hollywood actor playing the part of Gino in *Cheers* for three years. Then, after a big role in *Clueless,* he went off to South America for the summer to do volunteer work. While there he heard that *Clueless* had become a blockbuster. The discrepancy between the fatuous success of Hollywood and the reality of life in Bolivia made him decide never to go back to his former profession.

We all followed Josh out a few minutes later to go to the meditation session. Bruce was up on the veranda of the big house solemnly striking a large bell. We gathered in the meditation hall upstairs, chanted some Hindu chants, and then sat in silence for half an hour. These same men whose appalling life stories I had heard that evening, finished the day with prostrations to the altar, went to bed in silence, to rise the next morning for meditation again at 5:30 A.M. The Human Kindness Foundation, I realized, is not for dilettantes.

In the morning I sat in the office and read a few of the letters that pour into the Foundation from prisoners and their families all over the country. One man from the Bronx, twenty-two years old, is on bail for armed robbery in a residential drug treatment program. He has read *We're*

All Doing Time, and says, "I'm getting in the habit of praying for people I dislike. And I've been practicing saying I love you under my breath as I pass people. It's doing something to me."

Bo is on the phone arguing the case for Steve. Steve is inside for $1,000 credit card fraud. He got six years. Then he was raped by a warden and got eighteen months extra for reporting it, even though the warden had been found guilty twice before. They were about to put him on antiseizure medication. This is in Michigan, in the "Land of the Free." Happens all the time, says Bo, who is trying to get him sent to the foundation, though with little success. When Bobby was let out a few weeks ago, they had withheld his bag of personal belongings. We'll send it on, they said. This was in Montana. This morning Bobby calls and they say, laughing, "Oh we burned that trash."

On the wall in large letters is a copy of something the Dalai Lama said:

> *Never give up,*
> *no matter what is going on*
> *Never give up*
> *Develop the heart*
> *Too much energy in your country*
> *is spent developing the mind*
> *instead of the heart*
> *Be compassionate . . .*
> *and I say again*
> *Never give up*
> *No matter what is happening*
> *No matter what is going on around you*
> *Never give up.*

Bobby is disheartened by the news of his belongings, but he sort of expected it. "You can't dwell on it," he says. "Prison taught me that. It turned out to be the most valuable time in my life because it turned me to the spirit. There's nowhere else to go. And it made me start to care for others."

Later, we all did a few hours work together putting a new roof on a barn. Service, more than meditation, is the spiritual practice here. That can mean licking stamps, cleaning the copy machine, hauling boxes up from the warehouse, whatever is needed. No activity is more important than any other at the foundation.

Then Bo sat down with me to explain more of the ethos of the community. He said he had seen a lot of people change hugely in prison. In-

side, they had developed an incredible confidence in their own instincts
and sense of personal guidance. Yet everything they had developed in
prison could be a real obstacle in a community like this. In prison you develop a resistance to authority. Yet this place has a clearly defined leadership that you are asked to obey. There is a rule that you don't go to town
for your first three months. In fact those first three months are treated like
a retreat—no visitors, no suggestions for a change of menu, no secular
music. Now Bo might say to Bruce that he can go to town after all, and
Tony might object that he wants to go too. Yet he would just have to accept the situation and Bo's judgment.

The foundation sends out an initial letter making it clear what to expect. Bo showed it to me. It was not exactly inviting. It emphasized that
this was not a place to come and "do your own thing." There is very little
free time, and you agree to do whatever work is assigned to you, with
gratitude. Personal preferences are always subordinate to the needs of the
community, and who is best suited to fulfill them. There is no television,
no cigarettes, coffee, or alcohol. While the life of most Americans is
founded on the principles of personal freedom and self-assertion, life at
the foundation is almost the opposite. Everyone, including Bo, receives
just $50 a month plus room and board.

"Our foremost practice here is goodwill," explains Bo. "Where we
know and acknowledge that we don't mean each other harm. That's our
base, square one. We had two women who couldn't acknowledge that
with each other, so they had to leave. If they can't do that they should be
in a psychotherapeutic community. We have stripped down what it
means to live in a community to some very basic things. Our oldest
board member, Father Murray, a very wise Anglican priest, said that we
should keep our simple lifestyle absolute. Don't accommodate anything,
he said. That way, if people fit in they stay, if they don't, they leave, it's
that simple."

When I ask how they support themselves, Bo says that fund-raising is
the one area he refuses to be involved in, not liking the idea of nonprofits competing against each other. Who is to say whether their project is
more worthy than a battered women's shelter or an AIDS hospice? They
send out their newsletter, and people respond. One couple in Milwaukee
has been sending them $10 a month for twenty years, and he has never
met them. Most of their donors are like that. The base of their support is
about two hundred people. They don't ask, but it comes. And their
lifestyle is cheap—the whole residential operation runs on just $25,000 a
year.

This man's integrity is hard to fault. Some years earlier, he tells me, he was on a prison tour in Louisiana in July. It's like being in the slave era when you are in a Southern prison in the summer, he says, white guards watching black inmates working in the fields. He starts the workshop and asks them why they have come. One guy at the back says, his voice cracking with emotion, that he is there because he cannot believe that Bo and Sita are actually standing in his prison. He has been there ten years; read everything they have ever sent. He holds up a scrap of paper like a holy relic, saying, "You even wrote me a personal note one time, and I saved it all these years."

Then Bo did something that he had been doing many years, and that he was quite proud of. He deflected the man's devotion from himself by saying that what the man was really feeling was inside himself, and it was for God. Later that day, he realized for the first time what he had done: he had concerned himself more with needing to feel humble than with the other person's genuine experience of devotion. It was his own spiritual pride, he suddenly saw, that had been more important to him all along than any genuine concern for the experience of the other. In that moment he saw how well he had gotten his act down in his years of working in prisons; how charming he was.

He saw that such deep parts of his persona were implicated that the only thing to do was to stop working; to stop being Bo until he felt mature enough to go into a prison again. For three years he stayed quiet. He did many intensive retreats, months of silence, passed through long stretches of despair. For weeks and months the whole world seemed black and white. It was like he had stopped living. Then eventually he began to see the end in sight, to feel he would be returning to the world within the year.

When a friend asked him what the next step would be, Bo said he imagined some physical place to do their work, a Kindness Institute, though he didn't know how it would happen. The friend said he just had lunch with a guy who went to high school with Bo. Bo's name came up and the man said how guilty he had felt all those years for not supporting Bo's work. "Anyway, have a conversation with him," the friend said. "He's wealthy."

The following week the classmate called, and asked Bo what he wanted. Bo spoke of a property, and the guy said, "Fine, start looking, I'll pay for it." Bo was in no rush; he didn't feel he was out of retreat yet. He thought it might happen in a couple of years. He picked up the paper the next week, and the first ad they saw was this place. He didn't feel ready, he didn't feel he could do it. Yet they knew this was the place. Then a friend insisted on taking them to meet a visiting saint from India, Chidananda. Chidananda said, "You have all the blessings of the saints and sages. Do it."

So here they are, Sita and Bo, a couple of volunteers, and three ex-prisoners, four years later. "I didn't change as much as I hoped," smiles Bo. "No surprise there. But this place has helped a good number of people in those four years."

I wondered if the work could find a bigger platform, help raise public awareness about the way we treat prisoners and show how everyone could benefit by doing it differently. I am being a naive liberal, I thought. The truth is, if you want to get elected in any state, you have to promise to get even tougher on crime than your rival.

But then Bo says there are some hopeful things in the pipeline for television.

"You ever hear of Mr. Rogers?" he asks.

I hadn't.

"Well everyone in America knows Mr. Rogers. For the last thirty years or so his television program has made him the patron saint of children. So, this Mr. Rogers had been buying all our books and tapes for years before we finally figured out it was *the* Fred Rogers. He eventually phoned after we had asked a few times, and in perfect Mr. Rogers style, he said, "I quoted you recently in one of my talks. I said, I have a new friend. He's a writer, and he said something very interesting. He said the cause of all our problems can be summed up in a single sentence: human life is very deep, while our modern lifestyle is not. And then do you know what I did? I told them I would really enjoy us to be silent for a minute or two and think about that."

"He starts every talk with a moment of silence now," says Bo. "So. He asked me if I could do something on television to help deglamorize prison for kids. One of the heads of the Corporation for Public Broadcasting had called Fred saying she was startled and frightened by the response of an African American kid to her question, 'What do you want to be when you grow up?' "I want to be in prison," the kid said, "because you get three hots and a cot."

"Three hot meals and a bed for free. That image hit her so hard she phoned Fred Rogers and asked what they could do. So he said, 'I have a friend.' What we are planning is a documentary called something like *Families Doing Time*, with Mr. Rogers talking to prisoners and their kids."

It can't be true, but: Sita tells me that one in every fifty American kids has a parent in prison, and that in a few years it will be one in twenty-five. Since they began their work, she says, the prison population has quintu-pled. The prison industrial complex provides safe jobs for life, new bases of political power, and huge corruption potential with millions of dollars of building contracts coming up every year.

"You know what I'd love to be?" Bo asks me suddenly. "I'd like to be the carpenter at this place. Really, I'd love that. I have really gotten over wanting to be the spiritual teacher, though I am willing to do what I can if that's what's needed. I feel more like a manager. I feel I just don't have the spiritual depth this place needs and these people deserve. We're supernice people, it needs more than that, but I guess you do what you can do."

I guess you do. Even this man, whose work has helped thousands around the world, is full of self-doubt. God bless us all, we do what we can do. Or do we, I asked myself as I left the Human Kindness Foundation to head further south for Georgia.

Chapter Eleven

Georgia and the Theology of the Hammer

We need people who realize that spiritual ain't worth spit
without sweat.

David Rowe, president,
Habitat International

Floating down the freeway in a boat of a car to Americus, Georgia, I
couldn't help but notice that the tone of the radio altered percepti-
bly the nearer I got. The farther south I drove the more stations
there were broadcasting what I can only call fundamentalist propaganda
which bore less and less resemblance as the day wore on to any message
of Christ I remember hearing. I had never heard anything like this before.
One harangue after another by people with strident voices complaining
about the prevalence of Eastern practices like tai chi (!) on campus, about,
of course, the right to life, about one crusade or another that the listener
should really join now.

It wasn't the issues that struck me (except for tai chi), it was the
twinge of fear invoked by the tone of voice, as if someone were implying
I'd better do or believe this or else. Or else I wouldn't be saved, I'd be an
outcast, I'd not be doing my duty. I don't mean that fundamentalism isn't
everywhere; it is, and has always been. It is a cast of mind that all of us are
prone to, a literalism that is not even a wafer away from absolute materialism. It bestows indisputable reality on a set of beliefs, a political philosophy, a tradition, a position. It allows for none of the ambiguity and
possibility of imagination, which is problematic, since everyone, even if
he tries not to use it, has an imaginal world that largely governs his unconscious if not conscious life.

Even the most ardent fundamentalist, be he Muslim, Christian, communist, capitalist, or scientific materialist, is obliged, consciously or otherwise, to sit on a whole army of inner voices that constantly disturb the status quo. No, there is a fundamentalist in me somewhere who when he is in the ascendant will brook no argument. What is new for me here down in the South is the airwave exposure to fundamentalism of a Christian kind.

Religious broadcasting is a distinctly American phenomenon. When you float around in aimless fashion for months on end you are prone to many things, all the way from unforgettable chance encounters to apparently useless facts and figures that drop into your lap out of nowhere. One little statistic that has clung to my memory for a couple of months—I don't remember where it came from, I just know it is as true as Jesus—is this: in 1974 there were nine religious TV stations. In 1996, there were two hundred fifty-seven. In 1974, only 1 percent of all programming was religious; now it is 16 percent. Clearly, the folks like it. And I guess most of them must be down here, judging from my radio waves.

I'm not on my way to any fundamentalist gathering, which would be to stray from my chosen territory. I am looking for the fresh, imaginative signs of the spirit in America; ways of being human that, even when they are based on traditional religion, have an openness to the cultural climate that allows them to contribute to the spiritual tenor of the millenium. So, I am wheeling into Americus to encounter the work—why else would you come to this sleepy two-street town—of an American household name, Habitat for Humanity.

I met Millard Fuller in the dining room of the town's hotel. This tall, gangly man with a big hand outstretched to greet me, he is the one who started it all. Before we sit down he greets half the people in the room, striding in a plain and direct way from one person to another, his eyes dashed with smile wrinkles. Millard is a conservative Christian with a compassionate heart. That is what enables him to see beyond literal differences of color, race, gender, or denomination. Habitat has been his life, though he had quite a life before that.

Even in college he was a successful entrepreneur, and soon after he graduated in law he was already on his way to his first million. Even then, in the segregated South, Millard was always one to put his neck on the line. He was one of the only people in the county to help out at Koinonia Farm, a Christian community that took care of black people in trouble. A friend of his told me later that Millard was a very dangerous man to be around in the sixties because of his refusal to toe the discrimination line.

Over the years he has defended fifteen murder cases, with only one failure. That was a black defendant with an all-white jury. He went on his knees before them to beg for the boy's life. When the jury returned they were all crying. They said they had to convict him or they would be ostracized from the community. The boy was led off in heavy ankle chains.

Listening to him, I realize I am in a foreign world here. I notice all the waitresses in the dining room are black, all the managers are white. Millard then tells me the taxi story, which has become part of the Habitat folklore. There he was, back in the sixties, getting rich pretty quick, he says, when he suddenly got a shock of a wake-up call from his wife. She said she admired his success, but for all the second homes, the powerboats, and other toys, their life was less happy than it was when they had none of those things. He had no time for their marriage, for home, for simple enjoyments. Their Christian faith seemed to be shrinking to the formality of Sunday mornings. She said she was going to New York, that she needed to be alone for a while.

Millard was devastated. He began to see how out of control his life had become, how at the mercy of ambition and success he was. He flew to New York a few days later and improbably found her on the steps of St. Patrick's Cathedral. He urged her to believe him, that he had seen the truth of what she had said, that their life would change from now on. Now Millard Fuller is a very practical down-to-earth man, not given to miracles. But he hailed a cab, they got in, and almost immediately a golden light filled the back of the car. "Let's sell everything," he found himself saying, ecstatically. "Let's go back to the simplicity of our faith and let God do what he wants with us."

A whole life ended and began right there in that cab. They went back to Americus; Millard sold all his business interests and began planning a nonprofit housing scheme on behalf of Koinonia. Then the church sent them to Zaire for three years to oversee building work there. In those three years they began to sense their mission. The simple housing being built in Zaire could be a model for the housing needs of the poor in America. Millard saw in Zaire how building houses can help build people—that a family's attitude to life and to each other is dramatically changed when they are made to feel they deserve decent housing. Even more so when they are the owners of the house, rather than the recipients of charity.

"Don't you think human beings are the most sensitive creatures on earth?" Millard says between two spoonfuls of dessert. "If I deal with you in such a way that you are led to believe I have a low opinion of you, you will respond accordingly. And of course the same is true if I hold you in high regard."

Millard's plan, which is how Habitat still operates today, was to enable those in need to buy their own houses through the "Bible Finance Plan"—no profit, no interest, and a long-term repayment schedule. The prospective owners give "sweat equity," meaning they agree to work for a few hundred hours alongside Habitat volunteers on the construction of their own and others' houses. Having no government funding ensures the strength of their grassroots support. Habitat is now raising new houses all over the world at the rate of twenty thousand a year.

Millard's answer is revealing when I ask him if he can still remember the first house he put up. It was when he was ten, he says. He helped his father rebuild a shack on their land for a black family. The signs are there if only we look. The soul can whisper its intentions even before we have learned to speak.

Habitat works, says Millard, because it is such a simple and obvious idea: everyone needs a decent place to live. Providing it is simply elemental goodness, love in action, no big deal. Yet Habitat is radical, both in its common sense and in going against the stream of consumer culture. Our aim is big, he says, very big—to eliminate poverty housing in America; and even, ultimately—why not?—from the face of the earth. A simple idea, but also a big one, a bold one; one that stirs the human heart.

That's why, I realize, Habitat appeals to everyone, regardless of beliefs. The Habitat Diversity Department deliberately mixes volunteers of all faiths and minorities. Habitat has discovered that movie stars, Junior Leaguers, sorority sisters, bar associations, professional football players, civic club members, church groups, campus chapters, women only groups, and corporations all have one thing in common: they like to build houses. And the houses go up quickly and cheaply, in a couple of weeks; for around $45,000, a Habitat house can be ready to live in.

"This is a deeply Christian movement," Millard says as we get up to go over the road to the Habitat headquarters. "But strictly nondenominational. That's why the Promise Keepers don't want to be involved with us, or with other fundamentalist groups. Though, you know, one of my best friends cried for three days after attending a Promise Keepers meeting, he was so moved to see all those men searching for meaning. The trouble is," he says, "everyone knows the Bible contradicts itself all over the place, so how can you take it literally?"

The Habitat Headquarters is in a car sales warehouse that they converted with $4 million (all paid for) into a beautiful open plan two-story block with its own print shop and four hundred employees. A whole block across the street is filled with volunteer housing, while a show street displays the variety of Habitat houses built in different parts of the world.

In Millard's office we are greeted by a breezy young woman from L.A.

who recently left the corporate world to write a book on contemporary heroes, one of whom will be Millard. The book will be called *Unstoppable,* and she has plans for an Unstoppable franchise, though I'm not sure what the franchise will sell—business plans to develop self-made heroes, perhaps. We have hardly sat down when the coordinator from Haiti walks in, having just arrived from Port au Prince. After eleven years' work there she is finally retiring at the age of seventy-five. Millard listens to her update on Haiti, asks about this person and that, and determines to write to some of them with his encouragement. The woman tells the story of a Haitian Habitat man who nominated someone for a house recently even though that same person was trying to ruin him with voodoo. He chose him, she said, because he fit the criteria. Simple as that. The new house owner continues to use sorcery on him.

While we are all sitting there the phone rings. It is someone who took Millard and "Unstoppable" fishing the day before. After they had both gotten bored, given up, and left, the caller had caught a huge catfish. "Jacob's coming round to show us the fish he caught last night. Let's go see," says the president of this international organization, best friend of Jimmy Carter and a celebrity all over the country.

We all pile into the elevator, Millard and Unstoppable laughing and joking about how they would never make good fishermen, just not enough patience, and I can see, they are sort of two of a kind. Just as we arrive at the front door an old gray truck pulls up. The black driver, wearing a battered straw hat and working clothes, climbs out, says with a smile, "I said you should have waited." He throws open the back of the truck and there are two giant catfish squirming in a box. "Gonna have a fish fry tonight," says Jacob. "You'd better come," he says, glancing at Millard, "so at least you get to eat what you coulda caught."

Millard says I can't come to the South and not have a fish fry, so that is what we agree to do later that evening. I leave them to talk and go out for a coffee in the grill down the street. The waitress asks me what I'm doing in Americus. "Might have known," she says. "Do you believe all that nonprofit stuff?" she asks. "Folks round here say the president has a castle in Africa with dozens of black servants. Whatever."

I tell that story to Millard as we drive to the fish fry later that evening. He and Unstoppable roar with laughter. "I've heard a lot," he says, "but not that one." The fish fry is taking place in a van outside Jacob's store in the poor end of town. The store windows are all boarded up, the local youths having stoned them. Jacob is a devout Christian, and says that if you contradict the values and attitudes of the people in that neighborhood, you are their enemy. He is handing out lumps of catfish and cans of Coke, his wife and a few other friends sitting on crates around the van. Jacob is telling fish stories, everyone laughing more at his enthusiasm than the stories themselves.

"You hear the one about the guy from New York, the one from Atlanta, and the one from Texas? Millard, you hear that one?" Millard hadn't.

" 'Well, how big is your fish?' the other two asked the New Yorker. 'eighteen inches.' 'Mine is twenty-four inches,' the Atlantan said. 'Mine is twelve inches,' said Tex. The other two laughed. 'I mean eyeball to eyeball,' Tex added."

Everyone fell about laughing. I ended the evening talking to Jack, an old friend of Millard's who was once a county commissioner. He tells me that the men in power in Sumter County today are the same ones who used to hit blacks with ax handles back in the sixties. The old ways die hard, black people in Georgia and elsewhere face discrimination and prejudice daily. I looked over at Millard and realized that what he models is the way of the future. I had been aware all day of a deep vein of equanimity in him—he is the same nonjudgmental presence whomever he is with. He passes the flame of human warmth unthinkingly to any human heart; to the president in the White House one day, to Jacob and his friends the next. No difference. The essence of Christianity, I thought.

The next morning, before heading off to Atlanta, I am scheduled to join a volunteer party on a new house going up on the edge of town. It is the first time I have ever begun the day with hymns to Jesus, which is the way the Habitat Headquarters starts every day. Then I join the others for the theology of the hammer, as it is known here—sweat that spirit. Sweat we did, in ninety-five degrees and humid. There were maybe twenty of us on that site, half from a church youth group in Chapel Hill, the others from a school in Cologne, Germany.

That morning we nailed the floor down with the help of Erlene, the prospective owner, a young black woman of twenty-three with four children living with her mother in Americus. It is easy to feel why people of every kind love to do this. It is that feeling of belonging; being part of a community of fellow humans working together across all dividing lines on a concrete task for the good of someone in particular. You don't have to think, you just hit the next nail in and you're there, shoulder to shoulder.

Driving into Atlanta later that day, I got to see the antithesis of community. More than three million people live outside the city limits and call themselves Atlantans. The suburban sprawl goes on for fifty miles or more, a uniform spread of the tame without warmth or soul, stringing out from the periodic nucleus of the mall. A ganglion of human shelters whose design you choose from a book and imagine you are making a personal statement, nobody knowing the person next door. As in so many American cities, downtown is ghostly after office hours, business and pleasure having mostly left for the suburbs for fear of crime and violence. Atlanta is segregated in its own way. In recent years it has been a mecca for immigrants. Thirty thousand Russians have come here since 1989; there are Turkish communities, Indian ones, all living their own lifestyle in a separate part of town.

I stopped in a mall for a coffee in the Madeleine cafe, and the manager there was Russian. Dmitri said he had been here a year, having been an interpreter in Moscow, and now about to go to school to study economics. "I don't like America much," he said. "I went to Kansas City first, that was terrible. At least Atlanta is better than that. Hey, I have an English friend here, he says it's too expensive to survive in England, so he had to come here. Is that true?"

I agreed that it was. I sat down next to a woman of a certain age with very long legs and enough mascara to disguise her features completely. Celine, like most Americans and especially, in my experience, American women, was immediately generous with the details of her life without my even having to ask. This Southern belle told me she had grown up in a small town in Tennessee where dancing was forbidden because of the power of the local Church of Christ. It is still forbidden there now, she says. Of course, she now dances weekly, and did her stint in earlier years as a Playboy bunny.

When I tell her of the book I am writing, she volunteers that she is a keen member of the North Atlanta Unity Church, that most people find community through their faith. "God without the guilt, that's my path," she says, and I believe her. "Unity is a way of life, not a religion. It helps me to know me better. What I say is, I'm a child of God first, a Southerner second, and an American third." Celine slaps her thigh and doubles with laughter before carrying on. Dmitri is throwing us the odd glance.

She is revving up now, telling us—her eyes include Dmitri in the conversation—that people are crazy to think that heaven and hell are pieces of real estate; that they're not, they're states of consciousness. That's why, she says, in Unity they say be careful what you think because you just might get it. Religion, she explains, is for those who are afraid of hell; spirituality, for those who have already been there.

I am beginning to wonder whether Celine is a part-time preacher; whether she has learned all these sound bites by heart; but no, she's a senior manager in a communications company and just enthusiastic; she's enjoying herself. Dmitri and I are enjoying her too. The subject is clearly her passion. She goes on to say that her church tries to marry recovery with metaphysics, bridge the soul with the spirit. Because if you can't feel it first, you can't heal it, she says, quoting the recovery hero, John Bradshaw. Celine warns us, her eyes like saucers now, that there is a danger with the twelve-step programs—that you can tell your story for ten years and never get past it. That's why, she explains, so many Unity churches are filled with twelve-step people—they have been drawn to the spiritual path by the twelve-step program, and want to take it further.

"But you know," she says, addressing me directly, "I think one of the main reasons you will find so much interest in spirituality in America is because we are not living in the survival mode of the industrial era any more. Baby boomers just aren't interested in materialism for its own sake. We are moving into the twenty-first century with a different set of expectations about life. Self-reliance is returning. Look at the positive effects of downsizing. I know, it's happened to me. We are beginning to learn that there is no security in the outside world, in a job, a family, even in education. Evolution wants us to be self-empowered. It seems to me that in the end, the cause of all our troubles is that we don't love ourselves."

I draw breath, so much to take in there. And Celine is right, of course. She is right, too, when she goes on to say that only in loving ourselves can we accept and love others; that we would then look at other people's spirituality differently. We would see that, whatever the outer form, if it serves them, opens their heart so they can bring love into their life, then it just doesn't matter what their beliefs are. I think of my own prejudices, startled for an instant to think that I might even have any. Can I imagine a loving fundamentalist? More to the point, can I imagine loving a fundamentalist? If not, I am out of touch with reality, and that says more about me, I think, than about them.

This kind of meeting would never happen in England. You would never sit down and have someone pour out his or her personal philosophy to you in five minutes. Nor would you be likely to hear such good sense in such a short time. This woman spoke with a spontaneous authority. She was not laying a trip, I realized, she was sharing her joy. She had long gone beyond the gates of self-consciousness. She just didn't care, and why should she, why should we? Lalla, the ecstatic Kashmiri poet, asks

> *When will my shame fall away?*
> *When will I accept being mocked*
> *And let my robe of dignity burn up?*

Celine burned her robe long ago; she is on fire herself now. We're all on the edge of our greatness, she tells us, Dmitri standing taller as she looks his way; but we feel that if we step into it, life just won't be the same, and of course it won't. Usually only pain will push us over the edge, and her church has a crying room to help the process. Our fear is we don't know what life will look like on the other side, but we are not meant to know, that is the point, our ego is powerless in major life transitions.

"We just have to surrender to the greatness in us and allow that to guide us over the edge. That's the faith Peter had for a moment when he stepped out of the boat and began to walk toward Jesus. Then he blew it, of course," she said, slapping her thigh and laughing again. "What I have found is that as long as I try to figure it all out I just sink deeper and deeper. But then once I let go I just fly."

She's certainly flying now, as we get up to go our own ways, all our energies lifted suddenly. Dmitri hands us both a loaf of Russian rye, compliments of the management, he says. Celine slings a bag with a range of small compartments, almost like a gun cartridge belt, over her shoulder. When I ask her what it is she says it is her make-up bag. There is $1,000 worth in there, she says. "Our men like us that way."

I couldn't quite believe I heard what I just heard. But I did. No matter. Celine is her own woman no doubt about that, whomever she happens to wear make-up for.

I left the Madeleine and made my way to the Auburn district, old Martin Luther King country and still the black community end of downtown. I head straight for the Martin Luther King Museum and Memorial, next to Ebenezer Chapel where King's father was preacher for forty-four years, until 1975. King himself was co-pastor there for eight years, till 1968. His memorial is a white marble tomb set in a lake with fountains outside the Memorial Museum. Droves of black teenagers are sitting by the lake, many of them wearing T-shirts with the slogan, "Have You Considered The Lord Lately?"

I am here to honor the inspiration of King not only for the civil rights movement but in the deepening of the spiritual and moral roots of democracy for all of us. King was without doubt the conscience of America in the second half of the twentieth century. It surprised me, then, to see so few white faces around his memorial. In fact I am the only one. I imagined this would be one of the great shrines of the nation. I spend a few minutes in the museum looking at the personal memorabilia of the King family, and then make my way across the street to a building that houses a sobering exhibition on the civil rights struggle.

On the way over I stop for a moment in front of a sculpture of an African American man holding a child up to the sky. It is called *Behold*, and was made by Patrick Morelli in 1990. The sculpture was inspired by the African ritual of raising a newborn child to the heavens with the words, "Behold, the only thing greater than yourself." I was reminded of Celine talking about being on the edge of our greatness and needing to stand in it. Seems like the Africans knew about that a long time ago. Today, though, African Americans have to work to remember it.

When you look at the civil rights exhibition, you understand why. I had never seen videos and photos like this before. There were black men dangling from trees and white men standing by sneering; hard, jeering faces rammed in front of black students who were entering college for the first time; beatings and taunting; Rosa Parks sitting in her place in that bus. I am ashamed to say I did not know. Not like this. When Millard Fuller's friend in Americus had mentioned the men with ax handles in Sumter County, it registered, and I was sickened; but not like this.

This is a source of endless despair unless one knows an even greater power. Martin Luther King did. He knew the faith that Celine had spoken of too, the faith of Peter to begin walking in the face of impossible odds. The faith of the Dalai Lama who knows never to give up, never to retaliate against your tormentors even when they systematically try to erase the memory of your race. The faith of the African American people today, who, ravaged by drugs, violence, poverty and continuing injustice (think of the stories of ex-prisoners at the Human Kindness Foundation), still hold their heads up and sing out their praises across the land.

I went to my hotel room chastened that night, and spent the rest of the evening alone. The next morning I am rather late in arriving at the early service at Ebenezer Baptist Chapel, and slip into a pew at the back of the crowded church among women in cream suits and flower hats and men in gray pinstripe suits with wide lapels. A young preacher has been setting the tone, and the choir, all in black, takes up the mood, crooning softly a hymn to Jesus. Then the big man comes on, the Ebenezer preacher, and in a few moments he is striding backward and forward across the stage mopping his brow with a large white kerchief.

He quotes Thomas Merton, which surprises me in what I imagine to be a traditional Baptist setting. He quotes Thomas Carlyle, of all people. He brings in Augustine. Augustine wouldn't, says the preacher, get married because he was too lustful. What Augustine didn't realize, he says, his voice rising, is that we all have a broken leg in one way or another. If you are ill you go to a doctor, if you are in emotional pain you go to a therapist. Don't be in denial, he urges us; don't expect God to take away your trials, get a life and wake up to how you brought your troubles on yourself and how you can seek help to heal them. Just because he is wearing robes, he says in a rising crescendo, doesn't mean he is any different. He cuts himself off too; he feels depressed; he is lying on a stretcher paralyzed, just like the rest of us. Perhaps someone is paralyzed because they have been knocked down so many times that all they want to do is go in their shell. That's understandable, cries the preacher. We all need help to get up again. That's what neighbors and therapists are for.

He reminds his congregation that the paralyzed man was taken to Jesus by his neighbors, because he didn't have the will to go himself. That we all need neighbors, and to be that for others. The whole sermon rises to a masterful blend of the traditional "come to Jesus" call, the twelve-step program, and popular therapy; the preacher dancing around the stage now, prodding the air, reaching for a second handkerchief. All of us are wrung out when he ends with a plea to people to come out to the front and ask for Jesus. Anyone who hasn't got a church can just say so and they would be connected with one. The root of all our pain, he says finally, is that we're disconnected from God. And the connection is Jesus.

What a performance, I think, as I walk round to the church office afterward to meet Joseph Powell, the man himself, who took over from Daddy King in 1975. Joseph is a big man, comfortable in his skin. When I tell him I have just come from Habitat, he says that Ebenezer has built nine Habitat houses, the largest number contributed by any minority church. And when I say that there didn't seem to be any black volunteers on the project, he gives me pause for thought.

"See, for 246 years we volunteered in a system called slavery, so volunteerism is not exciting for us. Added to that, the kind of work we do doesn't give time for volunteerism."

I say how impressed I am by his blend of religion and therapy; how he seems to be staying faithful to the roots of his tradition and also acknowledging contemporary understandings of people and their needs. He loses some people because of that, he tells me, and also because some think he is too political. "Just give me the Word, plain and simple, they say."

But for Powell the literal translation of the Word loses its essence. It has to be contextualized. That is why he can't take or preach from it literally. Instead, he emphasizes incarnational theology, God within us, but also among us. Powell is firmly in the tradition of King: our spirituality must demonstrate itself in how we involve ourselves socially and politically. He is also in the lineage of King in leading from the front. He is here to move the critical mass, he says. It's a crime to speak for forty minutes without issuing a challenge, a wake-up call. He has to do that for his own sense of authenticity, whether there are two or two thousand in church.

He fills in the background for me a little, explaining that it is natural for his people to want the Word, because the black church stands in that strong Protestant tradition of preaching. After 1865 and the abolition of slavery, black people agitated so strongly to read in part so they could read the Bible. From 1831 it was illegal to teach black people to read. The drum was illegal too.

"Yet Christianity has to be incarnational," Powell tells me, "otherwise you get the spirit divorced from the flesh. That kind of split enabled the slave owners to maltreat slaves with impunity. The same men who beat people with ax handles were all in church on Sundays. Unless spirituality manifests itself in a wholesome life for the flesh, it just doesn't cut. What interests me is how our men in this church can go out and be missionaries in crack houses, not by laying religion on people but by letting the kids there know we care. Christianity is about real relationship. It's not about good deeds, it's about an open heart. We need to get to people where they are, and that's what I try and do."

Just as he did in his sermon, he impresses on me the importance of recognizing that all of us are vulnerable. What a relief that is, he says, not to have to be pretentious. We have to own up to the fact that we all screw up. It's alright to say we have a neurosis. It's alright to preach a set of sermons on the twelve steps. In fact for his community, he says, it is crucial to help people out of their denial, and encourage them to feel it is legitimate to seek help. For the black community, that is still a new concept.

Then he said an interesting thing that made me think, I'm not sure why, of Celine and her Unity church. He said that the danger of taking incarnational theology to the extreme of identifying with the Holy Spirit is that you walk around with the attitude, "I am blessed to do well." You then ride an edge of a big wave of narcissism, fueled by the capitalist ethic. That wave can wash right over the deeper current of our vulnerability without our even noticing it. That is the danger, he thinks, with some of the New Age attitudes, and New Thought Christianity like the Science of Mind. The Christian ideal of love involves something called sacrifice, he smiles. And we don't like that.

Yet in Celine's church, I thought to myself, that isn't so; and Unity is certainly part of the New Thought movement, a development of the Transcendentalism of the 19th century. They even have a crying room, and she also told me they have twelve-step classes. The twelve-step program seems to have permeated all kinds of religious contexts. The marriage of soul and spirit, that's what we are talking about, I remembered. How different these two approaches to spirituality seemed, Celine's Unity Church and the Ebenezer Chapel of Joseph Powell. But in essence, it seems they are using different language and styles to say very similar things. Powell's way was different from Beacher Hicks's in Washington, too; less likely, perhaps, to use terms like the balm of Gilead, more likely to tell someone to go to a therapist. Yet even there, the Metropolitan had its lamentations classes and men's retreats. Religion, even old-time religion, is not what it used to be.

When I ask Robert Powell which writers have influenced his thinking, he responds that his background is in liberation theology, though he is at home across the church—he draws on the early church fathers, on Eckhart, on the fathers of the Reformation. He is up early every morning reading devotional literature, Nouwen, John of the Cross, Augustine; Thomas Merton is always an inspiration. When I tell him I am going to Merton's monastery the next day, he says he wishes he had the time to go with me, though his time would come.

"I am no more locked into the African American thing than King was," he goes on. "King was deeply influenced by Thoreau, and a number of white theologians such as Tillich. Essentially, racial barriers are irrelevant. If someone has found the tap root, I resonate. God is bigger than race. We call ourselves the Church of all Nations, and the black church never excluded anyone."

He paused for a moment. "You know," he said, "I want to make it clear that what I have just said does not imply a unified theology. No. White ministers need to talk to their congregations about sin and the sickness of the culture. I don't. I don't have to talk about being greedy, or about lack of compassion in the workplace. Theology is culturally determined, though of course there are points of contact. I believe in pluralism. Our choir sings spirituals, but also Bach and Beethoven, who are great by anyone's standards, if they have any sense. We insist that God not be limited by our own idolatry."

Speaking of idolatry, I wondered what it was like to follow the Kings as pastors of the church. He admitted it was both a gift and a burden. He is inevitably in the shadow of Martin Luther King, and he makes sure he in no way tries to emulate him. Yet people are always slightly disillusioned because of whatever their expectations are. Part of the burden is precisely in trying to keep the church and all who come to it from idolatry. Many people are more interested in knowing if Coretta King is in the congregation than if Christ is at home. He smiles, ruefully. Yet he has a growing number of serious members. They even have classes that study the spiritual classics.

"We study African history, too," he says, gathering his notes to make ready for the next service. "We have a new pride in our homeland and the intellectual achievements of Africa. Swahili is taught in many schools here now. We are learning to appreciate what was not told in the schoolbooks about the contributions we have made to world evolution. Most white people don't even know there was a major university in Timbuktu during the Malian dynasty."

"No," he laughed, seeing my expression, "they mostly haven't heard of the Malian dynasty either. We now know that the Dark Ages had nothing to do with dark people. We no longer think of ourselves as being the last link in the Darwinian chain. Even so, we want to stay within the African tradition while opening our people to life in the global village."

At the beginning of 1999 a new Ebenezer chapel will open across the street, and with that final, magnificent gesture, Powell's work in the neighborhood will be over. He will have been pastor for twenty-five years. He is moving on to teach and write, not without a certain concern about what will develop after he leaves, since there is no single leader to carry on the work.

I glance at him briefly as he holds the door open for me to leave. I am looking at a man who has given his life to the service of others. He has stayed in one place, one community, and dug his furrow for God there. What finer successor to Daddy King could the community of Auburn have wished for?

Chapter Twelve

Gethsemane Abbey, Kentucky

> The sacred attitude is one which does not recoil from our own interior emptiness, but rather penetrates into it with awe, reverence, and with the awareness of mystery.
>
> Thomas Merton

> A monastery is an endeavor in reality.
>
> Matthew Kelty

I am landing in Louisville, Kentucky, on the very day of the Derby, to drive for an hour through a soft rise of hills and oaks past distilleries of fine bourbon. Along the way there are placards that tell us to vote for Carson as jailer, arrows pointing to Lincoln's birthplace, and little white ranches nestling in trees. Then suddenly, there in a gap in the foliage, is the place that Joseph Powell will surely come to from Atlanta one day, as I have come now. Gethsemane Abbey, a stern-looking pile if ever there were one, is all the more forbidding today in the persistent rain that has been falling since daybreak.

How familiar they are, these gray and white fortresses with crenellated roofs, rows of small windows, long corridors, and cold stone floors. The nineteenth-century European monastery, a common mark on the landscape in Germany, Switzerland, and France, transposed here in 1848 as the American foundation of the French abbey of Melleray. I remembered Bo Lozoff's comparison of a prison to a monastery, and realize he must have been thinking of these nineteenth-century heaps of dressed stone.

I have come here for the reason that most people do, on a pilgrimage of sorts to the Abbey where Thomas Merton lived the monastic life. Merton's autobiography, *Seven Storey Mountain,* was an immediate best-seller after World War II, and he quickly became the spokesman for a whole generation that wanted to build a new culture on fresh values. He was an unusual monk for having first lived a full and sensuous life as a student at Oxford, in England, and for being a gifted literary figure who was popular at society parties and gatherings. Yet when he decided to take his vows he chose the strictest order of all, the Trappists, who at the time, in Gethsemane, lived in absolute silence and seclusion.

Silence was what Merton sought, and in the more than two decades that he lived at Gethsemane he used it to plunge wholeheartedly into intimacy with God and to write a score of books on the inner life that attracted an international following. His *Asian Journal* was the first of his books to stir me, the account of the journey that was to end in his death in 1968 by an accidental electric shock in a hotel room in Bangkok. Merton was a pioneer among Christian monks to suggest that there was much to be learned from the Eastern traditions, and to point to a spirituality that transcended the confines of dogma and ritual. He was profoundly moved on that journey by his meeting with the Dalai Lama, with Indian saints, and by the great Buddha statues of Southeast Asia. In the silence of Gethsemane he had plunged below the outer forms of his faith to the universal well that nourishes all traditions.

I arrive at his monastery—strange to call it that, him being dead now for thirty years—just in time for the start of Compline in a thin, tall chapel with a monumental tapestry of Christ at the far end and a single candle burning below it. Thirty monks are standing in the choir stalls chanting a psalm, while twenty or so visitors sing along with them at the west end. We all file up to the abbot finally to receive his benediction along with a sprinkling of holy water.

As we troop out at the end I see that everyone is turning off into a side chapel where, I am told, Father Matthew Kelty is about to give his weekly poetry and spirituality ramble for visitors. As soon as I have found my room along a corridor of cubicles I slip in at the back and listen to the faintly Irish lilt of this elderly man of Boston-Irish stock. "Be Not Ashamed": he begins with a poem of Wendell Berry, the poet of the earth who apparently lives just over the hill on his Kentucky farm.

No, why should we be ashamed, Father Kelty asks us in the manner of a distracted bard in an Irish pub, peering intermittently over his glasses, looking down at his notes, fumbling with his paperwork, picking a stray leaf up from the floor. Why should we be ashamed? We are sinners all right, but look, our sins are already forgiven, so why be ashamed? Christ will never leave us, he says. Why would he? There's no need for guilt because our sins are already forgiven. All we need is awareness of who we are. That's only healthy, isn't it now, and confession helps us on the way to that awareness. Confession helps us to have an examined life.

We all notice, don't we, he says—three brief looks over his glasses in the one sentence—how the same things come up again and again. Well, it's just like weeding the garden. You just keep weeding. The essence of the whole thing is kindness. And how do you treat yourself? Be kind with yourself too. If you know you are a sinner whose sins are forgiven, that makes it easier for you to give compassion to others. Humility is no more than honesty, seeing our nature—nothing self-degrading about that. A few more poems on the same theme, then he finishes with words that become poetry because of the way that he says them

"I tell him that, you know. I do. I say, 'I love you, Lord, come into the shambles of my heart, the shack I call home.' And when I don't, I wish I did." Then, as a parting shot, already halfway to the door, he says, "You want to know how you are doing in your spiritual life? Ask your dog, or the lady next door, or your wife. They'll tell you."

And then he is gone, out the door shuffling his papers, dropping one, stepping on it, picking it up, then gone. The spirit is alive in this place, no doubt about that. I don't care if he uses old Catholic jargon, sin and sinners that we are even if already forgiven. I get his meaning, even so: everything's all right, as long as we own up, like Joseph Powell at Ebenezer said, to our vulnerabilities, and place them in the hands of a higher power. I get his meaning because, no matter what terminology Mathew Kelty uses, he is speaking heart language, undiluted. And that always goes like an arrow straight to the mark.

The next day I sit down with him for a moment in his office, an hour later than our appointment because that can happen in monasteries, they run on a different time. Father Kelty tells me he started out in a missionary order, which sent him to New Guinea in 1948 for three years, then brought him back to Chicago to run a magazine. He came to Gethsemane in 1960, and had Merton as his novice master for a couple of years.

"He was winsome, witty, and charming all right, very low-keyed, sensitive, gentle, and easily hurt. Very British qualities, I'd say. He was the hardest working monk in the community; never wasted a minute, yet he always had time for you if you needed it."

Such a beautiful, surprising testimony Matthew Kelty gave then of a man whose name is public property for quite different reasons. He said that Merton's real gift to him was that he truly taught him how to be a monk. He taught him acceptance, docility. He helped him to see that there was really nothing to do in this monastery but to make fruitcake—

how utterly pointless it was to have ambitions here. He was able to do that, Kelty went on in his marvelous softness, because he himself had grown up in a competitive world, and had left it behind.

He quipped that although the community made fruitcake in order to earn a living, their best product here was silence. The value of the monastery in today's world, he says, is that it can offer an oasis of peace and quiet within a climate of faith. Very different now, of course, than during Merton's day when the rule was absolute. Now, they use their own discrimination on when to speak or not.

"The church has been around for a long time, so it's not surprising it seems hackneyed to many," he concluded, someone else waiting at the door to see him now. "There's an antipathy to the church at the moment, but the church has known that often before. People have prophesied its demise for centuries. Still here, though, despite all the experimentation with other ways. Mind you," he said, a glint in his eye, "good Buddhists are better than nothing. I mean, Buddha experienced Christ the best way he knew how."

I didn't rise to his bait, I didn't have the time anyway. Instead I thanked him with a clasp of his thick warm hand and went out into the folds of the hill on the other side of the chapel under a white mist of rain. There in the lee of a leafy tree were a few rows of wooden crosses, low and white, leaning uncertainly this way and that and speckled with bird's lime. One of them had a small vase of red miniature roses propped up against it, and a sprig of evergreen tied to the cross. Blackened into the wood were the words Father Louis. Died 1968.

This is all that remains of Gethsemane's favorite son, remembered by his monastic, not his worldly name. An anonymous little cross among two dozen others. Just as it should be. A man of no rank, like any other monk, here to make fruitcake. Except this one also left words etched into the hearts of people around the world, even if he went only once far beyond the monastery gates, and then to his death. I stood for a moment in the white drizzle, remembering my origins and my destination, and went back inside to meet Merton's last secretary.

Patrick Hart is a beaming Friar Tuck of a monk with a glistening pate who was Merton's secretary during the last year of his life, and has been editing his writing ever since. Just a few minutes he has, the monastic life is a busy affair, as Merton often complained in his writings. Then, as now, the community earned its keep by making cheese, its famous fruitcake, and keeping a beef cattle herd. Merton would often wryly remark that it must be easier to be a contemplative in daily life than in Gethsemane, where the daily grind was under your nose all the time.

But Patrick has enough time to tell me that he has been at Gethsemane all of forty-six years, enough to see a lot of ideas for change come and go. The change he would most like to see is to have the abbey offer a two- or three-year monastic training for men before they got married. That would surely help with the divorce rate, he felt, people getting a little more conscious about what went on inside them. I said that was a practice they had long had in the East, with young men in countries like Thailand routinely spending a year or so in a monastery before entering worldly affairs.

"That is where the idea comes from," he says. "Though it's not easy to make changes like that. There are many here who would like to see the order back as it was in 1098. Though we do have an exchange program now with a Tibetan monastery. They join in our offices and we sit in meditation with them. That's something of a development."

It is indeed, but before I could ask any more Patrick changes the subject and goes on to say that he spent seventeen years in the monastery with Merton. In all that time the only thing you knew never to do, he said, was to disturb him when he was writing. That would be like disturbing him at prayer; it was sacred work. All his monastic life Merton struggled with the tension between the contemplative he was and the poet; between his need for both silence and images. Yet besides his books, his intellectual rigor, his profound faith, Merton's enduring gift to the community was his sense of humor. He was a deeply human, caring man, said Patrick, utterly appreciative of whatever anyone did for him.

I wondered what Patrick thought Merton's popularity in the world was due to. He answered by telling the story of Merton's revelation one day when he was standing on the corner of Walnut and Fourth Street in Louisville. Merton realized from one moment to the next that he was in love with everyone on the street; that his separateness had fallen away, along with the romance of the monastic withdrawal from the world. From that moment on, said Patrick, he began to address moral and social issues, knowing he had a duty to respond to secular needs. His gift to the world at large, added Patrick, was to articulate the meaning of suffering for the contemporary person and the way to the other side of it through faith.

"You will hear him now as you have your lunch," Patrick ended as he led me to the vaulted dining room to join the other guests at long tables for a self-serve buffet. "And when you have finished, I have arranged for you to meet with Brother Anthony. He is definitely in the spirit of Merton, at the radical end of the community. If there is anyone here who would like to move us on into the next millennium it is he."

As Patrick bustled off I sat down to eat and listen in silence to the thin voice of Merton over the speaker system. It is a Benedictine custom to listen to inspiring works read out loud at meal times, and today it was a recording of Merton giving a talk to a class of novices some time in the sixties. Hart was right, this novice master had his pupils chuckling every few minutes, joking about the foolhardiness of monastic life, the madness of persevering in such a boring, useless existence. On the table was a copy of the *Constitutions of the Order.* Forgetting Merton for a moment, I began to read.

"The monastery is a school of the Lord's service where Christ is formed in the hearts of the brothers through the liturgy, the abbot's teaching, and the fraternal way of life. The monastery is an expression of the mystery of the Church where nothing is preferred to the praise of the Father's glory . . . only if the brothers prefer nothing whatsoever to Christ will they be happy to persevere in a life that is ordinary, obscure, and laborious."

That is Merton's point, I realized as I got up to find Brother Anthony. The monk is a fool of and for God. There is no earthly meaning to his existence whatsoever. That must be why Merton had such a sense of humor: he had seen through the fallacy of trying to make something of oneself, of trying to be anything other than a "man of no rank," as the Zen Buddhists put it. Of course he was lighthearted. "Except ye be as little children . . ." Yet you can't start from there, except by unusual grace; the vale of tears has to be gone through, the successes and failures enjoyed and endured. Only when the heart is broken open can a love that is not of this world pour through the cleft. That, it is dawning on me, is the purpose of the monastic daily grind, to wear away the heart, rub it down and let the waters of a new life emerge. It can, of course, be the value of anyone's daily grind, if only we are willing to see it that way.

I didn't have to go far in search of Brother Anthony. He came to find me as I was leaving the dining room, a slight, almost gaunt man with a gray beard, penetrating eyes, and an almost nervous, electric aliveness. As we settle back in some meeting room down in the vaults he tells me he has almost left Gethsemane three times in the last thirty years. On his twenty-fifth anniversary he dropped out of the choir and now just goes to the liturgy when he feels like it, which isn't often. He has found it unceasingly difficult to feel at home in such a traditional context, especially since he has been aware of all the innovative developments in spirituality in recent years.

"As far back as 1985 I just had to get out and explore," says Anthony. "The abbot here is blessedly open, he allows each individual to follow their personal call, and he doesn't confuse the ends for the means. I owe my sanity to him, really. I started out going to a Zen Christian retreat, and that set me off on the path of meditation. Then for some years I studied with the abbot of Furnace Mountain Zen Center. There can be a lot of silence in Christian monasteries, but not necessarily a lot of inner life. It's so easy to get stuck in the form, the liturgy. Interior silence as a practice has only been valued again in recent years. The Catholic Church has been wary of subjective mystical states for centuries, partly because personal experience can weaken the hold of external authority. So for generations we have placed more emphasis on works and church authority. Merton, of course, was an important influence in restoring the value of inner silence, but he had to struggle against the stream in Gethsemane, as you know."

Anthony's experience of meditation put him back in touch with his body, another dimension of experience the church has chosen to ignore for centuries. He was shocked to discover how much tension he was holding, and that led him to begin massage, yoga, and gestalt therapy. Then he discovered the holotropic breathwork of Stan Grof, a synthesis of breathing and music that releases stored tensions from as far back as the perinatal life. He did breath work for some time with a local therapist in Louisville, and on discovering the depth of grief and abandonment he had been holding, he went into therapy for some years. Now he is about to qualify as a master Reiki practitioner, a form of subtle energy massage. How many monks like this are sitting in these nineteenth-century cells, I wondered.

All the while he was exploring, Anthony continued to feel a deep resonance with the Christian worldview. Except now he has come to a non-dual realization that God and Jesus are not separate from who he is. It is not just Zen that has shown him that, he explains, but the essence of the Christian message, too—"I and my Father are one." What meditation has done is to let him experience that directly for himself. He is on his own journey now, he says, and it is a path of healing. For Anthony, unlike Matthew Kelty, the language of sin is no longer appropriate today. We need, rather, a therapeutic language of sickness and health. The very perception that this is bad and should be avoided, and that is good and should be clung to, heightens our sense of separation.

I wanted to know how Brother Anthony's Christian faith had been changed by all the realizations he had had. My question unstopped the fountain.

"We must recognize that the Resurrection is the eternal now," he exclaims, eyes alight. "The eternal act. I as a person am a radiant act, and our identity is the creative act of love. Unless we empower people to re-ceive the fact that they are the Holy Spirit, Christianity will not be of ser-vice to contemporary times. We are the new incarnation of the spirit, expressions of the loving ground. And since we are all that, we are a com-munion of persons in God. God is all in all. I am in you and you are all in me. That is the energy of enlightenment, the energy flowing always through our bodies, our existential connectedness."

I had never heard quite such a fluent alchemy of Christian and Bud-dhist insight, and Anthony was only just getting off the ground. The Hindu nondual advaita philosophy of Shankara was in there too, with the frequent allusions to the indescribable ground of being pervading all.

"The only grace you need"—on he flowed—"is the question, Who Am I?" (Another advaita teaching) "I am not this body and mind, I am the supreme spirit of love moving through this body. This is the break-through into divine love. So grief can pass through, yet I can still know that the essence of who I am is love. I have a mantra. It is this: 'Om Jesu, Om Jesu. I am father, mother, of the universe, creator of all."

I wonder if the pope knows about this, I think to myself—or the ab-bot, for that matter. Anthony goes a long way out for a Christian monk. And he hasn't finished yet.

"Then the cross," he says. "The cross is a sacrament of awakening. It is a meditation for difficult times. We have to turn the projection back onto ourselves because unless it is a living truth it just isn't the truth. In the middle of your suffering, in that moment you return to your breath with the intention to know love. Becoming that surrendered breath, you let that total love of the universe transform you. You see the cross and you see the highest quality of enlightened mind; then you open to the same quality of mind in yourself. When you breathe love on the cross in this way, you heal all beings."

"Oh blessed night beyond all others"—Anthony was soaring now—"the Exultet sung at the Paschal Vigil. It was blessed because when Christ breathed forth his last in surrender, he knew his connection with the source within him. Because of that, in that instant, he transformed the world's suffering and human consciousness. He unleashed into human consciousness the power of reconciliation and love. That is what we are called to do and be."

He winds down by saying that in the end we can only see everyone in the same way, with the same question: How can I help you? What a beau-tiful, earthly return, I think. Yes, he ends, we are all being drawn by the inner mystery of the heart, and we are not the ones doing it. Have I heard of Rumi, he asks. I have, I tell him, by now not surprised that Rumi has penetrated even these thick walls. What wonderful lines of his they are, says Anthony, the ones that say, "But we have ways within each other/That can never be said by anyone."

If the unique insight of Buddhism is the nature of silence, says Anthony as we leave the room, then the unique contribution of Christianity is that we are the image of God. Then, as we turn to go toward opposite ends of the corridor, he to his yoga, perhaps, I to collect my belongings and be on my way, he turns and says, "Gethsemane is a blessed place, you know. I thank it every day."

Chapter Thirteen

A Christian Ashram in Oklahoma

From Gethsemane I have flown today to another world; to another, very different religious community, also blessed and unique in its own way. I am sitting now in my hut at Osage Monastic Ashram in Sand Springs, Oklahoma. Warm fingers of light run down the trunks of the trees. I have never seen so many slender risings, a forest of saplings with huts here and there between them. No sound here, but for the falling light among the trees and the new crocus pushing purple up from sandy soil. A spray of white blossom veils a deer. I have never spent time in woods before. They bring butterflies by the rainbow, click of woodpeckers, and the wind filtered through green. A dog by my door, a Labrador, longs to play ball.

I am in Oklahoma now, which means the land of the red man, and this isn't the only land that belongs to him. Not the first place you might think of for an experiment in faith. Sister Pascalene opened Osage nearly twenty years ago, on the model of Shantivanam, a Christian ashram in Southern India, on the banks of the holy river Gaudaveri.

Shantivanam was founded by Fr. Bede Griffiths, an English monk who left the abbey of Prinknash in England in the early fifties to begin an experiment in Christian community in India. Like everything else that tries to implant itself in Indian soil, Bede's experiment gradually took on more and more of the characteristics of the Hindu faith that surrounded him. The church has the appearance of a temple, with the apostles like gods emerging from the four directions. It is open on all sides, a flame burns constantly at the entrance to the holy of holies, the dark "womb house" at the eastern end made in the style of the inner sanctum of a Hindu temple.

Most important of all, Bede aspired to synthesize the Hindu concept of sannyasin, the wandering ascetic free of all belongings or abode, with the Christian concept of community. Following the example of the tenth-century Italian Saint Romuald, Bede had each monk live in his own hut in the forest by the holy river Goadaveri, and they would come together in community for meals and for liturgy. The monks took the formal *sannyasin* vow, dipping themselves in the holy river and offering Bede, the symbolic guru, the bundle of their belongings. Yet they would also take vows of obedience to the head of the Camaldoli Order in Rome, which was the only order Bede found willing to support this unusual alchemy of East and West.

Over the years, Shantivanam became an increasing attraction for those Westerners who sought a Christianity informed by the wisdom traditions of the East. One of the people who went there in the seventies was a sister from the Order of the Rosy Cross in Illinois. Sister Pascalene spent a year at Shantivanam, and was so changed by the experience that when she returned to Illinois she asked her superiors for permission to start a monastic ashram based on the Shantivanam model, though adapted for life in the West.

For the opening ceremony Sister Pascalene had a local chief come and bless the place. Tibetan monks were in attendance; Bede Griffiths came from India in his *sannyasi* robes.

Now the gong sounds, a Tibetan one, for vespers. I move only slowly, the daffodil light from the window sealing my feet in a pool on the floor. Osage is indeed a blessed place.

The chapel there is almost in the round, with large long windows that let in the trees. We sit in a round well, five elderly sisters, four guests, and me, on black Buddhist cushions while Pascalene gives a reading from the Upanishads followed by psalms and the hymns that tell of the coming of Easter. A young woman out of graduate school, here for a year, plays a small organ to accompany us. Then, as in the little monastery of San Benito, I remember, the Montana hermitage affiliated to the same order as Osage, we sit in silence for twenty minutes against a background of wood songs and the occasional barking dog.

The guests, as I find out later, come from all over the country to sit in this forest of peace in rural Oklahoma. One, a travel agent, here now from Dallas, always spends New Year at Osage. Another, from Miami, works in an AIDS hospice; then there is a Cambodian physician from Tulsa, and a nurse born and bred in Oklahoma.

In the dining room next to the chapel is a fine bronze statue of Nataraj, the figure of Shiva dancing in the circle of his own light. He used to be in the chapel, until a visitor from Texas wrote a vitriolic letter complaining about a heathen statue decorated with flowers. Someone else was shocked by the statue of the welcoming Buddha at the monastery entrance, and Pascalene has had to replace it with a figure of the Risen Christ. It is not easy to break new ground, even in the land of the free.

Sister Pascalene explains that you have to be very careful in the current climate if you want to stay within the Catholic Church. All the American bishops are conservative, she tells me, and to her knowledge there is not a single liberal seminary remaining. One Texan bishop has forbidden meditation and has threatened excommunication to anyone connected with Call to Action, the liberal movement that is seeking to call the papacy into question in light of today's world. Call to Action is lobbying for reforms in the American Catholic Church, which include the freedom of priests to marry and the formal assent to birth control.

Pascalene is a wisp of a woman, a gentle soul who has had to develop a courageous persistence in holding her vision of a contemplative community that, like Shantivanam in India, blends Eastern and Western styles of practice. A reduced form of the Western offices provides the structure of the day, but the nature of an ashram is present in the simple, unstructured lifestyle that is open to all religions and allows each person to follow his own rhythm. Every Monday is forest day, when everyone is alone in silence. One of the sisters lives the life of a hermit in a cabin off in the woods.

Isn't that something? What a year away from home can do, I thought, as I sat and talked with Pascalene the next day. How the absence of the familiar can wash you up on the shores of despair or set you down in the arms of love in a way that you have never known either. Sister Pascalene came back from India not only full of a new vision of Christ but also transformed by her encounter with Bede, who was to become the spiritual director of her life journey. She would hesitate to call him *guru*, her superiors would balk at that, but he was, she says, an extraordinary listening field. His listening was of the quality that allows the condition of presence to emerge. He was, she says, an icon of integrity.

The unswerving attention to presence is the entire point of the community, she goes on. It is a gift to have the conditions to be able to pursue that. It is painful to recognize how few people in her order seem to understand the experience of the East. A couple of the sisters have been with her for many years, others come and go. No young people seem to be attracted, and it can be a lonely path sometimes.

"But you know," says Pascalene thoughtfully, "I really don't plan or worry for the future. If Osage goes on, that's all well and good. If not, well and good. That is not my concern and not in my hands."

I remembered that the sisters at San Benito in Montana had said exactly the same thing. Part of the point of the contemplative life, I realize, is to develop a trust in the way of things that is deeper than one's own will or wishes. Today is a good day to die, say the plains Indians. Everything passes, the Buddhists remind us; thy will, not mine, say the Christians, Moslems, and Jews.

I walk that afternoon away on the Osage land between young oaks and ancient crags, up and down ravines, and always a hawk in the clean blue air. I see a woodsnake, and blue and white anemones open to the sun. I pass Mary's grotto by a stream and come to a green bench where Helen, the travel agent from Dallas, is looking down through the leaves to the silver glaze of the Arkansas River far below. I sit down alongside her for a few moments and we gaze over the land. Then out of the silence she speaks her true mind.

"What do you do when the longing is so bad you don't know where to turn? When you ache with it all over your body?"

Bang. Out with it. Just like that. What would you say? Quote a line from Rumi, or John of the Cross? Tell her to hang in there? Go get some spiritual direction? I hold her hand. It feels like my own. It is my own. My own question and the answer slipping right there between the fingers.

"When the spirit blows, the leaf shudders. It's all right. Everything's all right," I hear myself say after some time. And it is. In that moment, I know it is.

Chapter Fourteen

Boulder: The Spirit in Education

The molecule is so beautiful I guess the rest of my life has
been spent trying to live up to it.

James Watson, joint discoverer
of the double helix

On the flight from Oklahoma to Denver, I sat next to a young
African American woman who told me she was just finishing her
Ph.D. in eighteenth-century French history. She then added that
her brother was dying of AIDS, her sister was a crack cocaine addict, and
her mother was a Seventh Day Adventist who believes the world is about
to come to an end. How do you get out of that one, I wondered? She certainly seems to have succeeded, just one more witness to the ever surprising human spirit.

I am on my way to Boulder for the Spirit in Education Conference,
which is being hosted by Naropa Institute, a college specializing in Buddhist Studies. It offers unusual courses under the aegis of departments like
the Jack Kerouac School of Disembodied Poetics, started here by Allen
Ginsberg and Anne Waldman back in 1974. Naropa itself started then,
under the impulse of the Tibetan master, Chögyam Trungpa, who came
to America in the sixties from Scotland after he crashed his car into a joke
shop while his girlfriend, the story goes, was between his legs.

That, he must have thought, was a sign to move on. Trungpa was in
the lineage of the crazy wisdom teachings, so most of his students
thought it was all quite appropriate. He was in fact a remarkable and inscrutable teacher, breaking all the rules, yet founding, before he died, one
of the most enduring and influential networks of Tibetan Buddhist teachings in the Western world. The Shambala Training Centers teach Bud-

dhist practice and principles to the secular public in most major cities in America.

He founded Naropa to offer an education that balanced the outside with the inside, knowledge with contemplation, content with no content. The institute is named after the Indian sage who was for many years the president of Nilandra University in the eleventh century, and then left everything to find his root teacher. Naropa's life story, then, offers the challenge of a new view of education—the willingness to risk all, strip down and be open to the new—especially the new that can arise in the spaciousness of our own minds. When you do your masters in Buddhism at Naropa, meditation retreats are part of the course.

The conference is taking place in a large tent on the faculty lawn. The tent is crowded already as I come in, with John Cobb, the president of Naropa, telling us all that education at the institute is a tool to see your own face. Gradually, he says, we come to realize that there is nothing to be worshipped outside of one's own pure mind nature, which has created everything one sees in the first place. The natural mind, he continues, is what is fundamentally sacred. Pretty profound, but my own mind nature has another script and keeps telling me John Cobb is the very image of John Cleese; even the way he bends slightly to the left when getting to a punch line. Knowledge without wisdom, he goes on, impervious to my interruption, is like having a clear view without feet—you can see where you need to go but you can't get there. So we need both, and that is the purpose of education. Anyway, he concludes, what he is really here for is to thaw out with us all in the warm presence of Rabbi Zalman Schachter, who at that moment is sidling onto the stage with a big grin in his beard.

Reb Zalman was the inspiration behind the Jewish renewal movement I had seen in the Catskills. Born into a family of Hassidic Polish butchers in 1924, he was raised in Vienna and escaped the Holocaust via a French internment camp, arriving with his family in America in 1940. He was ordained in the Lubavitcher Yeshiva in Brooklyn, becoming increasingly disillusioned with Chabad orthodoxy. In 1966 he was finally kicked out after writing an article in *Commentary* magazine praising the sacramental potential of LSD. By 1975, after he went to teach at Temple University in Philadelphia, he was helping his followers to integrate the feminism, ecological awareness, progressive politics and egalitarianism of the havurah movement with a universalized Hasidic mysticism. Out of this brew came the renewal movement.

Today, he is the holder of the Naropa Institute Wisdom Chair, which suits him perfectly because he is a consummate generalist, and his position requires him to distill and dispense wisdom from beyond the boundaries of any one tradition. Few could do that today with the skill, humor and learning of Zalman, and he puts everything together in his own impish and heartfelt style in a program at Naropa called Aging to Sageing—how to become a wise elder in a culture that tries to deny aging.

He is wise elder and court jester now, standing on the stage in this tent before these educators of the young, playing the fool as one of his age has every right to do. Telling us Ginsberg jokes in honor of the poet who recently died, something about Yawheh, Allah, both hooknosed gods and circumcised. He ends his routine finally with a Ginsberg half song/half poem, which "if we are psychosemitic we can sing along to . . ." He urges us to "remember in all the discussions to follow over the next couple of days, that what we are really here for is to be real, to be holy, and laugh a lot."

There is so much hope in this tent, I realize, so much will to the good, looking at the laughing faces around me, several hundred educators in attendance from around the country. So much pain, too, the tribulations of working in tough inner city environments often without the support or empathy of a hierarchy that sees education as a career track more than a vocation.

Of all the speakers I am to hear over the following days, the one whose thoughts most stir my imagination is Parker Palmer, a Quaker who was for many years on the staff of Pendle Hill, the Quaker College in Pennsylvania. A tall, intent man, author of several books on education and spirituality, Parker begins by saying that what education requires is a transformative way of being in the world, one infused with soul, not with new techniques. The soul, he says, is an exceedingly shy, wild animal, and we are here to coax its life-giving forces into an enterprise—education—that is too often death dealing. Parker's images immediately have my attention. If education is dull, he continues, it is because we have driven a sense of the sacred out of knowing, teaching, and learning.

"I see the sacred," he says, "to be that which is worthy of respect. So the sacred is everywhere. Even when we feel anger, or jealousy, if we reach deep down for respect for the other, then something happens. Universities, unfortunately, only grant respect to text and competition. There is no respect for silence, or wonder, and I think that is because the academic culture is one of fear—fear of what might change or challenge us. Neither can we expect our institutions to carry these qualities for us. The sacred will not be carried by the Roman Catholic Church, or even Naropa Institute. These are things we ourselves are called to carry in our own hearts both in solitude and in community."

A moment to let the applause die down, and he goes straight to the crux: what all faculty members share, he says, is the pain of disconnection—from themselves, from their students, from their colleagues, even from their subjects. To acknowledge that pain is the first step. This is the beginning of the transformation of education. We need to speak the truth about the pain and fear we feel—he says it like a clarion call, every listening—and the next step is to proclaim what we feel in community.

"I tell people who think they are alone that they have not proclaimed themselves," he tells us. "We can't do it ourselves, and in proclaiming ourselves we invite community. Think of Rosa Parks, there is no better example of what can happen if you dare to speak up."

Parker Palmer has spent a lot of his time in recent years fostering community in academic settings by giving talks like this one at Naropa. Individuals will come up to him at the end and say they know exactly what he is talking about, but that they don't know anyone else on the faculty who feels that way. Then he points them in the direction of the other people who have come up and said exactly the same thing. What he leaves behind is the seed of a new community that can work for social change not by developing an action plan but by giving individuals the permission to connect to the soft truth of their heart in the company of others—no fixing each other, no critiquing, no interrupting, just listening in openness.

Pockets of possibility have opened up around the country. At the University of Michigan, some two hundred to three hundred of the faculty have offered each other community of heart over the last decade. Again, the institution is not going to do that, people must do it for themselves. Another illustration of grassroots democracy, I reflect; change from the ground up, like Jim Wallis's work in Washington. Similar initiatives to Michigan, Parker says, are happening in five urban centers through a program called the Courage to Teach.

He mentions Allen's School in Dayton, Ohio, which was transformed by the arrival of a new principal. In his first talk to the staff, the man said that what they all must understand is that their pupils have souls. Their job was to make those souls visible to the students themselves and to others. So we, the faculty, he said, must find the soul in ourselves. In five years that school was top of the league.

A good teacher, Parker, continues, has connective tissue with both her subject and the pupils. The words of a bad teacher float in front of your face, like the balloons in a cartoon.

He ends, finally, all of us present there with him, by giving the example of the biologist Barbara McLintock, as one who embodies a sense of the sacred in education. Her work of many years was the study of corn, and she said once, "All I can tell you about great science is that you have to lean into the kernel." In her relationship with ears of corn, she practiced the highest form of love, an intimacy that doesn't annihilate differences. To uncover that precious inwardness of the things of this world, including each other, is the essence of true education. That, he concludes, will come from the decision to live divided no more; to live on the outside what we know on the inside.

Parker Palmer's speech gave me a glimpse of just how much people in education were desperate for change and were willing to put themselves out to seek it. Another speaker, John Taylor Gatto, reminded us that the American genius was precisely to locate wisdom in ordinary people. In 1629, he said, the preacher of the town of Salem was chosen by the congregation. It became known as The Salem Procedure, the congregational principle that trusts that good things can happen when the human spirit is left alone to form its own curriculum. That is the kind of democratic ground swell that Parker is advocating in his call to community in educational circles.

This tent is crammed with people from all over the country determined to bring meaning back into their working lives, I thought, as I came away. It was a statement of solidarity about being human in the classroom, an arena where many might think the odds against change were hopeless. Neither was it just talk; even before the end, groups were organizing by area to put into practice some of the visions that had been aired. Since then the conference has become an annual event.

I was leaving to meet with three young people who were putting their own unique vision of education into practice. I drove the half-hour or so to the barrio district of Denver, and pulled up in a shabby street outside a house that served as the office of Peace Jam. I was greeted by Dawn Engle, Ivan Suvanjieff, and Julia Imado, the finance director. We sit down in some wicker chairs in a room otherwise bare except for a desk and a computer.

Ivan begins by telling me that through occasional work with the local young people in the district, he realized that while they were not all able to give the name of the president of the United States, every one of them knew who Nelson Mandela was. They all knew of him as a righteous, exceptional human being. One day a lightbulb went off in Ivan's brain—why not put kids from deprived areas like this together with the best role models you could think of, Nobel Peace Prize laureates like Mandela?

That was in 1994, Dawn said, taking up the story. Ivan knew of her connection with the Dalai Lama through her work as chairperson of the Colorado Friends of Tibet; he knew, too, that she had previously worked in

Washington as a lobbyist in Congress for the Tibetan cause. So he kept talking to her about his idea until she finally became as enthused as he was.

"We had, had, had to do this," she laughed. "We were obsessed."

They eventually put together a proposal and gave it to the Dalai Lama's people, who liked it so much that His Holiness immediately agreed to participate. From there, they cold-called every other laureate.

"Pretty wild when you think about it," said Julie, who joined them soon afterward. "We were nuts. Imagine, calling Desmond Tutu, and saying, 'You don't know me, but I live in Denver . . .' "

With the backing of the Dalai Lama, the others came along. They borrowed money from friends, used their life savings, got on planes, flew around the world, met every one of the laureates. Then they managed to get funding for the event itself. The plan was to put a few hundred young people together for the weekend with one or more laureates, and plan how they could bring the idea of peace back into their own lives and communities.

Peace Jam, as it is known—there have been six of them so far, and more are planned every year—is not another conference; it is an apprenticeship. "We see it as a transformational program for youth," Ivan says. "They learn from the Nobel laureates the skills and attitudes you need to bring positive change in your community. And they learn to see qualities in themselves that they had never recognized."

The students plan for a Peace Jam for months, studying the life of the participating laureate, and planning activities and projects through which they can take the work of peace back into their classrooms and communities. The aim is to generate a lifelong commitment to service, says Dawn; to have service be a natural part of your life. Laureates who have participated include the Dalai Lama, Desmond Tutu, Pres. Oscar Arias of Costa Rica, Rigoberta Menchu Tum from Guatemala, and Betty Williams and Mairead Corrigan Maguire from Northern Ireland.

Williams and Maguire received the Nobel Peace Prize in 1976 after they had organized some of the largest peace rallies ever known in Northern Ireland. Williams had knelt in prayer in 1973 for a British soldier shot to death outside her house, earning the derision of her Catholic neighbors. What impresses many of the young people about the two Irishwomen is that they are ordinary citizens who responded to what they saw around them.

"Every act of love is an act of peace. So we can all do something where we are. Blossom where you are planted," Williams tells the students. She urges them to recognize the violence of today's world and to build a nonviolent society for the new millennium. "Start small. Put up antigun posters in a classroom or two. It will spread to the rest of the school and the community."

I was beginning to get the picture. Here is an idea whose time has come, seized upon by three people—just three—and being taken already around the world. In 1998 they held a Peace Jam on Robben Island, South Africa, the infamous prison where Nelson Mandela spent so many years of his life. One hundred and fifty students reflected South Africa's racial mix, sleeping in the former quarters of the prison guards. What these three are demonstrating is that if you follow a mad dream with enough courage and guts it can grow into something far bigger than yourself or anything you imagined.

Julie hands me an e-mail from a pile on her desk. It is from Sarah Johnson, in tenth grade at Evergreen High, and it says, "When I was two my father died; my mother was killed when I was six. I moved in with my grandma, who died when I was nine. I have since been adopted, and all my pains, I believe, have made me a stronger person. Listening to Mairead Corrigan Maguire, I realized I didn't have to sit and watch the world die. I am going to touch people's lives. Probably not anything as great as Mairead had done, but like she said, touching one person's life is great too. I'm planning on volunteering in a nursing home and listening to their ideas of peace, and just getting to know and show my respect for the forgotten members of our community. When I grow up my goal is to work as a social worker and help others find peace. Peace Jam was so powerful I went home and cried."

I wonder if there is any religious underpinning to their work, whether they are fired by some Christian ideal of service. But no, Ivan is an Orthodox Christian, his background being Russian, but that was not a factor in the initiative. Dawn and Julie are not religious. No, what moved these people to risk their life savings, I realize, as I got ready to move on south to a place called Crestone, is the quality the Dalai Lama said was more important than any religion, available to any of us as soon as we become willing to step out of our self-preoccupation. The good heart, he called it.

Chapter Fifteen

The Crestone Community, Colorado

D riving south from Denver toward Santa Fe you will see, after a
few hours of lonely passes and big skies, the Sangre del Cristo
range of mountains following the black ribbon of your road a
few miles to the east. In the lee of those mountains is the tiny village of
Crestone.

Here, in the heart of a vast wilderness region, a developer dreamed of
turning two hundred thousand acres into a lucrative retirement resort,
the Baca Estate. The infrastructure was laid, some houses were built, but
the dream foundered. Then, in 1978, along came Hanne and Maurice
Strong with another dream. Their vision was to help the world move toward peaceful coexistence by creating at Baca a foundation that would
grant land to different religious traditions. The world's religions could
then establish centers of sustained spiritual practice alongside each other.

Baca today has a Christian monastery, a Zen monastery, a Hindu
temple, a Tibetan foundation, the Sri Aurobindo Learning Center, and
other groups representing Jewish, Sufi, and Native American organizations. It is the largest interfaith ecumenical community in North America. Maurice Strong, a Canadian oil developer and United Nations
diplomat, was the man behind the 1992 Earth Summit in Rio. While he
jetted about the world on behalf of the environment, his wife was establishing the Baca dream. Over the years, individuals and families who have
felt drawn by Hanne's vision have come here to settle and share the land
with the religious foundations.

Hanne is a warm, imposing presence, almost larger than life. When
she welcomes me into her house in the Baca I find her surrounded by her
grandchildren, Tibetan monks, and a famous Tibetan woman doctor who
has just immigrated to America from Lhasa. Other guests, from two or
three different continents, are strolling around too. An English film-

maker, Mark Elliot, lounges on the sofa. He, I discover, is a Baca resident, having moved here some years before. A Brazilian woman is talking animatedly with another Baca local. Here, at the end of the road, in the middle of the great open spaces of Colorado, different worlds meet.

If Hanne Strong has anything, it is magnetism. As I sit down to talk to her, I realize she has something much more; she has an absolute conviction about the Baca dream; and that it is far larger than anyone's personal vision. The experiment has hardly begun, she tells me; its future is still in the domain of prophecy. The native peoples of the area have always foreseen that the world's religious traditions would gather here to be part of a global harmonization.

As director of the Manitou Foundation, the umbrella organization for the whole project, Hanne oversees land grants at Baca and also heads up the Earth Restoration Corps, another brainchild of hers. The notion is to teach sustainable development skills and values to youth as they engage in environmental cleanup and restoration projects all over the world. A pilot project at Baca drew twenty-two participants from fourteen countries. Manitou also runs experimental projects in ecological farming and solar housing.

This big, blonde mama with the wide cheekbones of a Laplander—she is Danish—in weathered boots and flowing cape—everything she has cooking is enough to keep you stimulated and entertained for hours. But what really impresses me about this woman, as I sit with her there for an hour, is the way she is with her grandchildren. Hanne has clearly seen it all and met everyone there is to meet. Native teachers, Tibetan lamas, diplomats, magnates, film stars, spiritual seekers, and wise ones of every description—they have all beaten a path to her door in the Baca. She doesn't need to be impressed any more. Nothing special is happening, just life. So at the same time as listening to some seminal question or conversing with someone from the other side of the world, she plays with her grandchildren. If they ask her something, she will pause in whatever she is doing and give them a response. The most natural thing in the world, yet increasingly rare in our microchip times.

I leave them all eventually to their global conversations, though not before the Tibetan doctor, a serene presence who spoke no English, takes my pulse and gives me a pill made of precious metals wrapped in silk with instructions from her daughter to swallow it at the next new moon. I set off to find my cabin at the Spiritual Life Institute, whose Carmelite monastery at the Baca is one of their three communities of hermits, the other two being in Nova Scotia and Ireland. I am to stay here the night on my way south to Santa Fe.

A mile on down the road, at the end of a track in the tumbleweed, a long low building with a cross on its roof sits unobtrusively in the middle of a vast desert plain, the western mountains pink now on the far horizon under an endless arc of blue. The building is the community's communal area and chapel. The monks here—there are men and women—live in their own solitary hermitages in the brush, and guests do the same. My keys were in the library, and in moments I was putting my bags down in a wood cabin with a bed, a wood-burning stove, a small kitchen, and a view out to the mountains beyond the valley.

An age it seemed I was there, soaking in the fragrance of warm wood, my gaze drifting out on the blue to the mountains. Then the thought struck me that since none of the Carmelites was in evidence, this would be as good a time as any to visit the Zen Center further up the mountain. There Richard Baker Roshi started up a community again after he left the San Francisco Zen Center back in the eighties. Baker Roshi now spends half the year teaching in Europe, and the other half here in the Baca.

He is not here now, though, I discover after a rough ride up a rutted track that ends in the Mountain Zen Center. Instead, a man named John is frying tempe in a spotless kitchen of pine and stainless steel. He has been here five months, he tells me, having done time both at Tassajara and also at Green Gulch Zen Centers in California. This one is right, he smiles, and so is the Roshi.

Like most Zen centers, this one is beautiful, clarity everywhere. The bowls in the kitchen, the utensils, everything an object for contemplation. Not just the flowers, but the vases arrest my attention. The paintings on the wall are startling. A statue of Tara, the goddess of compassion, is an exact replica of the one at ground zero in Hiroshima.

Mark walks in, baldpate, clear large eyes that have been open since 4:30; he's the guy in charge, been here five years now. He offers to show me the zendo, and on the way over tells me that they sit twice daily, work being the main practice here. You learn to send the dishes back if you notice a spot, he says. The zendo, or meditation hall, is a long wooden room with a wide raised shelf that runs all the way round. You sit in meditation on the front plank of the shelf, which you see as the altar. You are the Buddha as you sit there. Where else could he be? Mark points to the two rows of drawers at the back of the shelf and says that one traditionally holds a pullout mattress and the other, your belongings. Here, it is symbolic, but in Japan all novices would sleep where they meditated in the zendo. No one would have any personal space.

We take tea for a while under a juniper tree, the hummingbirds whirring above our heads, cobalt blue. Another practitioner stops by; he is on his way to Aspen with his massage chair to make some money over the coming Easter season. Just half a dozen of them up on this mountain, Crestone Peak behind us, the Sand Dunes National Monument far below—a freak natural phenomenon, the sand picked up from all across the valley floor and dumped into dunes along the foot of the mountain.

Before I leave Mark says I should visit the Lindisfarne Chapel, just beyond the Zen Center. I have not heard of it, and he explains that Lindisfarne is a fellowship of artists, scientists, and religious folk back East, who are devoted to the study and realization of a new planetary culture. The most prominent part of their work is Christian-Buddhist dialogue, and it was they who founded the Zen Center back in 1988.

We went up the mountain a little and there it was, a wooden dome among the rocks. It is an interfaith sanctuary, says Mark, a sacred, rather than a religious, place, one that invokes the future more than the past. We step into a large round open space with light filtering in from a central skylight in the middle of a roof of intricately latticed slats. The silence is palpable; the geometry seems to act on the body, making me feel my feet on the ground. Mark tells me that the English architect Keith Critchlow followed the principles of proportion inherent in the seashell or the sunflower. In the center of the circle, beneath the skylight, was a stone ring. The floor was of baked bricks, which, he says, symbolizes the realm of transformed nature that is human culture. The skylight represents the meeting of the human and the angelic realms.

"People from all the Baca communities use the chapel at different times, for gatherings, concerts, special occasions," says Mark on our way back down. I thanked him for his hospitality, and made my way back to my cabin at the Carmelite Hermitage, gazing at the western sky all the while, purple, and rose now over the white-crested mountains.

The next morning I met Father Dave outside the Hermitage chapel. The Spiritual Life Institute was founded by William McNamara almost forty years ago, he tells me, and they moved here from Sedona when the Arizona town became too popular with tourists. Father Dave, in open sandals and wearing a brown habit, is the son of a Hollywood producer, and a Jew. Dave was expected to go to UCLA film school, but he met Father Willy, as he calls him, in the sixties, and has been in the community ever since.

The institute is unique in having male and female monks in the same community. The emphasis is on solitude supported by a community setting, with each monk living alone and eating communally only twice a week. One week in four is completely silent. McNamara and his co-founder, Tessa Bielecki, are also radical in using unapologetically erotic and passionate language to describe their purpose, in the style of the founder of the Carmelites, Teresa of Avila herself. They want to live, writes McNamara, "so vivaciously and mindfully that, in a loving kind of relatedness . . . they embody and anticipate the kingdom of God."

"Our life," it says in their rule, "is both militant and matrimonial. It demands an uncompromising ascetical combat—spiritual warfare—and faithful, passionate, spousal love for the divine bridegroom who woos and weds us."

Theirs is an ardent, full-blooded search for God in lands of remote wilderness, which makes them similar in temperament and outlook, says Father Dave, to the early Celtic Christians. McNamara has coined the phrase *refined ferocity* for their approach. The energy of sexuality is transmuted entirely into an erotic thrust of the whole being toward the embodiment of the kingdom: divine union. Eros is expressed in their relations between each other through the honest sharing of feelings, through trust, and the freedom of a natural eroticism that brooks no pretense and is liberal with laughter. Sexuality, Dave explains, becomes a symbol of their weddedness to God through Christ. They practice a special form of prayer, the spousal prayer of fusion, to intensify their calling to Christ the bridegroom.

Father Dave seemed to be describing a way of life in which nothing was left out. Well, a little something, maybe. For all the single-mindedness celibacy can offer (or does it?), I am still not convinced that the body automatically needs to be left out of the spiritual equation in the way that monastic traditions all over the world have advocated for millennia. McNamara will say that theirs is an embodied spirituality, and in a way it is. Yet as I heard Dave speak and read some of McNamara's writing, I couldn't help feeling that their celebration of the earth and the senses was less an embodied one than a spirituality of the passionate mind infused with faith—far more juicy, for all that, than a dry spirituality of the intellect.

On my way out of the Carmelite Hermitage, I was reminded of the story of Thomas Merton, who, not long before he died, was in a hospital in Louisville. A young nurse came and massaged his feet. It was a life-changing experience for Merton. For the first time, he wrote in his journal, he understood what embodied love really meant. He fell in love with this young woman, only just in her twenties and he past fifty, and they began an affair, which only ended when his abbot overheard one of their phone calls.

Now Merton had lived in the passionate mind for decades. Yet he had never understood the wisdom that the bodily intelligence can convey before he was introduced to it by a woman thirty years his junior. He received something from her at a cellular level that all his years of solitude and silence had never given him. I do not refer to simple animal pleasure. I mean an embodied love. And I do not mean that there is no place for celibacy. I mean there are many ways to cook a goose. Everyone to his recipe.

On my way out of the Baca I went up another mountain road for a brief look at the Haidakhan Babaji Center, another recipe for spiritual enlightenment. A Hindu temple stands there on a butte, with an earth ship administrative center berthed alongside. Earth ships are low adobe buildings made primarily of tires and aluminum cans that store heat and let it out slowly into the building. This one was bright yellow and blue with one man inside, wearing an Indian dhoti and a red dot on his third eye. He was spooning down a large bowl of fruit salad. He had worked in a shipping agents in New York, went to India, came out here, saw this place, and that was it, he knew this was home.

As I step into the temple I bang my head on a bell and trip over the carpet, falling flat on my face before the image of Haidakhan Babaji, an Indian saint whose ashram in India I had happened to stay in for a while in the mid-eighties. His was another intense and passionate way, I remembered. People there would be chanting through the night and building walls all day in the Indian sun. Wherever you go, the one common theme seems to be you have to work for God's grace; it doesn't come easy. Two other devotees are in prayer before the statue of Lakshmi, Goddess of Bounty and Wealth. She is bedecked in yellow flower garlands and looks happy. I make one perambulation of the central altar, and make my exit mindfully in order to avoid the bell.

There were many other centers in Baca that I never even saw, yet even the short time I spent there made me awake to the scope of Hanne's dream. Each of these different groups lived in their own world; I could barely imagine what the Babaji people would have to say to the Carmelites. And yet no, they shared something larger than their own private worlds: an ecumenical vision of unity in diversity on the same stretch of land. A model for the future, you might say, of the United States of America.

Chapter Sixteen

Santa Fe: Art as Joy

When you drive out of Crestone in any direction there is no need to rush because the flat straight roads go on forever and the sensation soon arises, as in a desert, that you are going nowhere. Only, on driving south, as you come into Antonito, after a straight stretch of sixty miles or so, is there a break in the skyline, the first hint of a hill, a few bluffs and canyons, red and white, the sagebrush sweeping the land now. New Mexico comes upon you gradually; but then, before you know it, the presence of the ages is speaking from the land on every side.

Already as I pass Ojo Caliente's warm waters I am deep in red rock country, and a few miles before Abiquu I stop at a lone hotel for a break. The owner asks if I have come for the sanctuary. When I say that if I have I didn't know it, he points to a red rock cliff behind the hotel and suggests I follow the path there.

As I approach the cliff I see that there are windows in it, long slender openings covered with Plexiglas. The path leads me to a door in the rock, and I open it to find myself standing before a flowing sequence of chambers that someone has sculpted out of the compressed sand. Not a straight line to be seen, no boundaries of floor, wall, ceiling, and in moments, of seer and seen. All soft shadow and enfolding curves in the heart of the earth, until there at a turn the walls funnel in and soar to an eye in the cliff top that pours down the light and the sky. As I follow the chambers deep into the cliff I come finally to an alcove where people have left offerings, flowers, photos of saints. Behind me in a nook a red rose floats in a round bowl of water. This is a hallowed place, and I sit there in the half-light letting it in.

The hotel owner tells me that he has guests who come just to be able to sit quietly deep in the cliff. When I ask him who the author of this remarkable place is he tells me the man's name is Ra Paulette, and he lives over in Embudo Station. I want to know how someone even conceived such a unique work of art and shrine all in one. Santa Fe can wait another few hours.

Over the back roads of an Indian reservation, across the Rio Grande up a dirt track into the hills, and there he stands before me, at the door of the guest quarters he is digging out of a cliff for a friend in Embudo. It is late afternoon, and Ra Paulette has been wheeling barrows of sand out of his new work since early morning. Having introduced myself, I make a comment about how tough the work must be, though his eyes are as clear as any I have seen.

"I wish people could understand that labor is not a macho thing," he says pensively. "It can't be sustained if it comes from that attitude. The only way you can push barrows of sand around all day is to relax and persevere. You don't aim to get the job done, you take one load at a time, and you surrender to the task. Then it is enabling. This work is a feminine thing, requiring a harmony of male and female energies. Then it becomes a joy to push those barrows, just as it is a joy for a mother to raise a child. It is a kind of cooperative play between the material and myself. That, I believe, is how male virility can best be put to use. It is such a magnificent energy, don't you think? Far too precious to waste in competition and strife."

I follow him in through the entrance, a vulva-shaped slit in the cliff. Smooth curves of sand soar away dozens of feet above me; below, another room is hollowed out to take in the sunlight streaming in through another feminine opening in the cliff wall. I feel I am standing in an earth cathedral, the like of which has perhaps never existed before. The caves of Lascaux in southern France have a similar feel, though they are darker, unshaped by the human imagination. The rock churches of Anatolia in Turkey come closer still, but the material is entirely different, volcanic tufts instead of red sand. Ra's work is defined by the New Mexico landscape, there being no red sand cliffs anywhere else that I can think of.

While I am gazing about me Ra is talking still on the theme of virility, and how apologetic men feel about their own strength today. The beauty of their power, he says, is distorted into violence and aggression; either that, or stifled altogether in a retreat into weakness and inadequacy. Better to dance, he says, looking straight at me.

Ra literally dances into every day, because for him life is art and art begins with the way we open our eyes in the morning. Ra Paulette dances; not just any old dance, but one that stirs in his body and soul the deeper feelings of what it means for him to be a man. He strikes poses and makes gestures that make him feel noble, dignified, powerful, and proud; he becomes a bullfighter, a Zorba, a wild dancing man with a heart larger than life.

For years he earned his living as a casual farm laborer, and then as a garbage disposal man. Every time he picked up a bag he would do a little jig before launching it into the back of the disposal cart with an infectious panache that spread to his fellow workers. The whole team ended up jigging in rhythm, and life at the back of the refuse cart became something to talk about. "Any true laborer gives himself emotionally to what he does," Ra Paulette says. "The whole point of work is the utter surrender to the task, nothing less."

Ra did his art training that way, the same way he does it today: he deliberately cultivates beauty and joy. He never went to art college. Ten years back he wanted to create a retreat hut for himself. Instead of building one, he decided to hollow a space out of a red rock cliff. He dug out the compressed sand with a pickax and smoothed over the surfaces with an iron comb. These, along with a wheelbarrow, are still the only tools he uses. He called the cave his Heart Chamber. It wasn't just another cave, though. It was a spiraling turning dance of a space, so beautiful that within a year or so two hundred people a week were flocking to visit it. He hadn't meant it to be that way; it was to be his own sequestered heart ground, but news spread of this soft womb in the rock that brought a profound sense of stillness and rest to whomever entered it. The chamber seemed to fill a deep public need, but when numbers grew to the extent that they were beginning to leave their mark on the public land, Ra decided to fill the in chamber.

"People thought I was mad," he said. " But everything has its time, and the Heart Chamber had brought beauty to people for a year or two. When the effects of so many visitors on the ecology of the land outweighed its usefulness, it was a question of seeing the larger picture and placing the overall beauty of the area above the beauty of the particular. My purpose is to make art, not to develop a personal investment in it. The public seemed to be more invested in the Heart Chamber than I was, but in my eyes the closure was part of the piece as art, in a way the summation of the whole project."

Ra lives and walks lightly in this world, I discovered. A simple yurt is enough living space for him, with no running water and no electricity. He can barely afford to buy a coffee at the local cafe. When he works on a shrine or a commissioned work, he still asks the kind of hourly rate one would pay a laborer. He never even contemplates fund-raising or grants, because it would take time away from what he loves, and because then, he feels, he would be invested in his work in a way that would compromise it.

Since creating the Heart Chamber, Ra has fallen in love with red rock cliffs and sculpted several shrines of beauty that have become well known and loved throughout the Southwest. The sanctuary I visited behind the hotel is one. He wants to make a network of shrines, sitting places, caves, to be used for the celebration and healing of people's lives through beauty.

"They would be perceptual beauty traps," he explained. "Thanksgiving shrines. That is what we humans are, after all—creation's thanksgiving element. We are praising beings, and what I do is pour my love and praise through my muscles into this work. Wouldn't it be wonderful to take sick people out to shrines like that? I have even designed a carrying device that would take them across the land, since there would be no pathways or roads, of course. Imagine what a positive use of male energy it would be, to have men carrying the sick to these places. Our culture has such a disdain for physical labor, but that kind of work would restore the true beauty of male strength; it would redeem it by transforming it into an act of nurture."

"You know," he went on, "the whole idea is to be possessed by the sacred, not the other way around. As soon as I think of this being 'my' work, 'my' artistic career, 'my' path, I am turning the sacred into a possession. Whatever our work, the essence of it is how we feel about what we are doing at any one moment, not the label of artist, sculptor, laborer, or writer. Nothing stultifies the imagination more than self-importance, and nothing frees it more than play."

These are the virtues in being self-taught, this man's words rising from his own deep well. I ask him what future projects he has in mind, and he says he would love to make a building for people to die in. He says it with a look so direct it passes through me and on to the world outside—as if he were speaking to the plants, the animals, to the air that moves between us all.

"That would be the ultimate performance piece, wouldn't it?" he laughs.

But his next big project would be a public one, ideally on public land, which is so undervalued in the States, he tells me, where everyone is beholden to the idea of public property. What he wants to do is to build a fifty-foot tree of life underground, with the branches fanning out over the roof. He wants to build it with a team of men, because it is time now in our culture, he thinks, for joy to have its say. And there could be few joys like that of men lending their strength to the common cause of beauty.

I stepped out into the open and was filled immediately with the clean desert light. This is Sacred America, I thought. This country, of all countries, seems able to generate passionate individual spirits like Ra Paulette. Ra's work is sacred art. He is one of America's gifts to the world, whether or not anyone hears of him beyond the New Mexico border.

Ra has work to do, but he says I might like to meet a friend of his over the mountain, Pierre de Lattre, whose own sanctuary in the hills Ra sculpted a few years before. I agree to follow the stream. Ra calls Pierre, who says he would be delighted to take me to his sanctuary. An hour later I am walking along dry riverbeds and ridges of soft clay far from anywhere with Pierre and Picasso, his dog. The odd cottonwood flames yellow among the green.

Pierre has been many things in his life, including the famous beatnik priest on San Francisco's North Beach in the late fifties, the one whose church was a coffee bar that hosted all the best poets and musicians of the day. He hit the front cover of *Time* magazine in those days; since then he has been a professor of creative writing in Minnesota, lived in Mexico for fifteen years, and is now an artist out here in the high country near Taos. We walked for an hour or more until finally we slid down a bank to a ridge of soft sand under a long flat capstone.

There, far out in the backcountry a double door opens onto an exquisite room with no edges and a Mexican Virgin in wood at one end surrounded by candles. "This is my church," murmurs Pierre. "I come here daily." We pour a brandy and water from some bottles in an alcove, light the candles, and watch the day fall behind the far hill. When he and his wife first came to the area, Pierre told me, they didn't know how they were going to earn their living.

"Then I remembered something a Zen master said to me once. When you don't know what to do, stop and look around you. The answer will come. I stopped one day on a walk in these hills and picked up a stone. 'Why don't you paint it?' my wife said. I did, and a gallery sold it for $250. So I asked Ra how much he would need to sculpt me a hermitage. "$3,500," he said. "But you can't pay that." I can, I shall paint stones, I said. That's what I did, and I made exactly $3,500."

As we closed the doors behind us eventually, about to walk off into the evening light, Pierre pointed to an ancient firepit on the sand ledge, complete with ashes. Above it an undulating snake was etched into the sand wall. From chippings he has found there Pierre estimates the snake to be at least fifteen hundred years old. And probably no one has seen it except for the few he has brought to his sanctuary.

How many more wild artists and dancing men are hiding in these hills of northern New Mexico, I wondered, as I drove into Santa Fe that night. This state has drawn people with vision and those seeking vision from all over the world for decades. The outsider tradition of Georgia O'Keeffe and D. H. Lawrence continues as ever, the red rock magnetism casting its spell over new generations now.

I was not long in Santa Fe the next morning, because although I stood for a while before some of the work in the galleries along Canyon Road, I did not catch the scent of any deep devotion, no shard of light on the edge of my vision, no work flung fully formed out of a deep unconscious wellspring. Santa Fe is the third largest art market in the country after New York and Los Angeles, and perhaps you can't expect that kind of shock from any art market. Better to go wandering in lonely canyons.

Which is what I did later in the day, in search of another keeper of vision a friend had urged me to see, a woman named Dominique Mazeaud. She lives between two pink ridges west of the city, a willowy presence whose tiny house is itself a ritual space, every nook and corner with its own meaning. A row of plastic fish, tiny ones, filled with the water from the confluence of two rivers, runs down the middle of a table. Twigs on a ledge spell the word *Estoy,* I am. An open cupboard is filled with Kachina dolls, a painting hails the Virgin Mary in an embrace with Hanuman, the Hindu monkey god, essence of devotion.

Dominique is French, though she has lived in the New World for twenty years or more. We sit down, the table between us a shrine of sorts, a tray of sand with a Kachina in the middle, a snake skin draped over the doll's head. For Dominique the source of creativity is the heart. What matters in her work, she tells me, is the connection or the collaboration with the participant. Craig Comstock has written of her in *The Elmwood Quarterly* that "Mazeaud is an artist, but instead of making objects for art galleries (or installing 'found objects') she was becoming more concerned with the revelation, via ritual and reverie, of being rather than doing."

Sitting there across from the snakeskin, I can sense what he means. Art, she tells me, serves to create a space where people can go deep together. Her work is participatory and experiential. In the eighties she lived for a week in a store window in Manhattan, just eight feet by five feet, weaving a performance on peace. She brought things from home, a wall hanging of the Virgin Mary from South America, the wedding gown of her dissolved marriage. She cut strips from the gown and did rituals of forgiveness with them, and people would come into the space and spontaneously talk about their own forgivings.

She is uneasy with the label of artist, implying as it might someone who is set apart by a special activity. Everyone has the potential to be in touch with his own essence, to make his own unique creative contribution to life, even if the form isn't one sanctioned by the mainstream. It is a question of keeping faith with oneself. She herself has no objects for sale, and though important critics and museums have noticed her work, her path is far from the beaten track of the established art world. Another Ra Paulette, sowing her corner with seeds of self-reliance.

She attracted the attention of mainstream critics when, starting in 1986, she began the Great Cleansing of the Rio Grande. For seven years she went every month to the river to perform a cleansing ritual. She would always wear the same clothes, and would pick up trash from the river as if it were so many beads on a rosary, stacking it in bags supplied by the city. The river would give her gifts—a statue of Jesus one month, a dildo the next, needles the next, and with these she created installations. She would find many heart-shaped stones, and would place them in spirals, joining any broken ones with a strip from that same wedding gown, fusing her own broken heart with the broken heart of the world. Now she is developing projects that use rivers as metaphors for interconnectedness for children of different cultures, and giving lectures on doing art for earth.

She is also at work on the Temple of the Heart, which will be four multisensory and interactive installations corresponding to the four chambers of the heart, all echoes on the theme of deep listening. She is a kind of shaman figure, this quiet presence, rubbing one of her plastic fish now between her thumb and forefinger; a woman who is using art to heal the wounded environment.

You might think she is teeming with projects and ideas, but no, Dominique Mazeaud is more lunar than that. Images steal up on her from an angle, she is never quite sure where she is going next, allowing as she does the thread of her work and her life to take her by surprise. Like you, or me, perhaps. As I leave Dominique I take with me the affirmation of that nighttime vision, the soft focus that lets us be reeled in by life, a willing, attentive collaborator. I take, too, the image of the snake skin.

Dominique's central work of art is her own transformation, being made good in the fire of her craft—like anyone whose heart is committed to what he does, whatever he does. Like Colleen Kelly and her husband, Robert Ott, who take top executives out into the New Mexico red rock for days at a time so that their hearts may be renewed in the face of the unknown. Colleen and Robert have lived much of their life in the wilderness of nature, and years ago now they saw how the wilderness could be a teacher for people who live their lives in the corporate jungle.

They set up a company called Living Systems and devised a contemporary hero's journey in which executives pass through an entire rite of passage. They make their own book of sorrows, in which they face their fears and acknowledge what is not working in their lives. They listen for their calling, which for many is the family, and service to the community. Colleen discovered that a surprising number of them do volunteer work after a twelve-hour day, and almost all of them are deeply religious. They spend twenty-four hours alone, opening themselves to guidance, and usually, they return to their familiar world with a new sense of purpose.

"Taking people out onto the land helps them to think 'outside of the box,'" said Colleen when we met later that day in a downtown cafe. "It helps them to revisit their core values. People really do want to make a difference; that's what gives meaning to our lives, and with a whole systems approach we help them to a new level of thinking about how they can make that happen. With nature as the model, for example, we study the principles of cooperation and strength through diversity. We help them to see how all problems are connected to a picture of their larger life and values, not just the symptom at work. This ritual is our art form. If it helps restore a sense of purpose and joy in their work, if it encourages harmony between nature and culture, the ritual has been a work of beauty."

That beauty can change not only the individual but the larger system, the company itself. One of their first journeys was for a group of Rank Xerox senior board members. Colleen and Robert always start their rituals sitting around a landfill, contemplating the way we as a culture are treating the earth. Suddenly, one of the Xerox group pointed down at the eyesore: "Look," he said. "There's one of our machines!"

The moment was such a revelation for them that by the end the vice-president, who was there, committed the company to researching and producing a biodegradable machine. Six years later, in 1997, that machine came on the market. It is 100 percent biodegradable, even the circuitry.

Since then Xerox have gone even further, greening a whole division of the company—recycling cans, banning polystyrene cups, naming different departments of their new office in Rochester, New York, with titles like the Rainforest Room as a gesture toward having a greater world awareness. They have done away with reserved parking—a powerful symbol—and jeans and tennis shoes have replaced suits and ties.

How easy it is to brand the whole corporate world with the values of the lowest common denominator. The inventor of Xerox was himself a committed Zen Buddhist who brought the first roshi to the Rochester Zen Center—the center that Toni Packer later left to begin her own version. The owner of the company, Joe Wilson, was revered as a saint in his day for the deep values he strove to put into practice. He committed significant funds in local community and educational projects. During the race riots in Rochester, he met the community leader, the Reverend Florence, and together they worked out a plan through which Xerox would hire local youth and build housing for people on low incomes.

The work of Living Systems and others like them is helping us to remember the meaning of sacred land. The great spaces of America have always been considered sacred, not just by the native peoples but also by the poets, explorers like John Muir, artists like Ansel Adams, and by many of the recent generation of ecological careers. Land is of itself virgin. In that sense it is always pure, sacred, utterly other. As we open to its power and beauty, it evokes those same sacred powers in us. Colleen and Robert are restoring an ancient ritual of initiation in a contemporary context, and doing so in a setting—the wilderness—that has always been used for that purpose through the ages. The land calls the executives to open to their own wildness—to the raw, raucous, wailing, joyous, quiet, longing soul in them that knows the true nature of power.

I am aware as I listen to Colleen that I have only been witness to the new New Mexico—the one peopled by white, educated artists, writers, entrepreneurs, New Agers, counterculturalists who stream into the enchanted Southwest from all over the country to start a new life for themselves. They tend to move on quickly too, discovering that the dream doesn't always match the reality. Red rock country is not easy to earn a living in. Though the people I have met so far happen to have lived here for many years, it is a local joke that if you have been in Santa Fe for a year you are an old-timer already. I know there is an old New Mexico, and I shall be going there soon. Yet before I do, I leave Colleen Kelly in the café to visit a place whose work is a bridge between the old and the new: the Institute of Medicine and Prayer.

Traditional peoples have always known that prayer is good medicine. What is new is the existence of an institute by that name in a city general hospital—no coincidence, either, that the hospital is in Santa Fe. I found the institute in a corner of the Cancer Treatment Center at St. Vincent's. It was started in 1995 on the inspiration of Dr. Larry Dossey, the author of *Prayer Is Good Medicine*. The treatment center invited it to share its premises because it needed help with pastoral care and also for the support of physicians. The institute runs educational programs on the efficacy of prayer for the sick and for medical staff, and conducts scientific research in the field.

The president of the institute, Frank Lawliss, strolls in wearing shorts and a baseball cap. Frank was always on the leading edge—even when he was on the staff of the Dallas SouthWestern Medical School he used to treat severe patients with drumming sessions and sensory deprivation

chambers. Before coming to Santa Fe he was president of the Institute of
Transpersonal Psychology (ITP) in California, which gave him a more
suitable context for his explorations into what he calls transpersonal medicine—healing methods that include in their frame of reference the psychic and spiritual dimensions of the patient. At the Santa Fe Institute he
is currently seeking funds for hard research into the scientific efficacy of
spiritual healing techniques.

"Quite a lot of research has already been done," he tells me, "but it
needs to be more specific and conclusive, and to be supported by a
methodology that is fully acceptable to the medical establishment. More
than two hundred and fifty studies already show that regardless of the
type of belief, the regular practice of religious or spiritual rituals means
one is likely to live longer, be ill less regularly, and have less cancer than
nonbelievers. Praying for others is even better medicine than praying for
oneself, it seems, according to research done by Sean O'Lear at ITP."

I was reminded as Frank spoke of the ancient Tibetan practice of
Tong Len, in which you visualize someone who is ill, or causing you
harm, and see his illness or bad feeling pour into you like smoke with the
in breath, while you pour light into him with your out breath. The person who is most immediately assisted by the practice is the meditator
himself, as I know from my own experience.

A fundamentalist Christian group recently offered the institute
$100,000 toward research if they agreed to convert people to Christian-
ity. That, however, is hardly part of the institute's brief. Many people
come in wanting to know how to pray, but not to a specifically Christian
God. Some say they are Jews, but they have their own beliefs; others, that
they were raised Catholic, and would like to restore some ritual in their
lives, but not religion. Most traditional cultures, Frank explains, define
disease as a break in the "geo-social-spiritual web of connectedness,"
though they might not put it that way; and they use rituals to weave the
individual back into the overall system of life. The institute offers a simple prayer ritual—one acceptable to any tradition—for the same purpose,
with a little formula based around the willingness to be peaceful and
grateful.

Interest in the work is running high. At a recent Spirituality in Health
Care Conference they cosponsored in Albuquerque, eight hundred
health-care professionals registered and three hundred were turned away.
The other sponsor was the Medical School in Albuquerque, which insisted the institute's name be left out of publicity because of the word
prayer. The term still raises objections, Frank says, especially in the funding world; so they are considering changing the name to the Institute of

Spirituality and Medicine. Spirituality, it seems, is acceptable, more neutral, somehow; while prayer can sound too partisan, with too many Christian connotations for Americans disenchanted with the church.

Here in northern New Mexico, I thought, as Frank and I parted on the steps of St. Vincent's, the two old worlds of native America and Hispanic Catholicism, and the new world of transreligious synthesis, spirituality in the workplace, the development of a personal credo or art form seem to exist side by side in equanimity, with the new drawing deeply from the wellspring of the old. I had yet to encounter the Hispanic world of faith anywhere on my journey so far. Fortunately, it was almost Easter, and I was about to see more than I ever bargained for.

Chapter Seventeen

Easter in Old New Mexico

In Chimayo, the New World equivalent of Lourdes, is the church of the healing earth where hundreds have hung up their crutches already. I had heard of this place of miracles and often dreamed of going there, I don't know why. That's what a name does sometimes, lodges in the imagination, accrues layers of images, won't let go. The big day at Chimayo is Good Friday, which happens to be tomorrow, and I am driving north out of Santa Fe to stay nearby at the village of Truchas, with my friend Alvaro Cardona Hine, his wife, and their two bulldogs.

On the way I pass the small pueblo of Tesuque, and my mind shoots back to the early fall of the year before when I happened to have walked into the pueblo on the very day of the Corn Dance. It was the first genuine Native ceremony that I had ever seen. The men of the community were dressed in white with fox pelts hanging down their backs, feathers in their hair, and shells hanging from their shoulders. The women were facing them in long black dresses with red braids and turquoise necklaces, juniper branches in their hands. Back and forth they went, the whole community, from four year olds to grandparents, stamping and hopping from foot to foot for hours on end without ceasing. The doors of the church were open wide, and, opposite, on the other side of the plaza, was a tent sheltering St. Francis, their patron saint, on a makeshift altar.

On entering the pueblo I was in a different world to the one just outside. I had stepped unwittingly into a ritual space where everything, every gesture, sound, item of clothing, had its meaning as part of the whole. People were quiet, the beat of the drum and the drone of thirty singers shook the air. I remember how it had pressed me down, that drumbeat, down into the earth where I belonged, my body swaying to the lilt of the singers, an affinity there with a communal world with ancestral continuity, one people. When I left finally, it was to step out of a dreamtime into a world where the clock was ticking again.

I think now as I drive past the pueblo of Frank Lawless in Santa Fe, what he said about disease being seen by traditional cultures as a "break in the geo-social-spiritual web of connectedness." It was a mouthful alright, but this was exactly what the Tesuque pueblo was doing—they were confirming with their Corn Dance the threads that bind the earth, the people, and the spirit together as one. The sun dancers I had seen in Wyoming were weaving the same threads, but from the spirit of sacrifice more than from a community celebration. As Frank Waters said in his book *Masked Gods*, "This was prayer, but not as we know it—not a collective supplication, but a unification and release of psychic forces through a specific discipline into a communion with all the forces of all creation. These were not men humbly beseeching the gifts of life. They were the forces of life made manifest in man as in earth, demanding by the laws that governed both an interchange of the energies potential in each."

The Corn Dance only ended, I assumed, once that exchange of energies had taken place. A different perception of life to the Catholic one I was about to enter? I am not so sure. I wonder what the physics of miracles are.

On my way to Truchas on Maundy Thursday I stop for an hour in Vilarde to meet Eulogio Ortega and his wife; and to see their chapel, itself the catalyst, it appears, of a miracle. Eulogio is one of the oldest and most respected *santores* in New Mexico—the woodcarvers who make statues of the saints. Their art has only revived in the last twenty years, as a result of private patronage. The old tradition faded away with the coming of the railroad and cheap plaster santos from Europe, though now there is a strong demand for them again, as much from art collectors as from devout Catholics.

I find their house down a track, and discover I am not the only foreigner to have knocked at their door. Someone from St. Petersburg was here only the week before, and the curator of a Prague museum also stopped by recently, everyone, like me, by word of mouth. Eulogio's wife opens the door, black hair drawn up in Spanish bouffant style, and ushers me into a room full of clocks with loud ticks and a life-size gold Madonna who bestows perpetual blessings from a corner of the room.

Eulogio walks in at a grandfatherly pace, welcomes me as if he were expecting me, though I have come unannounced. They have a patron saint for every activity, he tells me. In that way they sanctify everything. It is not a matter of worship, he says, but rather one of invocation, of drawing the saint's presence into one's life. They give people peace and tranquillity. He begins, unbidden, to speak of his own faith.

"I sometimes have doubts, you know, about the Resurrection and all, but if I didn't keep to Catholicism, what would I have? I'm too old to change now," he says, a smile breaking across his gentle face. "The essence for me is mystery, and that is in every tradition. I often get up at four, make myself a coffee, sit in that chair, and wonder about it all. Before I went to work, I would always recite the Twenty-third Psalm and the Hail Mary. One morning I said, 'Hail Mary full of grace . . .'" and I stopped, full of awe. What could that ever be like, I thought, to be full of grace? I was so struck by the wonder of it I could say no more Hail Mary's that day."

His wife had much more faith than he did, he went on, looking across at her with an affection that moved me. In 1980 she had cancer, and she asked him to build a chapel in their garden to Our Lady of Guadalupe. He thought it would be too much work for him, and suggested a grotto. But no, she insisted on a chapel. Soon after, three boys came by from Mexico looking for work. They were builders. So they built the foundations and Eulogio did the rest. His wife took one year to paint the reredos. She had her operation for cancer, and that was seventeen years ago.

He takes me out to see the chapel, a beautiful wooden building with a few rows of pews and an astonishing santo of Our Lady of Guadalupe near the altar. His wife follows us and kneels in the front pew. Such artistic devotion, all the work of one man. He points out the various santos, one, Nuestra Señora de la Soledad, is two hundred years old. He shows me San Isidro with the angel plowing the field with two oxen. San Isidro was a farm hand, Eulogio murmurs, but he was always late for work because he would get so lost in his prayers. The farmer could never understand how Isidro always managed to get the work done, until one day he went to watch him in the fields. He saw that while Isidro prayed, an angel did his plowing for him.

Driving along the highway you might think you were safely ensconced in the dream of modern America. The supermarkets are there, along with antique stores, cappuccino coffee shops, bookshops, *The New York Times* as well as the *Santa Fe Sun,* and the latest stock prices. New Mexico has all you need to sustain the middle-class fantasy of life at the turn of the millennium. You would likely never suspect that another, far more fervent dream sustains the imagination of the people in these hills. They live in two worlds, inhabiting, even now, a sacred as well as a secular mythic field; one handed down to them by an old Spanish culture for whom stories like the one of San Isidro are living realities, and to whom wooden saints still speak in the night.

Eulogio and his wife were my doorway into this other world. Just how alive it still is I am about to discover at the hands of Alvaro Cardona Hine. Alvaro, originally from Costa Rica, has lived most of his long life in America. He is one of the rare Renaissance men I have ever met, a consummate artist, poet, writer, composer, practitioner of Zen, a generous, compassionate heart. He runs his own art gallery in Truchas, and his bulldogs greet me at the gate. Alvaro is not in the best of spirits. He is in some physical pain, and he is missing his wife, who is away on a retreat. Even meditators, wise men, feel the absence, perhaps especially so.

Alvaro tells me that a few miles away in the village of Cordova there is a powerful brotherhood of *penitentes* (penitents), and that I would probably find their ceremonies over Easter more potent than the pilgrimage to Chimayo, which has become something of a tourist attraction in recent years. I had heard of the penitentes, how in the nineteenth and earlier part of the twentieth centuries these Catholic male fraternities had wielded enormous influence in New Mexico. They had begun in the early Spanish settlement days, when the local men whose communities had no priest would band together to uphold the Catholic rituals and tradition. They came to be feared as well as respected as time wore on, for their social and political influence, but also because of their custom of self-flagellation and penance during periods like Easter. The flagellation stopped some years ago, though more socially acceptable forms of penance, like fasting, are still part of their practice.

Alvaro has already made certain arrangements on my behalf. He has a friend in Cordova, a fine woodcarver, who is willing to take us to the *morada*—the church of the penitentes—this very evening, should I wish. We eat and talk and drink a little and head off to meet Terry, one of the only Anglos in the village, in Cordova. He leads us to the far end where a long low building stands on its own.

Short, burly men are passing in and out of the open door, most of them shouting a greeting to Terry and beckoning us in. The building has a bare wooden floor and a shelf at one end that runs the width of the *morada*. The shelf, evidently an altar of sorts, is teeming with wooden carvings of Jesus, of Calvary, of the saints, votive candles, and a statue of Christ bleeding. Violet lace curtains half-veil this holy of holies, and in the middle of the church, all on its own, is a wooden box that looks like a crib, except it is the tomb with a wooden Jesus lying in it. Every so often one of the burly men will come up to the tomb and walk softly round it. At the other end of the *morada* is a blazing fire, and through a low doorway comes the sound of men singing devotionals, ones I do not understand and have never heard the like of before.

One of the penitentes, seeing Terry, comes and talks for a few moments. He has a strangely brusque, at the same time courteous, even dignified voice. He tells me that all penitentes run in the family, with many lineages going back almost two hundred years. There are thirty-eight men in the Cordova morada, he says; as large as any group in the state, though almost every village in northern New Mexico has its morada. An old man, stooped, with a big hat on, comes in just then, on the arms of two twenty-year-olds.

"That's Mateo," says our friend. "He is ninety-six, the oldest penitente in the state, a woodcarver with work in the Smithsonian. He's seen some changes. He would know all about flagellation, though we don't do that now. By the way," he adds, "we have a procession tonight, some time after ten, to the village church. We shall have the Rosario there, then the Tenieblas, when we pray for the dead. The church will be open from sunset, so if you want you can go early, do some sacrifice."

We thank him, but no, we go back to Truchas for the interim, Alvaro to continue work on his opera, I to walk through the village in the tumbling light. At the far end of Truchas is another church, a Presbyterian one. I peek inside to see everyone seated at a long table reenacting The Last Supper. Even the Anglos join the story here, something I have never heard of in England, though it is true I never made a habit of going to church there. I back out quietly and watch the moon, just a sliver from full, floating over snow mountains washed with pink, the same Sangre del Cristos that I saw up in Crestone.

> *The silver glint of words in the mouth*
> *gives hint of an Easter message,*
> *yet nothing is said, only silence*
> *As I stand here in the full light of*
> *a crucified moon.*
> *Only silence rings in the body*
> *and tolls the knell of*
> *a defeated mind.*

When I arrive back at San Antonio church in Cordova at ten, having left Alvaro to plunge into his music, the church is less than half full. Three stout men with beards and bellies sit by the altar. There is no priest, the penitentes having preserved the custom of fending for themselves. The men begin a refrain in large hoarse voices, the women—there are only women in the church—responding. Half an hour later, the same refrain going back and forth, I step outside to look at the stars, feel the clean dark air, and as I do I hear the chanting of the procession making its way from the morada to San Antonio's. In a moment they are in view, led by a man with a lantern, and I hurry back to my place in the church.

As soon as the men enter the church the lights go out, except for the candles on the altar. Three of their number are bent double with cloths over their heads, led along by the others. Up to the altar they go and out of a side door leaving us quiet again except for the refrain of the burlies and the women. For an age they go on it seems, till finally, soon after eleven, the procession returns singing for all it is worth, swinging loud rattles and playing flutes. I can see now that they are mostly in their early twenties with bomber jackets and sneakers.

They all press forward into the sanctuary around the altar and the Rosario begins, a bellowing of prayers for loved ones and the sick. One of the young men has a logo on his back saying, "Sly, Slick, and Wicked." Everyone but me, I think, oblivious to the incongruity.

With every loved one and sick friend and neighbor prayed for, the Tenieblas takes over, and fourteen candles on the altar are snuffed out one by one between the chanting of psalms. I think of the stars outside, how even they are praising the dead and long gone, their ancient light seeping through the millions of dark years even now to remind us of our beginnings in the galactic turning. The rattles, a man tells me, are making the sound of the thunder that was heard at the crucifixion.

I am in southern Spain here, or over the border deep into Mexico. The somber intensity of the southern male is inward turned and resonant with the power of group authority. I have seen this in Andalucia, in Seville, during the Lenten penitence, felt its brooding heat in Córdoba, in the men around the old mosque with the Catholic Church inside. Like Rilke, I know of this fierce male bonding, feel an affinity for it, yet remain on the outside:

> *I have many brothers in the south.*
> *Laurels stand there in monastery gardens,*
> *and I know in what a human way they adore the Madonna*
> *I think often of young Titians through whom God walks, burning . . .*

But this is America, and I go back to Alvaro's that night shorn of my stock images and ready-made preconceptions. There is more to come the next day, Good Friday, and I return to Cordova to witness the Encuentro, the passion of Mary meeting Christ for the last time. As I reach San Antonio's, a file of villagers are walking slowly, step by step, out of the church, led by two women, one carrying a figure of the Virgin Mary and the other a *retablo* of the baby Jesus with his parents. A few standers-by are in the street, everyone silent. From the morada another procession, all men, is making its way toward us. The penitentes are led by a lantern bearer, and are then followed by men carrying a figure of Christ Jesus on a stretcher. This Christ is spattered with blood.

Step-by-step the processions inch toward each other, stopping periodically for readings from the Bible passage where Mary embraces Jesus for the last time. The tension builds, a magnetic field between the approaching figures, until finally they meet, and Mary is bowed over three times to Jesus on his stretcher. Then the figures and the banners and the various *retablos* are lined up and we all file by and kiss them one after the other. I do not remember the last time I kissed the feet of Jesus, or if I ever did, I an Anglican from a more sober world. Many of the women are crying now, and some of the men, too, ones who would look more at home on a Harley Davidson than weeping at the feet of Jesus.

Three of the men are barefoot; they are the ones who came into the church bent over double the night before. They have been chosen to do penance for the whole fraternity. Finally, Mary is processed back to San Antonio's and Jesus to the morada, and I make my way at last on to Chimayo, the last lines of that same poem by Rilke, another northerner, on my mind:

> *Yet no matter how deeply I go down into myself,*
> *My God is dark, like a webbing made of a hundred roots*
> *that drink in silence.*
> *I know that my trunk rose from his warmth,*
> *but that is all,*
> *because my branches hardly move at all near the ground,*
> *and just a little in the wind.*

The traffic back on the main road to Chimayo is bumper to bumper. People are hiking in twos, in threes, in whole families, some with crosses over their shoulders, other with images of Christ, most with just a backpack. Like most pilgrimages around the world, this one is traditionally taken on foot, and I abandon my car a couple of miles before the village to join the throng, many of whom have come from the far corners of the state and beyond. Many of the houses along the way have tables outside with fruit and drink for the hikers. I stop at one for a few moments and the family tells me what a blessing it is to be thanked by so many people in one day, everybody blessing everyone else and this is a true life it seems to me, a blessing blessed life.

These tens of thousands of people are converging on Chimayo this Good Friday because in 1812—the very same year that Napoléon met his Waterloo, and the year that Beethoven celebrated with his thunderous overture—out here in remote New Mexico a pastor, it is said, on one Good Friday morning, saw a light pouring out of the earth. He dug down into the spot, unearthed a green crucifix, and tried three times to take it away to the church of Santa Cruz, but it always mysteriously returned to the place where it was found. So the pastor had a church built around the hole in the ground and to this day people are healed by touching the earth there. As in any healing shrine around the world, the walls of the *santuario* (sanctuary) are lined with crutches.

When I finally arrive a couple of hours later it is with some relief to find that although Chimayo is teeming with people, a genuine community feeling seems to pervade, rather than the distracted buzz of a tourist attraction. A long line stretches down the lane of all those wanting to pass through the church and receive some of the blessed earth. Students of the New Mexico Institute for the Healing Arts are giving free massages to the hikers in the shade of the adobe church walls, everybody is smiling, the sun is beaming down, and it is good, it is all very good.

Just there in the line I catch sight of a friend from Santa Fe, Doug Conwell, and I join him to go into the church. Doug runs a program called Earth Walks, which takes people with AIDS out into the wilderness, and it doesn't surprise me when he says he has just walked ten miles to get here. An old iron cross is sticking out of his bag, and when I comment on it—Doug not being the kind of person I would expect to see with a cross—he says, "You know, this is one of the most potent community events in the state, a real family thing. I come every year on Good Friday because it really helps me undo some of my childhood prejudices about Christianity. My little cross reminds me to own my own troubles, and to place them under a greater light. Christ has come to personify that greater light for me now, not as some external figure, but as the larger wisdom that guides my life from within. And you must have seen how much warmth and companionship there is along the way. A day like today is a testimony to how and what we can be for each other."

He is right, of course, and my attention turns to the gathered atmosphere about me, the people just ahead in the church already now, some kissing Christ and Mary, others lighting candles, a woman weeping at the foot of a great wooden cross that leans against the wall. Such a place of beauty, the santuario at Chimayo, all adobe folds with no straight lines, old Spanish bells up on the roof, delicately painted saints and reredos inside. Everything is sacred, I remember, and I touch the feet of Mary and Jesus, the second time in a day, and not a hint of embarrassment.

I, too, file past the altar, take my portion of sacred earth from the box in a little plastic bag, and duck through the tiny exit past the crutches on the wall to let others take my place. Every now and then men come by and fill up the box again by the bucketload, the earth taken now from a nearby source, though it doesn't matter, the earth is sacred wherever it comes from. This is it, it strikes me; this is why all these thousands of people are gathered here, to recognize and venerate the simple sanctity of mud, of humble earth. And so it should be. Without it we won't get far, and gratitude is the least we can offer.

Chapter Eighteen

Cry Freedom in the Desert

From Truchas and the home of Alvaro I set out after Easter on my way out West to Barstow, California. I had a date in Barstow with one of the more remarkable people I was to meet anywhere in America. First, though, I was going to camp for a couple of nights in Chaco Canyon, one of the most remote of all national parks, and by all accounts, eerily beautiful.

Driving through Abiquu I stopped for a while to gaze on the crescent of pink and red rock streaked with white at Ghost Ranch, where Georgia O'Keeffe and so many others have stood for days and weeks and painted the changing colors. There was an art class at work when I arrived, elderly ladies, their easels set among the piñon pines, hoping to catch the color and light of the Southwest for their grandchildren.

For mile upon empty mile I drove along open highway past red rocks and scrub and the occasional hilltop settlement. After twenty miles on a dirt road in dazzling clarity and biting cold I entered Chaco Canyon at last, a wide and sinuous riverbed between two cliffs half a mile apart. The approach fosters the idea that you are truly in the middle of nowhere—which you are, since the nearest village is fifty miles away. But then you come upon a double row of parked cars, the visitor's center, and people eating dinner on picnic tables scattered among the rocks courtesy of the parks department.

In this great emptiness, a tame little corner. The campsite is almost full, even this early in the year. A square bordered with wooden slats and a private picnic table tells you where you can pitch your tent. The next site is twenty yards along, then the outhouses all in a row. As I am putting up my tent in the last glimmer of light I already hear the snores of the man next to me. Four women in an RV have their generator whirring. Two hours later, when they finally shut it off, the whole campsite claps. So this is the great outdoors in America.

The next day while the cliffs gleam in the sun I stroll over to look at the ruins of the Anasazi settlement, which draws so many people here. If you didn't know where you were you could be forgiven for thinking you had stumbled across a deserted Mexican village, except for all the people who are clambering in and out of the doorways with cameras in hand. No one knows why the original population deserted the valley so suddenly in the twelfth century, leaving their villages intact. Evocative of some ancient wisdom is the great kiva the Anasazi left behind, a huge stone well, some hundred feet across, set on the edge of the village and used for ceremonial purposes. Kivas are still used by the local Indians today for initiation and ceremony.

The women from the RV are sitting around the Anasazi kiva in serious contemplation, one at each of the four cardinal directions. I give them a wide berth and head up the cliff to a different view of the world—though not too far, because you need a special permit to go off the trail. An hour of silence I pass up there, with a full view of the canyon stretching before me. Finally a bunch of kite flyers arrive and I head off, without a pass, higher into the back country in a light so clear and warming now that I can see all the way to the mountains west of Durango in Colorado, 125 miles away. You would never see half that far anywhere in England. I never even knew it was possible for eyes to see such a distance. It changes the blood cells, casting a gaze that far.

A national parks survey says that 92 percent of all the people going to parks stay within half a mile of the campsite. Until I strayed from the path, the day was hardly in line with my imaginings—always the problem when dreaming life up before you live it. Even so, if anything needed redeeming, the sunset obliged. A purple glow on the horizon, pink shards of light streaking the cliffs, a tabletop mountain in the distance ablaze in the backlight. A nearly full moon gathers height, I stand there on a rise watching the last slip of light ebb away, and turn into bed finally just as the RV women begin a laughter competition. Yet even here, in this Motel 6 of a campsite, in the very heart, it seems, of Middle America, the land can still seep into your pores and soften the tightenings of civilized life.

At one in the morning I awake with a start to hear a woman's voice screaming for help. I falter. I know that, often, if you interfere in scenes of domestic violence, both parties may turn on you. I get up, even so, but seconds later a motor starts and a truck roars past the tent. Two dogs continue barking for the next hour. In the morning, as I am leaving, the park ranger tells me that a child had had a seizure and they had taken him to hospital, though he had recovered by the time they got there. Chaco

Canyon, microcosm of everyday America—the outer reaches of wilderness with a nucleus tamed almost to the point of absurdity. The parks have a tough line to tread, shepherding streams of people through in such a way as to keep them safe and happy while attempting to preserve the original face of the land.

Once out of the park the land seems all the wilder, and I drive for hours through the bluffs and the blue air until the evening light brings me to Arizona and the small town of Sedona, home of channels, clairvoyants, archangels, ascended masters who have descended to help us out in these trying times, pink Jeep energy vortex tours, and I am sure a great many ordinary people as well.

A night there and I am ready to move on to Barstow. First, though, I take breakfast in a coffee shop where a 250-pound transvestite psychic is telling another customer that she doesn't like to talk about it, but knows she is a reincarnation of the Lord of the Universe. Another psychic is complaining about the charges they have to pay at the local clairvoyant fair, and a young man walks in wearing a long black robe, a didgeridoo strapped to his back. In the local *Four Corners* magazine I see an ad for the Prophet's Conference, and another one for the Ageless Wisdom Seminary. An hour later, as I am leaving town, I see the Lord of the Universe plastering phone booths with his phone number. In Sedona, I am glad for my English realism; or maybe I am a cynic, like so many others from that ancient island that has seen it all.

On through the dry country I go, through Prescott, past Salome, past dozens of trailer parks with folks out to pasture, on over the border to Desert Center (a gas station and a grocery store) to the hot and dusty backwater of Barstow, California. I am here, en route to Los Angeles, to meet Byron Katie, one of those rare individuals who, struck once by the spiritual equivalent of lightning, has never been the same since.

She hardly seemed a likely candidate for the visitation of grace. She had lived for decades in the thrall of money and power, had made and lost fortunes in real estate deals, let her kids wither in drugs and alcohol, had sunk into fits of uncontrollable rage. An obsession with food brought her to a weight of more than two hundred pounds, and then to a halfway house for women with eating disorders in L.A.

Early one morning she was lying on the floor of her room when a cockroach crawled over her foot. She stared. She saw the cockroach as part of herself. She saw her foot move in reaction, her hand move, her body rise. In that instant she was animation observing itself. She saw the bed, and, as if she were watching an ancient dream, became aware of the belief she held that she was not worthy of a bed. In that moment, through her perception of it, the belief dissolved and she knew it was alright to lie on the bed. She had no way of distinguishing between where she ended and something else began. She was the All, and the All was her. It was 1986, and Byron was forty-three.

When her family came, she could see straight through their names and labels to who they really were. Her hands, her husband, children— suddenly everything was one body, adored and loved in this present moment without any reference to either past or future. Her entire structure for perceiving reality as she had known it had gone.

For three years Byron was in a state of continual revelation. Yet she was "a woman from Barstow," as she is fond of saying. "Women from Barstow don't know about spirituality and religious traditions." She had never studied religion or done any form of spiritual practice in her life. "We would only read about gurus and such things in the funny papers," she says. Yet what she did say, spontaneous and simple as it was, could have come from any of the great mystical teachings.

"To act without thought is divine," she would murmur, "unknowing is everything, there is no time or space, only love, and I am love. Attachment and the perception of loss is the only death. Life springs forth as we let go of attachment. What I am is a complete and total love that has never left this one."

The virtually cellular change she went through on that floor in her room left her radiant, and stayed. From then on, even in the halfway house, people started dissolving in tears in her presence. Yet she felt she had nothing to teach or even say. Word got around, and back home in Barstow people started turning up at the door for what they called healing, though Byron would not have said she was doing anything. People would ask what she did, and she'd say she didn't know. She didn't know why these people came, but they came, so it must be good. From that first moment in the halfway house, she has recognized that what is— whatever *it* is—can be nothing less than the highest order of good and truth.

One regular visitor to her house in those early days was the wife of an L.A. policeman. She came just to be in Byron's presence, without knowing why. Her husband eventually tried to forbid her to go, he was so afraid of losing her, but she came anyway. One day he followed her, burst into the house and ordered his wife to leave. He threatened to burn Byron's house down. Byron listened to him quietly, and asked, "How can you hurt me? You can wreck my house. It isn't my house. Take my house. It's yours." The policeman burst into tears and she held him in her arms. He had heard the truth.

And now here am I, another stranger turning up at her door. Several houses are on the lot, perhaps a dozen people living here now to administer the organization that has grown up around her in the last several years. I have arranged to spend twenty-four hours with the community. When I arrive I see two women in the hall leaning over a stack of audiocassettes.

"Just let's change it to say there is no copyright and people can duplicate them or use the tapes for whatever purpose they like," Byron is saying. A woman in her fifties, she wears a flowing dress and has her hair pinned back in a clip. She looks up, her face utterly open, as if she were saying, "I am here to serve you." Or not even that, just, "Here I am." I tell her who I am, and it does not appear to register; I imagine she doesn't remember speaking to me on the phone. Yet without a second's hesitation she stops what she is doing and leads me through to a conservatory that gives onto the garden. There is an immediacy about this woman, an utter simplicity and directness of movement, that leaves the air clean of any trace of motive. What I feel in those first few seconds is the presence of a being who isn't being anyone—not a teacher, a wise person, or anyone with anything particular to tell. It feels both a relief and strange at the same time.

We sit down, and she asks me if I would like to do The Work. I falter, having thought I was the one who was going to ask the questions. She explains that almost twelve years earlier, not long after people started seeking her out, she began to see how the projections people placed upon her could only serve to promote her as some kind of spiritual celebrity—yet she knew that she as a person could never help anybody. All she could offer people was a radical perception, an entirely new way of seeing, one that she had come to in her own experience. So she honed her own realization down to a process of four questions that challenged people's perception of reality. These questions she calls The Work, and she began inviting people to use The Work to heal themselves. Their healing, she smiled, was not her business. It was theirs.

What Byron saw on the floor of the halfway house was that we create our reality with our own beliefs, and that the most tenacious belief we have is that we are a separate entity in a world of separate entities. Our personal stories of hope and fear keep the illusion of separateness intact. Further, we genuinely believe that who we are is the drama of that story, its ups and downs, successes and failures, its search for God, truth, happiness, the perfect partner—at the same time believing other people's stories. Just like a Buddhist would say it, I thought, listening to her. Except Byron has no knowledge of Buddhism, or any other ism.

She created The Work by retracing her own thought processes during her time of revelation. She would be abiding in the absolute awareness of The One Life that lives us all, and a thought would come in from her past beliefs to suggest the contrary. One day she was in a mall. A ninety-year-old woman walked in and Byron became her, took on her smell, became aware of her own skin falling from the bone. She could see herself through the old woman's eyes, and knew there was no difference between them. The thought came in, I can't live this way, followed by the realization that I am living this way.

Her awareness would become the rocks, the sky, other people; she traveled through everything, became everything. Once her awareness went into a bird, and the thought came, but I don't know how to fly. The question followed immediately, can I really know that? and she flew on as that bird. For Byron, there is no story that we are not, even the story of a bird flying. There is only one life living us all, and only our limiting beliefs prevent us from seeing that truth.

A radical teaching, the kind you find in ancient yogic texts. Nothing less than the undoing of everything we think we are, we think the world is, life is; the return to what is there before thought, belief, and language divide up the world. Not a return to the unconscious merging of the infant, but to a condition of awareness that knows existentially the one life living us all. Yet Byron says none of this, teaches nothing, as such. She gives you The Work and invites you to perform the operation on yourself.

She asks me to think of someone I am having difficulty with in my life; to make a statement about something that irritates or saddens me, and to ask myself if it is really true. How can it be true that my partner and I are going our own ways? I ask. It certainly feels that way. I have come to America, she is in England. Yet our love continues as ever. It is as if the force of destiny has pulled us apart to follow our own myths. She looks at me, and smiles from somewhere far, far down. Then she says, "Hopeless," and smiles again.

"Is it true that there is someone else who is or ever was your partner? How can you really know that is true? It is your belief that she was your partner. Without that belief, you might realize there can be no arriving or leaving."

I sit for a moment opposite this woman who seems literally to ripple with joy, so much she can barely contain it. She is totally there, utterly without effort, pouring a love from her eyes not for me alone but for everything.

She asks me a third question. "What do you gain by holding the belief that she was your partner?" And then a fourth: "Who or what would you be without that belief?"

"Free," I laugh, "I would be free, free of an object by which I try to identify myself, give myself firm ground to stand on. I would be free to let life move through me without trying to hold on to it or push it away. And I would be closer to that same person than I could have ever dreamed of."

"No one has ever done anything to you, honey," she says, gazing upon me with an infinite tenderness. "We all do everything to ourselves, and we do it with our beliefs. They are your beliefs, no one else's. I am not saying you haven't parted from each other. What is, *is*. I am saying it isn't what you think it is, and nobody is ever creating the story except you. The Work helps you see through the fabric of your own beliefs, through the layers you put onto reality, onto what *is*. It allows you to lose control and that is the doorway to revelation. Can you even say it's a beautiful day and really know it's true? Without those conditions, we can know ultimate intimacy. The judgment, the construct that we put on reality sticks to it like Velcro and dampens the very intimacy we are seeking through our descriptions and theories."

There she goes again, I thought, paraphrasing the essence of Buddhist teachings without knowing it. Nonattachment is the deepest form of intimacy, they say. Except she talks about Velcro, uses the language of everyday America. She was moving on already, saying that until we drop our story we don't even breathe without a motive, every breath coming from fear. When we drop our story there is no longer a world, no existence—who is there to exist—no other worlds, no angels or devils. The Work, she says, is trickery, a trick to enable you to experience your own awareness of self beyond the story.

"Without The Work," says Byron, shaking with laughter, "I'd have nothing to say. The point is that through The Work, *you* say it. I don't have a message; for me, even to say the sky is blue is to speak dishonestly. I ask what your message is."

Who is this woman before me? I find myself wondering. In her presence, it is true, I can feel my own story slipping away—not for anything she says, not even primarily because of her work—but because she seems to be a sheer reflection of the innocence that is prior to word and concept. Byron is childlike, but with a fiery knowing that pares away my postures, both subtle and obvious, of who I like to think I am and what it is I think I am doing. I can feel that she simply doesn't connect to any aspect of my identity; yet she is wholly there with me, her attention pouring over me undiluted. In this gaze that sees me through and through, I am aware of feeling returned to a deep restedness, the peace that comes from knowing there is no one to be, nothing to hold up any more, at least, not in this moment.

We walk out to the garden, and she shows me the buildings, five of them, that house the offices, the people who live with her, a meditation and meeting hall. Back in her paranoid days, she used to own eleven houses on the block, part of a desperate attempt to control the neighborhood. It didn't work, of course, she laughed, she got more out of control than ever. For hours we talked, Byron a fountain of energy, unaware of time, food, or schedule.

People would come up to her as we spoke to ask about some administrative detail, to know what to say to someone on the phone, to arrange a meeting. Whomever it was, whatever they needed, she would turn the full beam of her attention on them until they had what they wanted. I was amazed to hear that she was expecting two hundred people the next day for a weekend retreat, this woman who was strolling around with me like she had all the time in the world. Which she did.

People came to live with her not because they were chosen, but as they turned up, and according to availability of space. Years ago, in the beginning, people would ask what she did. She didn't know, she said. Come live with me, do what I do. People would always think it was some kind of doing, so she told them to come and see for themselves. The people with her now manage her schedule, run the office, dispense her tapes, and seem to "get" that Byron doesn't actually "do" anything at all to be who she is. Maybe that's why they laugh a lot.

Byron's life is dedicated to going wherever she is asked, providing there is space in the schedule, which is rare these days since she has invitations from all over the world. She never charges, but offers The Work on a donation basis. What I notice as we stroll around is that she seems to say yes to everything and everyone. Isn't there ever a place for no, I wonder?

"Yes, no, same thing," she says. "What we are looking for is integrity, the truth of the simple heart. That's what I'm married to. I go and do The Work wherever I am asked because people suffer. If you suffer, I have an interest. That's it. If you care about it, I do, because I know it is an illusion. I lived that illusion for forty-three years, and I found a way through it. Someone who is tired of suffering can hear what I am saying and will do The Work for the love of truth."

We would have turned to the matter of love anyway, though with my own story so close to the surface, it was bound to emerge sooner rather than later. Byron is unequivocal. There is only one way you can ever join anyone, she asserts, and that is in awareness.

"You experience what is usually called love with someone who is a reflection of your own wonderfulness." She seems to smile with her whole body. "Someone who is agreeing with you. As soon as they stray from that role, then love goes and we try everything we can to fit them back into the place that we like. What you love, then, is your own story of the other. Connection, joining, marriage, all those things are about your own nature, nothing else. If you were clear you would be happy living with Frankenstein."

I can hear the truth of it, clear as a knife slicing through an apple. Yet I feel a tension, too, between the truth and the wish to hold on to my own story anyway, some mad attachment to the drama of my own suffering. If there is only one awareness, I say, that must mean the end of sexual desire, which needs a sense of other to arise.

"When my husband, Paul, would ask me if I wanted to make love," Byron responds, not even a hint of self-consciousness, "I would say, I don't know, touch me and we'll find out; every moment is a deep surprise. My own experience is that I have no interest, but if I say that, people can make a dogma out of it. So I say, inquire, ask the question: is it true you have no sexual interest? What do you get for holding that belief? There's no formula, no better or worse. It's none of my business whether I have a sexual desire or not. It just is, or it isn't. But I don't, that's my experience."

We have been talking for hours, the sun has gone down, and I realize I am hungry, not having eaten since early morning. Byron would have gone on all through the night, oblivious of food, sleep, or any other natural calls. Yet when I ask if there might be some food in the house she stops, totally giving herself to that, handing me things out of the fridge, warming soup. Everything is organic now, her old junk food days long gone.

Over dinner I ask her about evolution. The whole story of Western civilization is founded on the idea of progress, the gradual development of our knowledge and intelligence to the point of having a society founded on wisdom, moral intelligence, and the power of justice. The ideal of America is wholly founded upon this view, as is the dream of an evolving spiritual democracy. Yet Byron has more of an Eastern eye, one that sees existence to be cyclical and repetitive.

"No, nothing is going anywhere, that's my experience," she says when I ask. "Nor do we go anywhere; we are already. You know, I work with a toxic waste corporation with branches in Dallas and Chicago. I ask them how they think they can clean up the planet if they don't clean up their own minds. Everything begins and ends with us, and the bottom line is,

What Is, Is. Everything else is a story about what is. Your life is a story about what is. All the issues we get excited about are stories we lay over what is. The highest truth, if you can bear it, is that God is what is, and I mean all of it. I see no darkness anywhere, and I know people find that hard. At the same time, it doesn't mean you don't care, that you don't respond to suffering. I am moved to respond to suffering at the root. That's all I know. That's why I go where I am asked."

I am astonished to learn that Byron is invited into large corporations, yet people in the most unlikely of settings seem ready for what she has to say. She tells me she has just been invited to speak to five thousand United Steel workers, an endangered species now, who fear for their jobs. These kinds of men are the backbone of America, they support home, church, and country, and they are the original good guys. All they have done is work, play their expected part, and now they don't feel heard; they are confused about their place in this changing world. Byron will do with them what she always does, use The Work to stop the mind, investigate, and try to cut through that confusion.

I am beginning to wilt now, with so much to absorb from our hours together, but she jolts my attention when she goes on to say that just the previous week she went to a prison in Texas, where there was only one white prisoner among three hundred inmates. The prison psychotherapist had invited her to come and do The Work. When she started, she could get no eye contact with any of them. An hour later it was different.

"I'd ask them what was not okay in their world. They'd tell me about their wife cheating on them. I'd say, "Your wife is meant to be loyal, is it true?" We'd go through the inquiry, and they would start to see the death of a sacred belief, one they would have killed for without a second thought. The reality, I'd say, is that it happens. How can it not be true? As long as you fight with reality, you are going to lose."

"Another thing. When I went in there, they were all innocent. When I left, some of them were guilty—they were acknowledging that they were the ones who had gotten themselves into prison, not society, not Mom or Dad, not the system. We are the ones doing it to ourselves. We are always going to have a story, which's what our life is. If you have a good story, I say keep it, just be a witness to it and let it roll on without a motive. If you are in a nightmare, then better to wake up, since you are the only one hurting."

As we close up the dining room and bring an end to the night, she adds one more thing. The prison pastor came up to her as she was leaving, said how inspired he was by what happened. But was there a place for Jesus in this, he asked, with more than a trace of concern. She looked at him and said yes, there was a place for everyone. He was visibly relieved.

The next morning I join Byron and the community for a couple of hours in the meditation hall for their daily session with The Work. This, I realize, is where the glitches of community as well as personal life get ironed out. The sound technician can't find the usual music, and when he apologizes, Byron says it is good we don't have it. Everything is good for Byron if it is happening. She speaks with people one after the other, facing with them their projections onto others, their avoidance of their own stories and their creation of them.

After the session she asks me if I would like to meet her husband. She and Paul have their own house on the property. She explains how difficult her sudden change had been for him, how he would wail that he had lost his wife, that he had been abandoned. All these years he had held on to that story, she says, though now he has acclimatized to it. She hasn't tried to affect his story through The Work, because it is all he has, he loves it, and he wants to keep it.

It might sound as if she were unfeeling, speaking of her husband this way; yet I sensed it to be compassionate wisdom. She could not leave the place she had fallen into by some mysterious act of grace (or misfortune, depending on your point of view). She could not do other than be truthful to it. At the same time, she could not change anyone else, nor could she have any wish to. She has "gone, gone far beyond," as the Heart Sutra says. You may fall suddenly and without apparent reason through the net of time and space to the condition she lives in, but you cannot evolve to it. You are there or you are not there. So however much she may or may not want her husband to join her—and from where she is, it wouldn't matter either way, except to relieve his suffering—she would be crying in the wind upon deaf ears.

She assures me Paul is always happy to tell his story, so I follow her into their house to find him sitting in a chair reading the paper. He is a large man with a large belly held in with a big belt, soft eyes in a ruddy face. The kind of man you might expect to find in a no-frills town like Barstow. He is seventy, Byron had told me, some fifteen years older than her. After she has introduced us I ask him what it is like to live with this extraordinary woman. He exhales, half laugh and half sigh, and says it was like getting a divorce and then living with the same person.

"Everything we used to do and enjoy together has gone," he says, sighing again. "She was the love of my life. I thought I had found what I wanted, and now she is gone. I used to have a drinking, smoking, fishing, hunting buddy, and I've lost them all. She would wonder why I didn't do The Work—what do you expect, I was pissed off with The Work, it took everything away from me. It even took away my chance to care for her. Now she is self-sufficient, and others look after her needs. But you know, I put up with it now because I watch all the people and see the difference in them in the time they stay here. She does a great deal to help people, and I'd be selfish to feel any other way. But it's a weird thing, having to stand in line now to hug your wife. Really, that's what I have to do."

I'd find that difficult, I tell him. I am amazed he is still there with her. Nowhere else to go, he says, and anyway, he loves her. She loves him, he thinks, but just like she loves everyone else, which isn't quite the same. Still, you just have to accept life as it is. They have a funny relationship, for sure, he says. He will drive her to L.A., some three or four hours away, and say two words. The car is her quiet time, almost the only time she isn't with a crowd. If he dwells on it all too much, he gets depressed and scared. Then, he says, looking at me with a gentleness you would never imagine coming from a bulk like his, he will go fishing. He'll sit there all day and watch that pole and suddenly it's dusk.

What a fine man he is, I think, moved and grateful to hear his story. It all sounds so unfair, but who is to say it should be any other way. It can't be any other way, since this is how it is, at least until it changes. His sadness stirs my sadness, even so.

As we leave Paul to his paper, Byron says it might be fun to take a walk in the desert for a while, continue talking there. I don't believe her, it is midmorning and her group will be arriving in the next hour or two. I can't stay myself, since I have an appointment in Studio City. As I am about to leave this secular American equivalent of a great Indian or Buddhist sage, she sends me off with one last shot from the hip.

"You know, I don't pray because I already have everything," she says, looking at me again with those fathomless eyes. "But if I did, it would be, God spare me from the desire to be loved and appreciated."

Wham! If anything is the teaching, it is that. Byron Katie is so undeniably what she talks about. If she were in India, she would be hailed as one of the masters of nondualism, in the lineage of Ramana Maharshi, the great sage who died in the 1950s. (He also woke up spontaneously while lying on the floor, though under much more normal circumstances.) But she isn't in any lineage. She just happened, out here in the desert. No accident, either, that she is a woman. In America, it often seems to be women who are cutting through established forms and making new tracks of their own. And these women seem more naturally free of the need to be teachers, to establish a hierarchy in which some know and others don't.

Byron's everyday language, her lack of any religious baggage, her utterly individual experience of awakening, exemplify an emerging form of quintessentially American spirituality. One founded not, like so much of the New Age phenomena, on a new and more exciting set of beliefs, or on wishful thinking, but on the radical experience of Being. There can be no better antidote than this to the American obsession with Doing.

Chapter Nineteen

City of Angels

I thought Hollywood producers chewed cigars, had bulging bellies and sweating brows. Not so; not, at least, in the case of Barnet Bain. Barnet is lean, with sharp, intelligent features, a keen gaze, and drinks mineral water. Perhaps he is a sign of a new breed. Young he may be, but not green: he was producer of the Robin Williams movie *What Dreams May Come*, and is producer of a major cable television series on the evolution of consciousness, with many more projects in the pipeline.

Unlike many of the critics, I was moved and surprised by *What Dreams May Come;* moved at the way profound ideas were expressed so simply and directly, surprised that such material was even accepted by a major Hollywood star and studio. But then, I know next to nothing of Hollywood, and Barnet, sitting across from me now in the kitchen of his home in Studio City, is in the process of enlightening me. For many people around the world, Los Angeles epitomizes shallowness, greed, and crass materialism. The story goes that the look rather than the substance is what matters in this town, where there are as many plastic surgeons as there are aspiring actors.

All of this is true, yet Barnet is telling me that L.A. is also one of the most beautiful and vibrant places you could live anywhere; full of the energy it takes to fulfill dreams, with endless potential, where people's strengths and passions are embraced. It is indeed the ultimate dream factory, he assures me, though in a positive sense, rather than in the disparaging way the term is normally used.

"See, what people don't think of," Barnet is saying, "is that Hollywood is a community of very bright, educated, successful people who have proven as much as they are ever going to prove. At their best, they have made an art out of commerce and commerce out of art. So all their needs are met. When you get to that place in life, you are suited either to alcoholism or to asking the big questions. A lot of people here are beginning to live an examined life."

"In the eighties these deeper interests were reflected in an interest in therapeutic relationships. Eventually, though, the therapeutic context leads you to ask questions that are bigger than the context itself. There comes a time when your life is working fine, yet still the deeper issues of what it means to be alive at all are unanswered. In the last few years there has been a great interest in spiritual practices, and a significant return to religion of all kinds. Many of these people are the ones who buy the material for the studios, and their broader view of life is bound in some way to affect their choices, especially as they are a reflection of a general cultural trend."

I was aware of this with Barnet's own film. *What Dreams May Come* embraces big spiritual ideas and presents them as mainstream entertainment. The film takes place in the afterlife and demonstrates through Robin Williams's character that we are all making our life—and our afterlife—up with our thoughts as we go along. So we ourselves are responsible for being in heaven or hell at any one moment. Using special effects rather than polemic, the film shows that thought is prior to and more real than the physical world, which itself is the creation of thought. Byron Katie would say the same, that we are making our story up as we go along, though she would add that who we are is beyond even thought, in the unconditioned domain of being. One step too far for Hollywood to follow, perhaps. Yet when the studios are willing to make an investment of such magnitude in stories of this kind, one of three things is happening. Either they are cashing in on a cultural trend, or there is a genuine wish emerging to be involved in more meaningful material, or, more likely, a mixture of the two.

In the case of Barnet and his producing partner, Stephen Simon, the second possibility applies. Stephen bought the rights to the original novel by Richard Matheson in the late seventies, and has stewarded the project for all that time with a rare tenacity and vision until it eventually materialized. That, if it is anything, is a labor of love. For them the producer is the visionary, always looking to the horizon, the dreamer dreaming realities that he wants both for himself and for others and finding those dreams reflected in stories. Sooner or later they find a story that expresses the essence of their dreams, and they become that story's champion, its midwife.

Barnet points out that *What Dreams May Come* is in a genre with a long Hollywood tradition, though earlier films—*It's a Wonderful Life*, *Field of Dreams*, *2001*—were rarely made with such a conscious intent to challenge the public with big and new ideas. One exception, Barnet suggests, may have been *Groundhog Day*. Usually, these films are successful disproportionate to all the statistics and expectations. Yet unlike films with a standard success formula that can be repeated, the successful ingredients of films with a mythical or spiritual dimension cannot be so easily identified. They are not made to a formula by a committee in the usual way, everyone stirring in their point of view and then baking for an hour at three hundred degrees. An authentic movie has to come from an authentic origin; and formulation by committee wouldn't fit that requirement.

"That films in the spiritual genre are being made more and more," says Barnet, "points to the increasing appetite there is for such material. Another example currently being filmed is the movie of the novel *Ishmael,* with Anthony Hopkins. You know, I have a theory about all this." Barnet leans back in his chair, muses for a moment before continuing.

"I think there are two trends in this century of filmmaking that have conspired to make this the right time for this kind of movie," he goes on. "First, the development in the consciousness of the movie-going public in regard to their willingness to suspend disbelief. This has been nurtured now for a hundred years to the point where we have reached a high measure of sophistication. We provide them with the rules of the game and they will suspend belief about physics and enter into the world you offer and abide by its own rules. Then, technology is developed to the point where we can do incredible special effects cost-effectively. So what we have at this particular time is the conjunction of technological development with a developed suspension of belief."

"What that does is allow us to present in a mainstream way the most esoteric concepts and ideas that mystics all over the world have sought to model for millennia, with only modest success. We now have both the fertile ground and the technology to deliver esoteric ideas in a highly accessible way. These same ideas that were once the prerogative of a privileged few are now the stuff of Hollywood matinees. Not that I have an agenda about converting the masses: I don't. I just want to be part of stories that are wise, compassionate, and model new ways for people to become empowered in their own lives."

I can just hear the objections rising in the ethers about spiritual materialism, and the ghost of de Tocqeville whispering, "I told you so, the danger with democracy is that it can reduce everything to the level of the lowest common denominator." People say the same about popular books with spiritual themes, like *The Celestine Prophecy.* Yet just because I couldn't finish that particular book does not detract from the fact that in some way admittedly inscrutable to me it touched something in millions. That a book sells in millions does not mean it is a good book by literary or philosophical standards, but it must mean it has struck in some way the chord of a collective wish or story.

I suspect the collective wish struck by *Celestine Prophecy* was for a life more resonant with meaning than that of our everyday mundane experience. The material itself did not need to be deep to strike that chord, but it did need a language that could access the reader's own interiority by awakening an aspiration, however inarticulate, for a deeper life. If the life of just one of those millions was mysteriously turned toward a deeper sense of purpose through reading the book, the author's labor was not in vain.

A spiritual truth can be heard at many levels, and the resonance it sets up in someone with a young inner life will not be the same as in the contemplative on the mountain. But the experience of the one does not invalidate that of the other. What makes a difference in the book or the film with a spiritual theme is the motivation it is conceived and executed with. If the intent is to cash in on a trend, that will, even imperceptibly, make its mark on the public. If the intent is authentic, it is likely to set up a resonance with the authenticity of the audience, as long as the story is strong enough to carry the intent home.

In the case of *What Dreams May Come*, I have no doubt about the motivation after being with Barnet for an afternoon. Not just the producers, but Vincent Ward, the director, and Robin Williams, were both profoundly stirred by the material and saw the film as a service they could perform by making it available to millions of people. Working with Williams was in itself a spiritual teaching, Barnet observed. Williams is one of those people who can speak in depth on almost anything, and is so wildly gifted that just to be around him is a constant lesson in self-acceptance and humility.

Through the medium of film and movie magic, the audience is able to sidestep the conceptual process and actually see directly how Williams moves through a reality of his own making. And how he becomes aware of it to the point that he has dominion over the outer world by virtue of the thoughts he holds. Because the visual element is so immediate, sophisticated concepts can be communicated directly. When Williams finds his wife and decides to stay with her in the nether world reserved for suicide cases, we see that his decision to share her place of suffering immediately begins to transform the situation. Joining someone where he is, rather than trying to fix him, is redemptive not only of the present but also of the past. I can think of no more direct and accessible teaching on the nature of compassion in any spiritual treatise. At the same time, the whole thing is wrapped around with the classic Hollywood love story.

Barnet was saying something about how the medium of film takes us beyond the paradigm of teacher and student; how, like the old medieval mystery plays, it works through modeling.

"We have modeled our own negative fantasies for long enough," he continues. "Surely it's time now for more creative, empowering visions of the future. What if we were to imagine a time, say in twenty years, when everyone was functioning at his or her best? That's the movie I want to see. We have a whole language to debate the story of despair. What we need is a language to share joy. Let's log in some time in a reality that works. That is the gift that we as a culture need to give to ourselves. As we expand our vocabulary we shall expand our sense of who we are, and then we can have more compassionate, generous stories."

Even in the midst of the mind-numbing mediocrity of American television, I thought, as I got up to leave, such generous stories exist. I was thinking of Oprah, and in particular the show when she cried with the author of the book *Simple Abundance,* acknowledging how important it was for her to be told to be grateful for five things every day. In that moment she was modeling a positive image for millions. She subsequently made a whole program where she asked people to keep gratitude journals and to come on the program and share their experiences.

What is so powerful about TV stories like that, or Barnet's film, is that as we watch we are immersing ourselves in the morphic field of what is being shown. Watching TV or a film is a whole body experience, a psychic and intuitive as well as a biological one. That means we are open to deep primal learning, absorbing information through the pores of our body; which is the reason *What Dreams May Come* can convey sophisticated ideas simply yet profoundly. It is also why we are able to suspend disbelief and enter the world on the screen: the medium itself creates a hypnagogic state. All the more reason, then, why we should be so much more attentive to the quality of the material we transmit. It is a sobering thought for an Englishman, at least, that the average American watches twenty-five thousand commercials a year.

That evening, I was sitting with a friend in a Santa Monica restaurant discussing the beneficial influence that Hollywood could have if only more people like Barnet Bain would walk their talk. Someone across the room waved to my dinner companion. It was a friend of his called Dorothy Braudy. Dorothy, it turned out, was compiling her own photographic essay called *Sacred L.A.* She had lived in L.A. for most of her life, and had become dispirited with the common image of the city as the ul-

timate materialist playground. For her, L.A. is a visionary city, a microcosm of the world. How could it be otherwise, with 108 different languages spoken in L.A. schools? Every ethnic group has its own religious
practices and places of worship, and she decided to make a photographic
art book that would celebrate a city whose vibrant spiritual diversity is
second to none.

We went home with her later to look at her work. She had photographed the Vedanta Temple in Hollywood; the great mosque on Ex-
position, frequented mostly by African Americans; the breaking-ground
ceremony for the new Catholic cathedral in the presence of representatives from dozens of races. She showed us pictures of another ceremony
for which the head of the Greek Orthodox Church had come to St.
Sophia's and led a procession to St. Anne's Presbyterian Church as a ritual
of connection. She showed us the nine sages at Hsi Lai, the biggest Buddhist temple in the Western Hemisphere, and the one where Al Gore gave
his fund-raising speech; she showed us the shrine where some of Ghandi's
ashes are kept in the Self-Realization Fellowship on Sunset Boulevard in
Pacific Palisades. The portfolio was a tribute, not just to Dorothy's pho-
tography but to an idea whose time has come, one belonging to no one
and everyone: the idea of celebration and praise rather than perpetuating
the image of what isn't working.

To hear Dorothy's passion for her work was enough in itself. But another, altogether different connection emerged from our meeting. She
mentioned during the evening that she had a friend whose work she
thought was central to my own theme. All she would say was that the
woman, Lyn Evola, was an artist with a unique sense of mission. She
phoned Lyn, who agreed to meet me the following lunchtime. It was in
that way that I went from dinner to lunch the next day in the same Santa
Monica restaurant.

Lyn Evola was sitting at the table already when I arrived, the kind of
woman who gives you the immediate feeling she has time only for
straight talk. As we settle in she tells me she is from the south side of
Chicago, and that she had come to Los Angeles some years earlier with
her small son to develop her career as an artist. She became highly successful, the galleries vying for her work, which was strongly in the tradition of art for art's sake. She was a material girl, and was reaping the
rewards she had always wanted.

Then something happened that changed her life forever. She paused;
her matter-of-fact tone softened, she looked at me searchingly. "I really
don't know why I should be telling you this," she said, vulnerable suddenly. "I have told practically no one the background to what I am doing

now. People wouldn't believe me, they would think I was mad. I don't know, somehow when Dorothy phoned I responded directly to meeting you. I have had to get used to trusting that in the last couple of years."

I sat with her, saying nothing, listening as deeply as I knew how. I was happy for her to tell me exactly what she wanted and no more. She fumbled with her napkin, looked down, and began speaking with an openness that opened my ears even further.

She was sitting in a room with a friend one day, she said, looking out over a garden. Suddenly, out of nowhere, she saw an angel figure on the lawn just outside the window. It was seven feet tall, bent on one knee, with a long face and piercing blue eyes looking straight at her. Her immediate reaction was anger. "I don't see this kind of stuff," she thought. "The only reason I would see an angel is that it was coming to take me away, and I'm not going anywhere, I have a son to look after."

She was an artist, with a highly visual imagination. Yet in those first few seconds she was struck by the realization that she could not be making this up because the angel had wings, not of feathers, but of white fur; she would never have conceived that image in a hundred years. A few seconds later—that's what it felt like, time had already disappeared—she became aware of other angels all around her in a circle. Her friend could see some of them too, though Lyn counted twelve; all of which she could see in the most minute detail, sinews and muscles rippling like Michaelangelo bronzes.

For the next two hours the angels moved around Lyn and spoke to her in a way she could only call holographic. The words they used entered her awareness through her whole body rather than through her ears alone, and they were silent, yet clear as day. She stopped, looked at me hesitantly for a moment, gauged my reaction.

"They told me three things," she said at last. "They said, 'We are just; you need have no fear, and we want something from you.' I said—not out loud, I just thought it—I have two conditions. Nothing must happen to my son, and this must be the greatest art I have ever done. I knew they wanted art from me, though I couldn't think why, because I'm a professional, I'm not into so-called 'spiritual' art. They said I had made a contract to do what I was going to do before I was born. As they said that, another angel appeared, a white one that I remembered seeing as a child. That made me shiver, you know, the feeling that life is already planned out. I had lived my life thinking I was the one controlling it with my conscious intent."

I thought of the Robin Williams movie, how it shows that we create our world. I saw no contradiction, though, because the choice and creation of our life happen less through the conscious ego than through the deeper intentionality of the soul, which can take lifetimes to materialize. The ego, anyway, is not around before we are born. It is, as always, a matter of who we think we are. Levels within levels. Ultimately, as Byron Katie would say, even the soul is another story, and who we are—can we bear it—is not a story at all. Only awareness is, and it belongs to no one. A few layers need to drop away before we can hear that one.

Meanwhile, however relative such visions and experiences may be, this one changed Lyn's entire life forever. Along with the birth of her son, it was the most magnificent few hours she had ever known in her life. It caused a deep internal change in her, and she sensed a whole era was over. From then on she knew she could not afford the luxury of a single bad feeling for anyone. She began to see through people to their deepest intentions. She stopped socializing. She felt like she had discovered gold, and knew she had been summoned to express the best of herself.

Two days after the visitation she got in her car and heard a voice say "twelve angels in L.A. and one in D.C." She thought the radio was on but when she turned the dial she found it was already off. From that day on none of her work sold, and she was unable to create any new work. She stopped having shows, and when the gallery owners would call and ask why she was no longer sending any work, she could not even reply to them. The only thing she felt able to do was to draw the angels she had seen, over and over, day after day. Lyn has full visual recall, and for two years she researched the figures, discovering that they were the twelve archangels. Throughout those two years, she sold nothing, and money worries began to crowd in on her.

From the beginning she knew that she was to sculpt the angels, even though sculpture was not her medium. She saw life-size figures installed in public places around L.A.; figures that would evoke the virtues that human beings strive for. She knew that in all cultures angels represented our deepest qualities, the potential of humanity. The angel sculptures would be a contemporary way of modeling the best of ourselves to the culture at large, in the same way that eighteenth-century artists sculpted the Apollo stance for the aristocracy.

There was more. In the first days after her vision Lyn had the intuition that the sculptures were to be made of guns handed in by the different L.A. gangs. The angels would be like magnets leeching the violence out of society, a metaphor for warring factions to come together and lay down their arms. Then she discovered in her research that guns were made of junk metal, a formidable challenge to any sculptor, and that a better material would be the titanium from nuclear missile casings. Even so, the symbolism of gun metal was central, and she eventually found a way to incorporate it. The whole point was to change the way people felt both about their weaponry and about themselves.

When the image of what she had to do became clear, an art critic friend said she knew a foundry in Berkeley that might be willing to help. Lyn explained the project to the foundry owner, who said she could do whatever she wished. He offered her his assistant, and insisted on charging her no rent. For six months she worked in the foundry with no income, making six moquettes—three-quarter-size models.

One day she screamed at the sky, " How do you expect me to do all this on no money?" The angels partly emerged, repeating, "We are here, we are here." Another time during the foundry period she was having a massage and the masseur suddenly leaped back, saying, "My God, there are three angels above you and they are telling me in the fiercest tone to be very careful with you."

Listening to Lyn Evola in that Santa Monica restaurant, I wondered about faith—my own—and how, despite all the moments of grace I had known, it evaporates at times into thin air. Faith, not in the protection of some parental or angelic power, but in the unfolding process of the unseen itself; its telos, the wisdom of its intentionality. I had no doubt whatsoever that Lyn had experienced everything she was telling me. Yet the effect on me was less to instill a "belief" in angels, than to deepen my own faith without an object; faith in the intelligence and inherent purpose of life itself.

As soon as she had finished the moquettes, she got a call from a woman who said she had heard that one of them looked just like her son, and that she wanted to buy it. "It's expensive," said Lyn, "$20,000." "I'll send you a check," said the woman.

That was in 1995, the first money Lyn had earned from art in two years. Before then she had a part time job that required her to drive all over L.A., and in the course of that she began to realize she was being shown where to install the twelve L.A. angels. They would each be in a different ethnic area. To begin with she thought L.A. would be the sum of the project, though gradually she became aware that the scope of the work needed to embrace the world. It has become known as the Peace Angel Project, and there will be an angel in recurring trouble spots around the globe. Lyn intends three to be installed by the end of 1999—in Los Angeles, New York, and South Africa. As funds emerge from the sale of the moquettes and from foundations, they will be followed by angels in Belfast, Sarajevo, Jerusalem, Istanbul, Korea, and Vietnam.

"There is a moquette installed a few blocks north," she said, "at the

Crossroads School in West L.A. We can go and have a look if you like. It's on my way home."

It was also on the way to where I was going that afternoon, to a celebration for the Season for Nonviolence being coordinated by people from Agape Church at Santa Monica High. They had already performed a ceremony that morning, Lyn told me, around her Peace Angel. We drove a few blocks north, and there it was—a figure several feet tall with an intensity of expression that held me still for moments on end. Without even a trace of sentimentality, this angel commanded by its very presence; demanded even, that we lay down our violence at its feet. I marveled to think that this woman had never sculpted anything before the Peace Angel Project had seized hold of her life. But then Lyn Evola has been lifted out of a life of self-preoccupation to one in which she is utterly given to the service of a vision. When that grace happens, anything is possible.

Chapter Twenty

A Season for Nonviolence

"Never doubt that a small group of thoughtful committed citizens can change the world: indeed it is the only thing that ever has."

Margaret Mead

In New York at the end of January, on the anniversary of Gandhi's assassination, I had joined a thousand others in the United Nations Headquarters to celebrate the start of A Season for Nonviolence, a nationwide campaign to promote nonviolence not just as a political strategy but as a way of life. Kofi Annan, the secretary general, had launched the season by telling us how the sixty-four days between then and the anniversary of Martin Luther King's assassination in April would be celebrated across the country. He had explained how they wanted to excite the imagination of the American people with an idea whose time had come—the vision of building a society (Dr. King had called it "the beloved community") where the dignity of every human being was honored and fostered. Religious congregations, community groups, and other local organizations would sponsor a sixty-four-day calendar of public events around the country to promote nonviolence.

Jesse Jackson was there that cold January day, so was Al Sharpton, which surprised me, but then nonviolence requires the abandoning of all prejudice; Arun and Sunanda Gandhi were also on the stage, along with a Native American from Canada who sang some prayers. The retired dean of St. John the Divine Cathedral, the indefatigable James Park Morton, was emcee, while the hall was full of representatives from groups across the country. A hundred and eleven U.S. cities and fifty states had committed themselves to the season.

And now, on the anniversary of King's death, the season's last day, I am at the closing ceremonies in Los Angeles, in the sports hall of Santa Monica High. Three hundred local community organizations have taken part in the L.A. area, and most of them are in the hall now. Perhaps a couple of thousand people, from every conceivable cultural and ethnic background, of all age groups, many of them waving banners, are singing along with the Agape Choir, a multiracial group of men and women from Agape Church, which seems to be blessed with a high degree of local Hollywood talent.

Michael Beckwith, minister and founder of Agape Church—its full name is Agape International Center of Truth—steps up with a smaller group, singing his heart out in an a cappella number, "It's a Fire That You Can't Put Out," followed by "Burn for God." What else can burn for God, I thought, tapping my foot to the rhythm, but our resistance to life, offered into the fire of a deeper longing?

Local celebrities take their turn to address the crowd, with KFI talk show host Maria Sanchez sharing the emcee role with Michael Beckwith. Sen. Tom Hayden strolls up in an open shirt and a white scarf given to him by the Dalai Lama to tell us that if we act for nonviolence we have to act for justice too. Right now we are spending more on prisons than on schools and community colleges combined, he says. We need to make a stand against the demonization of young people here in Los Angeles as well as across the United States. He tells us there are 105 square miles of officially designated poverty areas in the city and that there are young people out there, in this hall and out in the neighborhoods, who have dedicated themselves to reducing the fear in this city. We need to honor them, he calls. It's time for peace in America.

As Tom steps down to a roar of applause, Beckwith telling us that we have reached the interval, I slip out to find Eisha Mason, the woman who has put the whole L.A. end of A Season for Nonviolence together. I find her in a back room, a tall, graceful African American. Eisha tells me she is director of community outreach for Agape; that she coordinates their Peace Ministry, which holds an all-night vigil every December 30 for peace, and prayer vigils through the year for different world crises.

"So Season for Nonviolence was a natural next step for us," she says, looking so relaxed you would never guess she was responsible for the complexities of the event down the hall. "We see it as a bridge between spiritual life and action in the world. We are spiritual activists, and at the same time we trust in the perfect activity of God."

I remembered Jim Wallis in Washington, how he had responded when I had asked him about the danger of burnout. He had been spared that trap, he had said, by an experience that had led him to know that however things turned out, there was always a bigger power at work than himself. He was a spiritual activist too; yet like Eisha, he acknowledged the larger context. I want to know what nonviolence actually means for Eisha and the people she works with. It is a term, after all, that is wide open to interpretation. She laughs.

"We spent months discussing that," she answers. "Should we call it a peace or a nonviolent event? During that time we came to appreciate the philosophy and practice of nonviolence, which probably has a tradition stretching back to the birth of humanity, though Gandhi articulated it more fully than ever before. What we came to is that nonviolence means honoring the dignity and worth of every human being; living with reverence for life; recognizing our responsibility to and for each other; being willing to stand for a just and peaceful world. It means that no person is your enemy, but activities and beliefs that run counter to nonviolence are your enemies. Then there is the broader dimension: it implies a belief in the power of the spirit in us to overcome any obstacle; the spirit of love."

Here is the American version of *salaam*, I am thinking; the Muslim peace that Sayed Nasr described so eloquently in the conference at the American University in Georgetown. The essence of nonviolence, the lack of any impulse to harm, lies in the peace passing understanding at the heart of all of us and of every religious tradition. From that peace ensues trust in the unfolding process of life, at the same time as action to the greater good. It is the source of action because compassion naturally arises from wisdom, and wisdom is the nature of that peace. Compassion is being moved, literally, to act for the greater good.

"So," Eisha is saying, "all the different organizations here have sponsored an event of some kind that places their work in the context of nonviolence. The Watts Century Latino Organization had sixty kids clean up the neighborhood. Taking responsibility for your community alongside others is a nonviolent principle, and they did the work within that context. It was very empowering for them to see what they often do anyway in this new light."

Then Eisha tells me about the *caminata* organized by Father Greg Boyle of the Dolores Mission. East L.A. residents do a *caminata*, a walk, through the neighborhood housing projects every fortnight to encourage the young people to keep the tenuous peace there. During the sixty-four days of the season the *caminata* was dedicated to the campaign and connected to the national effort.

"The Season for Nonviolence has also served as a catalyst for the young to step into leadership," she adds. "One kid on community service with us started a Nonviolent Assembly at school which the staff and other students joined. The whole point is not to wait to be saved, but to be an active citizen. They discussed how they could make a difference in their school, where one boy has already been shot this year. So anyway," she finishes, getting up to go back to the hall, "today we are celebrating what we have done together these last two months, and making a covenant to continue working for peace. This is just the beginning."

As the music was starting up again in the sports hall I stopped to talk to Tom Hayden, who was standing at the door as we came in. Tom has a long history of activism, starting back in the sixties when he was imprisoned as one of the Chicago Seven, along with the likes of Abbie Hoffman and Bobby Seale. He's not in the mood for talking, but he does anyway, saying when I ask him why he is in politics that the whole point of political life is to make a stand for soul. The nature of our system, he says, tends to rob individuals and communities of their soul, and the role of the politician is to defend against that. Never, I thought, have I heard such a noble description of politics.

"Ask anyone who has had to fight against local government," he goes on in his gruff manner. "You will hear that the soul is not recognized, that people are turned into citizen zombies, and they give up. The gangs are a symptom of the same problem. They are made up of people who are never heard; they are the kids of people who never benefited from the war on poverty. You may not know that the first gangs in L.A. were mostly made up of Vietnam vets who came back to unemployment and disrespect."

"The Salvadorean gangs, the most extreme in the city, are all kids from the war in El Salvador that our government funded and perpetuated. They were born in war, saw their fathers murdered by death squads, came here in the trunks of cars, and formed gangs to protect themselves from other groups. Now we are deporting them back to El Salvador, so it's a whole circle. The only way to break the cycle is to recognize that these are people like us, and their presence here is a mirror onto our own failures. It's not a question of feeling guilty, it's a matter of dealing with it."

That means recognizing the value of people, he goes on, rather than typecasting them as hopeless and violent. Violence and anger are not racial or genetic—the Irish in America are mostly highly educated and middle class, whereas they used to comprise the worst gangs in New York. Violence, Hayden says, festers over generations in inevitable reaction to an assumed attitude of superiority on the part of the more fortunate. Let's stop any policies—his voice is passionate now—that continue to cause the deepening of shame, and create opportunities for jobs and training instead.

"Talk to Duane," Tom Hayden says suddenly, gripping the arm of a burly young African American by his side. "He'll give you the inside view on American justice." With that, Tom goes back onto the stage to join the other presenters.

Duane tells me he met Tom while serving a seven-year sentence in Wasco State Prison. Duane was one of those responsible for the cease-fire agreement among the gangs in 1991. Before the cease-fire a movement had been organized to deal with police brutality and the violence in the Watts area that grew out of the police murder of Duane's cousin, Henry Pico. They began to establish committees to draw attention to police misconduct, and the cease-fire agreement came out of that.

"The media propaganda, however, fueled by the L.A. Police Department, turned the story round to say the gangs were coming together to attack the police and take over L.A. That gave them a way to target me and railroad me into prison. I became the scapegoat because I had initiated the cease-fire agreement and because my cousin had just been killed, which would make it seem like I had a motive to do harm. I served four years for a robbery I did not commit. I had a hundred witnesses who said I hadn't done it, and many people like Jerry Brown and Jesse Jackson who came to support my case. They did reduce the sentence from ten to seven years, but my support was overwhelmed by my background and the DA's desire to have me removed from the streets."

Rough justice like this is not unique to America, I tell him. In Britain in the last few years a number of convictions have finally been overturned after the wrongfully imprisoned had already spent more than a decade behind bars. I was thinking of the Birmingham Seven in particular, the Irish who were imprisoned a decade ago for bombing a Birmingham pub. The Irish question, perhaps like the L.A. gang scene, puts pressure on the police to get results, even if they are sometimes the wrong ones.

Tom Hayden heard of Duane's case through his mother, a community activist who founded Mother's ROC—Mothers Reclaiming Our Children, in response to Duane's plight. Tom came to Wasco for a few hours in 1994; they talked, and he asked Duane if he had plans for the future. They discussed how they might bridge the gap between the community that Tom represented, the San Fernando Valley and Santa Monica, and the Watts/Compton neighborhood Duane grew up in. Tom continued to write, sent books, and maintained the relationship when Duane was released in 1996. They began to work on issues, Duane giving voluntary time, Tom mentoring him, until finally Duane became a full-time member of the district staff.

"I do everything," Duane explains. "Everything from helping to draft legislation to lobbying for or against different legislative measures. I still work on gang issues, and mostly youth issues. I have to say that Tom is a guy who really walks his talk. He has four members of staff with a criminal background. He has been willing to take a chance with us, and everyone in the office has a profound respect for him."

I am not surprised. Tom Hayden may be feisty, difficult even; you may not agree with him, but there is no doubting he is a man of principle, of soul; and that is a rare thing in the political arena. I believe in this grassroots spiritual activism, I thought, as I left the celebration to go to my hotel. Here are three hundred groups in Los Angeles practicing what they preach along with all those in every other big city in America. That must surely create a resonance, an energetic field to support further steps in the future. I remember something Eisha Mason said just as we were parting, that people don't act because they don't feel like it matters. They don't feel powerful. The fact is, she said, we are powerful. All we have to do is remember that and act. When people stand together with an intention to act, they can move the world. That is just what they have been doing this afternoon in Santa Monica High.

The next morning is a Sunday, the one after Easter, and before leaving L.A. I have time to join in the morning service at Agape, the spiritual inspiration behind the Season for Nonviolence activities in L.A. Some fifteen hundred people are already in place, both black and white in roughly equal proportions. Someone is leading the congregation into a silent meditation, while playing softly on a piano. I go to the men's room and on the mirror is a sticker saying, "Behold, the face of God."

As I come back in a group of musicians is striking up on stage, to be followed by the Agape choir, and we are into third gear now. More musicians and solo singers follow, this being Hollywood, I realize, so much talent available and ready to go, like being at a first-class blues and folk concert. Then the affirmations, everyone in unison, "I am grateful, grateful, grateful, the kingdom of God is at hand, and I live there now." I remember the Agape purpose statement I read on the way in, "to create an environment where we realize we are all unique expressions of God, and to actively practice this in life."

Then Michael Beckwith bounces onto the stage and begins a message to end all messages. "We don't believe *in* Jesus"—he almost croons it out. "But we believe Jesus when he says, '*You* are the light of the world.' Jesus spoke to the greatness of us all, to our divine possibility, and his life was a template for all of us, sons of God that we are. I tell you no life escapes the Crucifixion, Resurrection, and Ascension. No one goes through life without loss, betrayal, and crucifixion. We all know how we think life is meant to look one way and it turns out another. The mark of Judas is on all of us, and when that mark calls our name a hidden talent or strength can arise within. It can draw the Christ presence out of us; that's its gift, and we can cross over into a greater dimension of living."

He is warming up fast now. He urges us to give up the stories we tell about ourselves that aren't working; because underneath every story like that is a place where we have not forgiven. Some of these stories are so well rehearsed we see them as our identity, he cries. The point is to replace those stories with God's story—that's when you resurrect into Christ, who is a state of consciousness in full bloom, fully who we are. That is when we see ourselves to be on an ascension process, where every part of life is permeated with God. The Ascension, Beckwith urges us, is when you realize all your life is God's, that there is nothing left outside of God. The only price to pay for that is the loss of our sense of limitation and mediocrity.

I could feel the tempo lifting me up, raising my attention, sharpening my senses. I could feel, too, the truth of his words, Byron Katie in a different form, clothed in Christian language, the same message, you are it, nothing else. I could sense, too, the narcissistic shadow to the light he was casting, the ego's wish to be crowned in spiritual glory. There's always a risk, whichever path you tread. The danger with this one is that it's easy for the mind to assume the reality of the words without the body and emotions having incorporated it. Resting in *salaam,* the peace in which you are no one and everything, that is the saving grace, I thought.

Michael Beckwith has the same thought in mind, though he says it another way. As long as we imagine we are doing it, he says, nothing will happen. The attention needs to be surrendered in spirit, and if you don't recognize the presence of Christ above all, then you open the door to hubris. The point, he says, is to be present for something greater than self, rather than trying to hoist oneself into greatness; that is the opportunity of the Crucifixion.

"So when you go through that Crucifixion," he implores us, "don't ask how this can get any worse, because the universe is infinite—invoke the recognition factor: how awesome is the God I serve. This is his work. Then nothing can break you. You will bless the loss, the seeming betrayal, for something was born in you, and you will no longer need to rely on anything outside of you for joy. Yet it had to be taken away from you to know that. There is no nobility in being superior to another, but there is great nobility in being superior to your previous self."

His arms are raised to the heavens now, urging us all to say with him, "I and my Father are one. My mind is the mind of Christ Jesus."

"Remember," he ends finally, "if you want to make it through another day you have to let go. Let go and hear the divine presence who says 'I am with you always.'"

The choir starts up, people standing now, singing their hearts out, joy in their faces. What an inspiration it is, close enough to home for anyone to hear. When I see Michael Beckwith for a moment afterward, he tells me that of course he has doubts, he is human. Sometimes he wakes in the morning and wonders whether he can go on, and he just notices the thought, has mercy on himself, and starts into his day. He knows now with a certainty that there truly is something in us deeper than doubt, deeper than fear, and it is love, there for the remembering, who we are.

Chapter Twenty-One

Whidbey Island

I took a flight the next morning to Seattle from Los Angeles. A friend had offered me her house for a few days on Whidbey Island out in the Puget Sound. I could not write a book called *Sacred America*, she had added, without going to Whidbey. I had meant to fly from L.A. straight to San Francisco, where I was going to end my American year, but she was so emphatic I decided to go to Whidbey first. Anyway, I thought, it would be good to be on an island again. All this time traveling the vastness of the continent had given me a renewed respect for the more narrow confines of Britain.

I drove north out of Seattle and in less than an hour was settling into my place in the line for the ferry. I was out in rural Washington here, far from the sophistication of Los Angeles or even Seattle. A quiet was on the land and the water, a lone goose flapped a path through the clean blue air. Even the twenty minutes it took for the ferry to cross the Sound to Whidbey was enough to make me feel I had left America. As I drove ashore I had the impression of being on intimate land again; land whose limits were clearly defined, and which gave me in turn a more tangible impression of my own physical and psychic borders. Islands can restrict, but they also contain; they can rigidify but also strengthen the life they are host to by giving it clear parameters.

I spent that evening alone under the stars in the hot tub of my friend's house, the lights of the mainland twinkling off in the distance. The next day I returned from a trip to the local store to find a naked man and woman walking through the living room. "Hey, mun. We've been using the hot tub," said the man. "I'm David Abram, and this is Greta. We have just moved in over the street. Peggy told us you might be coming."

David Abram. My friend Peggy Taylor had said there were a lot of people I should meet on the island, and that some of them would be using her hot tub, the only one in the town. She had mentioned David, and I knew of him through his book, *The Spell of the Sensuous.* This willowy, sensitive man, a sleight-of-hand magician and a leading voice in the ecospiritual movement, stood there dripping wet before me in the shadow of his tall, magnificent partner from Belgium. Greta was the perfect counterpart to David, a quiet, powerful presence who, as a biodynamic gardener, used her hands rather than words to sculpt meaning.

It's a fine way to meet someone, no clothes, no disguises, no embarrassment, no surprise, as if this is the way it always happens. Just the time for them to dry off, get some fresh clothes from across the street, and David and I are threading our way between Langley's low houses to the beach. We are clambering over bare logs already, great trees long since stripped of their bark, tossed up on the shore by the swell like so many matchsticks. I had never seen so much driftwood on a single curve of sand, nor so many sandpipers, gray and white, probing the shoreline with saber beaks and tiny whimperings, moving as one body through the thin curl of foam that divided land from water.

We stop to watch and listen. They advance toward us, all eye and beak; then just a foot or two away they swing back in the other direction, no leaders or followers, just some intelligence that knows.

"We are the same in a way," murmurs David, as we watch them scurry back along the shore. "If we take the larger perspective, nations, and the whole of humanity, move this way and that, up and down, in a single wave. It is only from the limited perspective of the individual, or the microview, that we go our own way."

I had always felt as much. However wholeheartedly I might have swallowed the Western—and preeminently American—myth of self-determination, it is equally obvious to me that we move as a culture, and ever more now, as humanity. The hundredth-monkey metaphor—the idea that a behavior, attitude, or discovery can leap across geographical boundaries and be picked up around the world by members of the same species or cultural group—has been stretched wildly to validate all manner of dubious claims. The original point, though, remains clear: we are at least as prone, if not more so, to both the mood swings and illuminations of our culture as we are to our own.

"We are so anthropocentric," Abram went on, "that we act as if we are aware of other life forms, without considering how aware they are of us. We can only dream what those birds saw as they approached us—they may be aware of us in a way that we have not even begun to imagine. We think we are looking at nature with our own all-knowing eyes, without ever stopping to consider that everything has its own knowing, equally valid and intelligent. The world is as much one of living subjects as it is of objects. Our bodies directly experience things around us as animate powers. We may not have noticed, but our bodies were responding to that flock of sandpipers as much as they were to our presence here: on seeing them, our skin temperature will have altered, ours senses woke up, we were aware of the light on the water behind them suddenly. To the extent that we speak of these beings as objects, we are not only denying their intrinsic aliveness, we are negating our own direct sensory experience."

He paused for a moment as we sat astride another slippery tree trunk, the damp sand sucking at our shoes. "See, right there is the deepest impulse that motivates my work: I am making a plea for the renewal of that experience which has been at the heart of every traditional culture throughout time—the experience of being immersed, embedded, in the depths of a living world. That's what deep ecology is all about."

A very different kind of postmodernism, I thought. Post-Sartre, Camus, and Becket, postanxiety, postalienation; a philosophy of belonging and wonder. I suspect that more than anything we want to belong, we whose ancestors slunk heads bowed from Eden. Yet could it be anything more than a mental trick, a sleight of mind, to take the stance of belonging with a self-consciousness that had, like ours, been refined over thousands of years? Surely, in our untransformed, ordinary state at least, we belong and don't belong, and to deny either side of the paradox of being human is to deny our humanity altogether in preference for either the state of the angel or that of the animal.

> *That you and I were constantly joining,*
> *I never knew.*
> *I never knew that even to ask*
> *Who are you? or Who am I?*
> *Breaks the harmony.*

But for Rumi to know that essential truth about being human, he had to die. He had to die in the fire of love. It wasn't a matter of espousing a philosophy of deep ecology or anything else, but of submitting his mind to the kind of radical unknowing that bursts it open. In that fissure, perhaps, true belonging—the essence of Abram's deep ecology—can be known. In the meantime, Abram's position is not a bad one to take, as positions go. Perhaps it can even soften us up for that ultimate eruption of knowledge to end all knowledge that Rumi sings of.

"What I am doing," Abram went on, nudging me out of my self-absorption, "is to walk the path between the New Age philosophies, which so often abandon the sensuous world by assuming the primacy of spirit and mind, and the detached objectivism of the scientific main-stream. What really perpetuates the separation between human beings and the rest of the living world is language. The moment our alphabet became divorced from its connection with the natural world, our words became dissociated from our perceptions. How we speak has a profound influence on what we see and hear, and our writing even more so now that we are a visual and not an oral culture. The first alphabets omitted the vowels, the breath that gave life to the bones of the consonants. Then the Greeks inserted letters for the vowels, and desacralized the air and the breath. Think, when the Jews spoke the name of God, JHVH, they were sacralizing the breath—God breathes us in and out. What can be more of a celebration of the world than that?"

What more tangible a sense of the sacred could there be? I pondered; the spirit as breath that we pass between us; that moves through all and everything that lives and breathes. At the same time, the Jews had much to answer for in sweeping the spirits of nature out of the temple and re-placing them with an ill-humored image of themselves.

I imagined that Abram might feel rather distant from his religion of birth, yet when I said so he laughed and replied that the contrary was true. He was lucky, he felt, in having parents, both artists, who made their faith highly personal and home centered. His bar mitzvah occurred at home, not in the synagogue, and his parents would always make the values of the faith relevant to their life in the world.

"So I was never soured by traditional religion, he went on. "And you know, the Judaism I celebrate is embedded in nature. Even my name, Abram, espouses that, because that was Abraham's name before he gave the alphabet to the people. No, Judaism dances and sings, and the Shekinah, the light of the world, shines in everything. And your comment about an ill-humored Jehovah"—we were taking our shoes and socks off now, and splashing along in the wet sand leaving a trail of foot puddles filling with water—"Jehovah is like any tribal god: rough, tough, and gutsy, full of threats and thunderstorms. Indigenous people are rambunctious; their gods are tricksters, unpredictable, territorial, like the elements and the land we live on. I do think we need to be informed again by the spirits of the land we inhabit. We need to engage again in a deep relationship with our locality and learn its ways. Any contemporary spirituality must embrace the earth in its feeling for the divine, not in some abstract sense, but in a way that shapes our daily relationship to our surroundings."

Overhead the clouds were drifting in, the mainland over the water in shadow already; in the distance Mount Baker shone white and luminous still; the gray water was freezing my feet, the gulls were shrieking their complaints and diving fiercely into the Sound.

Abram gave me a brief but steady glance. Some people had criticized his book, he said, for giving too strong an emphasis to the immanent here and now at the expense of the vertical dimension of spirit. Well, he had no apology for reclaiming the horizontal dimension from so many centuries of eclipse in a climate of disdain for both body and nature. To reclaim the immanent divinity of all things was not to flatten the world—far from it. It was to deepen it, he felt; to help reveal the levels within levels that were in every living form.

"You know, that is what I find so hard about Buddhist language," he went on. "Getting detached, nonattachment, everything coming and going and we being the space between. No, no, that's the same life denying language as in any monastic tradition. Surely we need the language of belonging now, not of standing apart. We *are* this world, not different from it. Then, what an arrogance to imagine we are the highest of all births, the pinnacle of creation, and that we have labored for thousands of lifetimes through the 'lower' species to get the body we have now. How do we know that the ant or the cow isn't as intelligent as us; just intelligent in a different way?"

"Well, there is this remarkable blessing-curse that humans have called self-reflection," I ventured.

"But we don't know," he replied, "that animals, or even mountains, can't think. We need at least to allow the possibility that they might have a different thinking modality to ours, to give them the respect and benefit of the doubt. The Buddhist attitude has relegated the rest of creation to the lower orders. It is true, though," he added, "that the Dalai Lama has questioned that doctrine recently."

Not just the Buddhists, I reflected, but all traditions of perennial wisdom, East and West, place life within a hierarchy; a chain of being from more conscious and organized to less. Were they all simply products of patriarchal linear thinking, reflecting the dominant cultural perspective of their time, or had they to some degree at least hit on some universal order of things?

"The Buddhists I know don't see the doctrine of nonattachment to be a separating thing," I told him. "Though it's true the language sets it up to be taken that way. In fact I think they would say that the more one frees oneself from reactions of like and dislike, the more deeply intimate one can be with life as it presents itself. Far from separating us from creation, the act of seeing through our own automatic reactions frees us to be truly participative and empathic. That's why they talk so much about compassion—it's a natural result of being free from one's conditioning, though of course that freedom is lost or renewed moment by moment."

Suddenly I saw the two of us, there on that beach, discussing the nature of the world, talking about participation, the immanent here and now, the great chain of being. Meanwhile, the clouds were gathering heavily, rain was in the wind; Greta was at home gardening. I think we both felt our words float off in the wind at the same time. We turned to make our way back along the shore. David took my hand suddenly, looked into my palm, saying he loved to study hands. I was aware in that instant of the friendliness that had grown between us in that short time, of the vigor and life that can pass between people through the medium of words and the art of conversation. Here is a man, I thought, as he looked in genuine wonder at my hand, truly in love with the things of this world.

Back at the house there was a message from another David whose own love for this world I already knew from his poetry. David Whyte is an Englishman who has been living on Whidbey for twenty years, with a reputation in corporate America for bringing the language of the soul to traditional business. I had met him once at the Body and Soul conference in San Francisco where he had given a talk on finding meaning in work. I had not forgotten his opening words. He had paraphrased an old Zen saying: "Why are you unhappy? Because 98.9 percent of everything you say and do is for yourself. And there isn't one." The self that is truly alive, he had gone on to say, is the one that is in conversation with the world—meaningful work requires you to come out of hiding. Yes, a thousand times yes; I had known in my own life that game of hide-and-seek, its palpable exhilaration and terror.

David and Leslie, his new wife, had invited me for dinner that evening, and I walked up the street to the one house that was surrounded by a white wooden fence with an English stile. David opened the door wearing a red apron and brandishing a pot in his right hand. His shock of dark hair and intense blue eyes instantly made me think of Ireland, and sure enough he told me that his mother was a story-telling Irishwoman, though he had been born and raised in the north of England; his father was of that pragmatic stock. He had recently remarried, and his Canadian wife was feeding their baby.

As we raised our first glass of wine he told me that what he loved about living in America was the way people here were so encouraging of a person's gifts. He missed the conversations you could have in England, and he missed the land terribly, but his primary experience was that of so many English people in America: they could flower in a way that seemed so difficult in England. He was aware in his corporate work that there really was a new wave here, though it hadn't quite yet become the collective norm.

I replied that for me, on the other hand, the kind of conversations I was having in America would be hard to come by in England. Perhaps, David admitted, he had been away so long he was romanticizing the European imagination.

"Easy to do," I said. "Only a few weeks ago I was amazed to hear an Irish poet say, on an English television arts program, that the central theme of *Lolita* (which had just come out again as a movie) was the meeting of the sophistication of the European imagination with the crass vulgarity of America. I was staggered to hear the old clichés still being given credence. We are so arrogant I can only think it to be a last line of defense against the truth of our own estate and the contrasting creative outpouring of the New World."

I wondered how he had come to be living on Whidbey, and he explained that his first wife had come from the area. When they had come over on the ferry some twenty years before, he had been aware of how quickly that short ride could shift the mind. Mainstream America was far away already, and he had a sense of an earlier, simpler life. It also reminded him of home: the weather, the trout streams, the woods. By the end of their first day on the island he had asked his wife what he needed to do to stay there.

They had found work at the Chinook Learning Center, and quickly became involved in its growth. He was a self-taught Celtic scholar even then, and he would give evenings of stories and poetry and tales of the Celtic world. Then he was invited to speak and recite at a large annual event in California called the Asilomar Conference. He fell ill, and had to lie at the back of the hall, shivering. On the morning of his talk he was still sick, and he took a pile of books on stage with him, he was so worried about forgetting his lines.

"Anyway," he continued as the wine started to flow, "I got a standing ovation, and at the end, looking out over that hall, I knew that was how I would spend the rest of my life. I resigned from my job with Chinook, and with nothing in the bank, made myself available for talks and readings. Things went on for a few years until in 1987 Peter Block, the consultant who wrote *The Empowered Manager,* came to one of my talks. At the end he came up and asked me to join his team. He said that the language of corporate America just wasn't big enough to understand the changes taking place in the global workplace. He added that the kind of poetry I was reciting could help give a new shape and perspective to the struggles of people trying to make sense of their working life. I have discovered since that the poetry of people like Eliot, Naruda, Dante, Mary Oliver, Frost, Keats and others gives not only the language of change but also the experience of it. It is impossible to build a vital creative work force today unless every member of the team is asking germane questions about their own lives; finding what really moves them and bringing that passion into their workplace. Poetry can help that process."

His job now wasn't to give formulas for change, he explained, but to remind people that they were born with unique gifts and talent, and that their task was to share these with the world. He had learned that lesson himself, in his twenties, on discovering why he had been offered a job as the naturalist guide in the Galapagos over ninety other finalists. The interviewer had told him that the extracurricular activities on his application were the very thing he had been looking for. Rock climbing, scuba diving, learning foreign languages—everything he had pursued outside of academia had landed him the job.

"In the middle of the interview"—David was in full swing now—"I knew intuitively that I had it, and I felt a strange exaltation mixed with sadness at the small faith I had shown in my own desires and longings. I was flooded with the realization that everything I needed for this outrageous step in my life had only ever been done out of sheer joy. For the commonsense side of me, it was crazy: what I loved the most was what had qualified me for the job! In that moment I felt an almost physical resolve never to lose faith in those personal passions and desires that had led me to this place of fulfillment."

"How do you get people to have faith in their longings in the midst of a corporate atmosphere?" I asked. "I can imagine that if they were true to their calling many of them would just quit, go and be potters or caregivers."

David cautioned that it was too easy to have a clichéd view of business. He had soon found that his own images of contemporary business were as dated as the business world's image of poets in garrets. He had responded to Peter Block's call after reading Dana Gioa's essay challenging contemporary poets to come out of hiding and have an impact on the real world. He discovered the world of business to be an incredibly creative place, and that you couldn't ask for the creativity, adaptability and vitality that companies were expecting today without making a connection between the soul of the person and the work they were doing. The old days of leaving yourself at the door when you clocked in, he said wryly, and picking your real life up again when you left, were gone forever. Those divisions just didn't work any more, he realized, either for the company or for the individual.

When I asked which kind of companies hired him, he mentioned Honeywell, AT&T, Boeing, and companies around the world. They were all asking him to share poetic images that were large enough to embrace the kind of life people were wanting for themselves at the beginning of the millennium; a life that included the soul, its desires, longings, and aspirations.

"The point about great poetry is this," David said, looking up from the food he was placing on the table. "We have no defenses against it; its language liberates the soul. I am someone from outside of the business environment saying that there are other ways of looking at how we do things. We simply have too much time and emotional energy invested in the workplace to declare it a spiritual desert. I don't have some all-embracing vision which people have to buy. I am simply trying to work with the struggles we all deal with every day while we are trying to live out our personal destinies and make a living at the same time."

David had cooked a local salmon, and it was getting cold. Their baby was pulling at his hair and Leslie took the opportunity to play some music. The intensity of our conversation ebbed away and we sat together eating and drinking in silence. I wondered if there were intuitions, half-lights of understanding, that no poet had ever captured in words, that would remain forever pristine in the inchoate world of the preverbal brain, never to be marketed in the business world, to publishers, or anywhere else. I wondered if I myself could dare to give birth to a jewel of a word or a line without needing to show it to anyone.

David was saying something again, though it came to me through the haze of my daydreams; something about the word *desire,* how it meant of the stars, *de-sire,* keeping your star in sight. I remembered David Abram's complaint about Buddhist language, how it ran the risk of separating us from nature. I thought of how the word *desire* too, had suffered from its Buddhist translation. Our whole culture is constructed upon desire and its gratification, and of course the Buddhists are right when they point to the unhappiness caused by chasing our whims and obsessions. But desire—it has a deeper root than our daily hungers and wants, and Whyte was pointing to that now. True desire is the surge of the soul into life, and as Westerners we are imbued with the idea that every individual has a destiny waiting to flower beneath the preoccupations of the personality. True desire is the call of that destiny, and Whyte was saying how his work in business was to help people hear and respond to the call of their soul for an authentic life.

"I help people in business to ask how we can use the strategic mind as a servant of the soul's desires, not as an amnesia for them," said David, picking up the conversation again. "I ask them what they love to do, and what practical forms that can take. I ask what kind of people they love to be around. Yeats had this wonderful line on seeking and longing: 'Throw fuel on the fire at the center of your being, and the fire will take you where you want to go.' The more you discover your true work and give time to it, the more you are unearthing your gift. And as you do that, you will notice that people want it; they want the aliveness you carry, because that is our true gift to each other and to the world: our joy. What could be more spiritual than the sharing of joy?"

"Not that it's simple," I laughed. "Joseph Campbell, the mythologist, said that if you can see your path laid out in front of you it's probably someone else's. And in my experience we don't find it by trying to organize our lives more. Most of us start where we are, in our awkwardness. It seems to me that the aim of the soul is not to get rid of suffering and obstacles, but to belong. As I go on, I realize that doubt, fear, and so on don't fade away, they begin to happen within a larger ecology of experience."

David nodded vigorously, and added that he always told people in business that the first step was to rest back into oneself, to come to one's own earth. He encouraged executives to stay still a while, go deeper in, take the lonely road, confront their fears, their grief, their loss, and through the work of the poets know that they were not alone. I asked him which kind of poetry he made use of.

"Oh, there's no one like Rilke or Naruda to show how important it is to find one's own way. Antonio Machado, the Spanish poet, tells us "to make sweet honey from all our old failures," and Dante, of course, recounts the entire soul's journey through heaven and hell. In his *Divine Comedy* he says, "in the middle of the road of my life, I awoke in a dark wood, where the true way was wholly lost." I must say I have been astonished at the discontent and longing for something beyond the daily grind in men approaching fifty."

"As for Beowulf, he was an eighth-century management consultant; a prince who hires out his services to a king for a mix of personal honor, self-education, and personal gain. He dares us to confront our deepest fears. He was hired to fight the monster in the lake against whom all weapons are useless. The dark lake is the individual soul, and the challenge for managers is to recognize its place in business. Managers are often fighting their own monsters at work without even recognizing that they are doing so. It is imperative that people question the degree of fulfillment they find at work, and face their feelings honestly. True courage in a work situation would be to share those feelings with others. In the right conditions, a peer group doing this kind of work together can transform their business environment."

"The road seems to turn round and round," I said, "this way we have of making a home for ourselves in the world and then being exiled from it, only to return again. Isn't it strange," I added, "how just as the blessing is being given you are also broken open to the world again, and then as you are broken open blessings will come from even deeper still?"

"Yes, yes, it is just like that," Whyte replied. "If I could say it another way, I would say that life moves us again and again from the act of leaving to the act of arriving, of giving ourselves to the arrival in every moment, not just to the sorrow of the leaving. Every moment is an occasion to look for the gap, the sliver of light on the floor. That's what I go in and say to companies who are downsizing."

Did he ever despair of there being any real change of values in the corporate world? It was hard for me to imagine a board of directors discussing what would be good for their employees' souls.

"They wouldn't use that language, but it is certainly happening," came his reply. The soul isn't just about poetry and the scent of roses, it's forged more often than not in a vale of tears, in making a stand for the truth. No, I am full of hope. There is nothing more transforming to the American workplace than the thousands of daily decisions now being made that put an authentic life above the abstractions of organizational life. It is a grassroots thing as much as a boardroom concern."

Many people, he explained, now refused the wrenching transfers to faraway cities that had at one time been necessary for advancement. Many ignored the constant demands for more of their time, demands that robbed their families of their presence and set up a tension between home and work. In the eighties the climate had been different, people had done what was expected. Now the expectations themselves were changing, quality of life was being seen as intrinsic to quality of work. The old divisions just didn't work any more, David Whyte affirmed; and people knew it, even if they didn't always act on it.

The evening had flown by on the run of our words, and I left finally, taking the longer road the better to see the crescent moon. The next morning David and I went for a walk through the woods along a salmon stream of red water past the outdoor classroom built by the parents of the local school. We peered over the culvert but we saw no leapers, and we passed through the grounds of the Chinook Learning Center where David had started out all those years ago. New building was under way, and the center had recently been reborn as The Whidbey Institute.

The institute was no New Age dreamland. David assured me. Senior professionals from around the country and from a variety of fields were on the board. These people were passionately committed to new cultural patterns of justice and environmental wholeness; to a way of life that drew from spiritual traditions without being bound to past beliefs and practices; to a nondogmatic and inclusive spirit; and to a faith in the unique contribution of each individual life. In short, a manifesto of spirit in action for the new America. Right here, in the backwoods of Whidbey Island, they were already sending out ripples across the country in business and other professional communities.

"The institute draws on the model of the early monastic community on Iona, in Scotland," David explained. "The Celtic monks saw all of creation as a seamless whole, and learning was as much a part of their lives as praying. Whidbey is an extraordinary community," he added. "It's a seedbed for ideas and initiatives that are having an influence far beyond the Northwest. Our small town of Langley, too, is a community in the real sense of the word; partly because it is still small enough, just five thousand people. There are a disproportionate amount of artists and poets, a cybercafe, and initiatives like the Giraffe Project, which recognizes people who 'stick their neck out' and take risks—social, financial, or physical—for the good of the community. They have honored close to a thousand people who have overcome apathy and cynicism and have shown what an average person with courage can do. They also organize seminars to help businesses bring a 'giraffe spirit' to their work, and a Standing Tall program that teaches schoolchildren about caring, courage, and community. Then there's Ross Chapin, the architect who's creating a new kind of sustainable housing on 3rd Street. You should meet him."

I should, though my head was spinning already. We drove back to town and David showed me his writing cabin, all big windows, cedar, and a log fire. A biography of Wellington lay open on the table. Just after we arrived, Brendon, his son by his first wife, came through the door laughing and spattered in mud and I let them be, deciding after all to saunter on up to 3rd Street to find Ross the architect. I have long since learned on my travels through America to follow directions that come unbidden, as if out of the mouth of some unwitting oracle—and always without expectation of a particular outcome.

Ross was standing in the street with Jim Soules, his business partner, facing a new development of eight houses round a common green. In the middle of the commons a plum tree spiraled strikingly out almost horizontal with the ground.

"We heard you were coming through Peggy Taylor," he smiled with his hand outstretched. "Welcome to Langley, the village with the big city energy!"

Peggy had certainly prepared the ground for me. And I was beginning to have a feeling for what Ross meant. Langley seemed to have all the advantages of a small town with the creative and cultural fire of somewhere like Seattle. I asked Ross if he was a recent immigrant from the mainland, and he replied that he and his wife had been on Whidbey for twenty years. They had come looking for a place where they could live out their values, and all that time ago they had seen in Langley the potential for a local community whose mix of people would encourage the interfaith spirit they were seeking.

"It's very helpful," Ross continued, "that there is no one group or leader here whose voice is dominant. The town could have gone Americana, but fortunately tourism is less of a priority here than the concern of the local community for the kind of environment they live in. Some years ago I collaborated with a local developer to express those priorities in the downtown business area. We designed a site where each building was different, with its own character, and was oriented toward people rather than function. We wanted to create a workplace community where each person was passionate about their work, and that passion would generate a synergy, which everyone would benefit from. We went out and found tenants who shared our perspective, who cared about the beauty of the site, and whose business was geared to the needs of the community rather than tourism. It worked, as you can see if you go downtown."

When I asked what had led to this new housing development, Ross explained that he had worked for years in a large architects' office designing big houses for retired couples; bathrooms everywhere, and devoid of any real life. Then he had met Jim Soules when he was giving a talk in Seattle on Strategies for Designing Smaller Houses. Jim threw down the gauntlet and suggested they get started. Soon after that they were looking at Pine Street Cottages in Seattle, workers' cottages built in the 1920s and recently renovated. There were ten, four hundred-square-foot houses round a common green, with the only private outdoor space being the front porch. Yet the whole complex felt so intimate, so safe. They decided to do the same in Langley. They wanted to encourage a sense of community, but also to show that simplicity and economy of space could work.

"Just think," said Ross, "the average American home is over two thousand square feet, yet 25 percent of households are single people, and 40 percent are singles and couples combined. And we have a large and increasing population of single women that was unknown thirty years ago. In 1947 the average house was less than one thousand square feet and the average family had four children. Today, Bill Gates has a $60 million, forty thousand-square-feet house on the shore outside Seattle, and people flock to see it as if it were some kind of trophy of success, rather than what it is—a monument to the disastrous ego aggrandizement of our culture."

Yet it was also true that people were coming from all over the country to view their development in Langley, interjected Jim Soules, laughing. None of the houses in their development were more than 650 feet on the first floor or more than 975 feet including the second floor.

"As you can see," he said, pointing across the street, "every cottage is adjacent to the common area, with all the porches and kitchen windows facing in to the plum tree. If we don't have safe streets it is partly because houses are not built to look out onto streets or communal areas. Our idea is to have an old-fashioned neighborhood woven together with sidewalks and gardens. Huge garages dominate most streetscapes. You drive straight into the house and have no interaction on the street. Here, there are no garages, just one place for off-street parking. Each house has a different interior design, though they all have nine-foot ceilings and high windows, so they feel much larger than usual. They are for singles or couples, though not the elderly because the loft ladders are steep."

"We are not trying to create some sort of intentional community," Ross added. "There will be no one set of values or beliefs expressed by the people who live here. It's an organic community, rather, one that will find its own level. It's a bit like cohousing without the meetings, since we developed and sold under a condo-type ownership."

Jim added that when a woman across the street heard about the plans, she had written a stinging letter to the local authority about the impact of the density on the area. She had refused to talk to them, so they invited her to the opening celebration. Afterward she came up to them with tears in her eyes and said, "Jim, Ross, I'll eat that letter I wrote. What you are doing is so beautiful, a wonderful addition to the neighborhood. I may even sell my house and buy one of these cottages."

"That, said Ross, "was when we really knew we were doing something right."

We walked round along the paths and into some of the houses. It was true; they seemed so much more spacious on the inside than one would imagine from the exterior. This was housing for individuals who like to feel there are other individuals close by. There was a common project building with a wood burning stove and an upstairs deck where you could mend bicycles or make pots. Ross and Jim had already sold every unit, mostly to single women.

"So what's next?" I asked them.

"I am designing the One Drop Zen Center for Harada Roshi," Ross replied. He is moving here from Japan. He had a vision twenty-five years ago that the teaching would thrive in America. I guess he's right, from the number of Buddhist centers that are sprouting up everywhere."

We parted warmly in a light drizzle and I made my way back to Peggy's house, with clouds in the far distance that looked like mountains, or mountains that looked like clouds. Then for a moment the horizon cleared a little, and I could see it was Mount Baker, all white and trailing streams of vapor. Later that afternoon, when the clouds had cracked open to let a warm light fall in, I went over to the west side of the island. There, out of the sheer air beyond the mainland shore, rose the ghostly white form of Mount Rainier, the American Mount Fuji, the axis that people in all corners of the state can see. In the other direction the Olympics broke the sky into a jagged edge. In that moment on the pebbly beach I could see that Whidbey had its guardians in every direction, mountain presences who had watched over the Sound since it had come into being. Driving off the ferry the next day, back on the freeway to Seattle and mainstream America, I thanked Peggy Taylor out loud for bringing me to Whidbey, that other world over the water.

Chapter Twenty-Two

Feminine Spirit in Action

Passing through the portals of the Golden Gate Bridge I entered the land of the gods, Marin County, out into the blue from the fog of the city. Then I began to understand why so many people with an artistic or spiritual sensibility congregate here. There is a powerful spirit upon the land. Deeply feminine, it nourishes and inspires. It returns the human to a sense of proportion with the sheer scale of its grandeur. The folds of the hills roll into the biggest expanse of ocean on the globe, the needles of the giant redwoods drink in the morning mists, houses nestle among woods on the waves of the ridges.

This is a blessed land; yet for all its beauty, it can never replace the spot that gave a person her first sense of belonging and home; not, at least, for Susan Shannon. I was introduced to Susan by a mutual friend, Dale Borglum, whom I had first met in India years earlier. He told me he could think of no one better to exemplify the ideal of the everyday mystic; that in his mind, Susan was the embodiment of the feminine spirit of compassion in action. So it was that Susan and I met in Marin soon after I had arrived in the Bay area from Whidbey.

Until recently, and for fourteen years, Susan was the letter carrier for the town of San Anselmo, fifteen minutes north of the Golden Gate Bridge. She has lived in the area since the early eighties, but she was conceived during her parents' honeymoon on Orcas Island, one of the San Juan Islands in the Pacific Northwest. Her parents lived on the mainland, and would often visit Orcas with their young daughter.

When she was barely three, Susan was out playing on one of the island beaches. Her mother says that at one moment she stood up, looked over at Buck Mountain in the distance, and with an old look on her face, pointed to it and said, "I'm going to live there someday." When she was nineteen, Buck Mountain was where she made her first home.

Susan was sitting across from me in Dale's kitchen, a warm, clear presence with blue eyes that looked deep into me as she spoke. "I remember how even as a child I was aware on the ferry ride of a thousand shades of gray in the sky and the rocks pouring in on me, and of the shifting green of the trees. I didn't have the language for it then, of course, but the impressions entered me and stayed. Even now I use those images daily—the comfort of being on the ferryboat, the sound of the waves, the gusting winds. It is as if my DNA gets activated just sensing those sights, sounds, and smells. Even the way the light would hit a rock or a tree, or an eagle's head, would trigger an aliveness that was almost orgasmic. Returning as a child on the ferry to the island, I felt like I was walking back into the estate that was myself. A hundred rooms in my body were lit up and available for me there, whereas here it might be ten. The muse was alive in every cell."

The community Susan returned to on Orcas when she was nineteen lived by a different light than that of mainstream America. People's lives there were directly influenced by the rhythms of nature; their livelihoods all had a common connection to the elements. People shared an acceptance of their dependence on each other and on the cycle of the seasons; caring for each other was natural. A man on the north shore once helped out a Lummi Indian from a neighboring island with a boat problem. From then on the Orcas man was to find a fresh salmon on his porch every Friday for the rest of his life. That kind of respect was alive then. Susan had no need to go anywhere to nourish her spiritual life. It was all there; in the people, in the natural rhythms of the elements, and resonating inside her; the deep peace of belonging, within and without.

She left, she tells me, for love—that fresh wind that changes the course of so many lives without warning. Her new husband lived in Marin. She knew, too, that life was bringing her down here to learn lessons she could not learn on Orcas. She knew instinctively that whatever we have in front of us is exactly what we need to deepen our spiritual life. Orcas had been the Great Mother; it was time, she knew, to step away from that embrace. Her opportunity, and challenge, lay in cultivating consciously the belonging she had known naturally on the island.

Susan began her Californian life with hard physical labor, building their house and clearing the land. "I had cultivated a deep love for physical work in my work as a gardener on Orcas," she said. I loved the endorphin rush of heavy labor combined with a spiritual approach to my work. That for me was as good as it gets. I had three and a half years of going to my limits. I built stone walls, milled lumber; one summer I mixed over thirty tons of concrete. I loved it, that big machine going round and round like a prayer wheel, shoveling twelve sand, two lime, and three cement consistently to the rhythm of my mantra—by that time I had taken on some Tibetan Buddhist practices through the inspiration of the Dalai Lama. Nothing brought me to a place of blissful stillness like mixing concrete; pushing my physical limits like that opened me up to an endorphin ecstasy that would last for hours."

The only way she could sustain that level of effort was with a focus that included all of her. To do physical labor well, she explained, you have to be conscious of your breath. You need to watch over your mind, purify it from thoughts like, I'm tired; this is too heavy; I could be doing something more creative. It requires a depth of motivation that can then be applied to any other task. "If I can focus my mind and body to lift two hundred and fifty pounds above my head, then nothing will stop me from visualizing those around me as embodiments of love." The woman sitting across the table from me was no Amazon; a soft, gentle presence, rather; though with the will to move mountains. Here is another Ra Paulette, I thought; the artist in New Mexico who also makes a stand for the dignity and nobility of manual labor.

I was beginning to get Dale's meaning. Susan made no division between everyday work and spiritual life. Her story, though, had hardly begun. In 1986, she found herself a single mother. She needed a job with benefits, and though she had no inclination to take on a blue-collar job—intending rather to train in a profession—she ended up becoming the letter carrier for San Anselmo. After a couple of years she was glad to be able to support her child, but frustrated that she did not have a job of more benefit to humanity. She began to pray to be led into the right livelihood—either a new one, or into dimensions of the mail job that she had not discovered, that would enable her to live for the betterment of whomever she came in contact with.

Susan was blessed—probably from birth, and fostered during her life on Orcas—with a rare altruism that has always guided her days.

"Within days of my prayer, I was walking my route as usual when I saw this thornbush; two legs were sticking out of it, with orthopedic shoes and baggy nylons. An old lady had fallen off her porch, and couldn't get out of the bush. At the very moment I started helping her, I realized this was an answer to my prayers. I was being shown how much opportunity I had to be the right person turning up at the right time, if only I was willing to be open to it. Every day I was walking in and out of four or five hundred different people's lives."

From then on it became her first thought in the morning, to be of help to whomever crossed her path. Life took her up on the offer quickly.

It might be helping a child tie her shoe, or putting the chain back on her bike; picking up a paper for someone who couldn't go and get it; carrying a boy with a twisted ankle into the doctor's office; breaking up a fight; bringing a dog back home. There were endless ways in which she began to affect people's lives for the better, and they let her know it. As she gained energy and enthusiasm for her job, she began to see how much opportunity it offered for the living of a deeper life.

"Every day I would walk the same route, and I would get so used to it that I would not need to pay attention, so I devised tools to stay awake. When you do the same thing every day, people wonder how you can do it, it seems so boring. But I saw that a routine takes care of the body's need for regular rhythm; it enables you more easily to have your attention free for a deeper awareness. Some days I would simply pay attention to the rhythm of my feet and see what prayer or mantra would come into my mind as a result. Or I would promise myself that whenever I reached a certain corner I would observe something I had never seen before—and this was after years of reaching the same corner every day."

There was one particular gate that was difficult to open, she continued. She swore at it for years until she finally realized she had a choice to do something different. From then on she would review the words, "May the way begin for everyone," as soon as she saw it. When someone approached her wanting to chat, instead of hoping he wasn't going to talk her ear off, she would say under her breath, "May I welcome this person's presence into my life." People would want to engage with her every day; she would find herself not giving advice so much as being a true listener. Dogs, kids, the elderly: everyone responds to an open heart more than anything, and the community began to embrace her. Every day she would find herself accepting two or three gifts.

"I used to imagine my thoughts were on ropes that were only ten feet long." Susan laughs a long, almost raucous laugh. "I would see that only a few seconds would go by before one of those thoughts would convince me it needed a rope fifty feet long. Then all the other thoughts would say, 'Well, if that one can be on a fifty feet rope, so can we.' Then before you know it, you have spun off somewhere else altogether; and maybe you have passed up an opportunity to see a flower, or a kid who wants to come and show you his new stuffed animal."

"Cultivating this attitude gave me something I could apply anywhere whenever I could see my mind was distracted. Over the years, I realized that if I can keep my thoughts on ropes ten feet long, there's no reason for me to think I need to change anything or do anything different. It showed me that everything just keeps evolving exactly as it should. That was one of the beautiful fruits of being a mail lady; it gave me the chance to cultivate deep mindfulness. Now I see that any job can do that. I know now the value of a routine. If we are content within a structure, we can know the infinite. Being content with a day job doesn't mean selling out; it means being at rest in the limitations—the structure—of daily existence. The fruits of my job only emerged as I became at rest; at rest in the knowledge that I was making a difference, both to myself and to others."

Suddenly I heard the subtext beneath Susan's story. She had recreated in a more conscious way the belonging she had felt in the natural environment of Orcas. She had made use of her job to settle more deeply both into herself and into the community she served. I was reminded of Kristen Ragusen in Boston; her dream of the two stones that fit into each other.

"It's true," she said, when I voiced my thoughts. "I have been a fringe person all my life; living mostly in a shack with no TV. By nature I want to be invisible, and the job obliged me to come out. When I had to wear the uniform—I hated it at first—I was forced to interact. Suddenly, I had a place in society, and my job took away the sense of separateness that I had. Now, having been immersed in the Norman Rockwell world of America for so long, I can't ignore the fact that we're all the same. The mail job is one of the few jobs left that still gives daily personal contact like the old milkman job did. It opened my heart, showed me the insecurities and judgments I was carrying, and helped me let go of them."

The whole point of her job, as Susan saw it, was to be accessible. That was the reason for the uniform, she realized—everyone can look at you and know you're the mail lady. They can talk to you because you're a public person.

"You're right," she continued. "The peace I knew on Orcas, the inner and the outer being one, I have come to know through the mail job. My job took the contentedness deeper, even though it didn't offer the same resonance with the natural world that Orcas did. But it did give me a sense of belonging and a context in which to practice being human and experience my commonality with others. I have always been poor, yet I have come to know that my desire to be awakened does not require the money to go off on retreats. It simply needs the willingness to step into what is in front of me with the intention to awaken."

Susan Shannon had to retire from her work recently due to physical injury, so she stands at the beginning of another new era, not knowing how her being-in-the-world will express itself next. She has learned, though, that the quality of her inner life is determined less by the content of her day than the knowledge that wherever she is, there is always an opportunity for wholeness. What she does know is that she is volunteering herself to the big world, to be used as life wishes to use her. With that motivation, she says, whatever uncertainties lay ahead, she cannot help but be excited.

Dale came in just then, and over tea he suggested that we all might like to visit Calistoga later that week, the healing baths there. Neither Susan nor I had been to Calistoga before, so we agreed to go a couple of days later. There, unknown to us then, we were to meet an angel in the mud baths. In the meantime, I had a date with someone in the city who lived an entirely different life than Susan, one that was shifting people's attitudes to money; yet a life, even so, given to others.

What is remarkable about Lynne Twiste is the breadth, the audacity of her vision, the dedication she applies to it, and the love that pours from her tiny body into this world. For twenty years she has run the Hunger Project, which is committed to bringing about the end of hunger—not with a meal on every table, but by helping to usher in a whole life picture around the globe that awakens the spirit and enables a healthy, productive life. In an entirely unique, though related way, she stands for the same feminine presence that Susan embodies so differently. A healing presence, which in her case works in the West to transform people's relationship with money and the act of fundraising.

I met her in her house in San Francisco. Some Bangladeshis were visiting, and a couple of Ethiopians were occupying the guest room. Just a normal day, Lynne told me; there was always someone from around the world staying in their family home, for the Hunger Project is worldwide now, with thousands of people involved. Spiritual practice for her, she tells me as we sit down, means living in a way that is consistent with the deepest principles of love she can find in herself.

"That's what sufficiency is," she explains. " An act of love. It's what investment is, an act of love; and what fund-raising is, because to enable people to move their money toward their highest commitment is an act of love. Fund-raising has a bad name and people don't like to do it, but I tell you for me it is a total privilege and joy. I know how nurturing it is for people to give, so I have no fear about it. Fund-raising is holy work for me, nothing less. It is unlocking the energy that has become trapped in a reality void of humanity, the reality of money. I'm always fund-raising, whatever I do; it's just a part of me. Yet I don't spend any time at all fund-raising in the traditional manner. You fund-raise to nurture dreams, but only in a way that serves and unlocks people. And you never sell out for the money. I've learned that if you make a mistake you give the money back."

How was her work any different to the traditional concept of charity, I wanted to know. In her view, she said, charity heightens differences; it is based on an unequal relationship; and that, Lynne thinks, is why it is dying. In the long run, it simply hasn't worked. It is based primarily on feeling sorry for someone, on pity, or guilt. The idea of the wealthy Westerner giving to the illiterate mother will always separate and divide the two. In that sense, she says, charity is ultimately insulting to everyone. It is an interim action that has validity, but it won't even address the root of any world problem.

The only way to do that, she continues, is to change the systemic malfunction, the context of beliefs and assumptions within which a culture and its individuals perpetuates its problems. We know from child psychology that people fit into the expectations of the family system around them. It is the same with whole cultures. Unless we become conscious of what is happening, we act out the image others have of us.

"Take our work in Dharmapuri, in India," she said. "Until we started there, women literally did not know they were people. That had been beaten out of them for centuries. They considered themselves chattels, property; cows were more important than they were. If a woman had a daughter she would kill her because she was valueless, like the woman herself. Their only meaning was to bear a son. They wore the veil, they dragged their body around like a sack. Now these same people look you in the eye, they know they are human beings whose hopes and dreams are as important as anyone else's are. Fundamentally, the change began because someone stood across from them and related to them in that way."

The women would always pray for a son, she explained, because a son would give the husband status in the village. When they killed a daughter they would be traumatized and bent over even more. So the Hunger Project's first action was to invite the women to dialogue groups under the trees. They asked the village council (all men) if some of their local volunteers from Madras could come and be with the women. The council agreed, and they identified one woman who was the female power source of the village, knowing that if she came, then others would follow. At first there was little response, then more, till finally all the women came.

"By the time I visited the village," said Lynne, " some fifteen women were sitting in a circle under the trees. All of them had killed at least one child and had assisted in the killing of others. We would sit with them until they were able to forgive themselves. Until they did that, they had to keep making their actions right to themselves, and to keep doing it. Once they finally began to speak about the trauma and the horror, they couldn't do it any more. They started making vows that they would no longer assist in smothering newborn girls. Then peer pressure accelerated the process."

"Then of course, we had to start working with the men, and those who wouldn't go along. It was a very untidy process, and very painful, though eventually—by staying with the vision of who people are, and being there for them—change began to happen of its own accord. That is the essence of our work. The end of hunger—the spiritual hunger as well as the physical one—is all of us experiencing the power and beauty of our human spirit, and of that same spirit in others. So the men can't be left out of the picture. I mean, they don't make the women that way, the whole culture is complicit. Yet it can take just one person to break a conspiracy like that, and sometimes the men break it first."

She wasn't pretending that when the conspiracy did break everything was fine. There was always a backlash, she explained; an upset, just as any change is an upset. But the men did come to see that they were demeaning themselves by demeaning their women—people know these things deep down, she said. And it doesn't happen by talking, or lecturing, but through a manner of being that can shift their perception of themselves. When, as happened in this village and many others later, the women start to enjoy a coequal relationship with the men, everyone's life is uplifted—ontologically, spiritually, and materially.

"The next thing that happened, and it was like a miracle," Lynne went on, "was that the women started to want things for their future baby girls. They talked about how they would immunize them, educate them, bathe them. Gradually there was this complete turnaround from a girl being a throwaway to being precious. Then we met with Tamil Nadu's biggest male and female movie stars, who were married to each other, and who had a daughter. We got them to make a public service film in which the woman is giving birth, and the man arrives just in time to see his child is a girl. 'How wonderful! A girl!' they both cry. Then we see her grown up, on a motorbike with a briefcase on the back. That film was shown before and after every movie in Tamil Nadu for four years, and infanticide is now almost nonexistent there."

Through this one initiative the entire life of these Indian villages was transformed. With the growing sense of self-worth that came with their new attitude to their daughters, the women started to want to take care of their families, to begin farming or little businesses, and to have their daughters participate in the livelihood of the family. They moved out of poverty into a climate of respect, reverence, and relative prosperity. That, suggested Lynne, was the end of hunger at all levels; and it was hard not to agree with her.

Here in the West, however, Lynne's spiritual ministry is fund-raising. She raises money not just for the projects abroad but to heal people who need to give. She doesn't ask people to give to a particular project, but to fund their own vision for a world without hunger. She explores with them what that means, and helps them to invest in their vision with money. In the West, after all, money is one of the most powerful voices we have. It shows what we take seriously. It says I matter; I make a difference, and I'm willing to say so with my money. So the Hunger Project only raises money from individuals, not institutions, because individuals have a face and a heart—and that, not their bank account, is what Lynne Twiste raises money from.

"It has to be clean, though," she says. "We have to be sure that the money isn't being given to dominate, manipulate, or control the action, but to empower and encourage whatever action is appropriate—and only the resource poor people know what that is. Near the start of the project I was in the office of the CEO of a large food company, and he pushed a check across the desk to me. It was for $50,000. In those days that was a great deal of money. I took it, but I was uneasy. That night I knew I had to give it back; somehow I felt we were being used. Later, though, he gave a large sum of his own, and that worked. Once I even gave back a check for half a million dollars, which was very hard, we could have used it in so many ways."

How does a woman like this, with activities and concerns all around the globe, manage a family life, I wondered—I knew she had three children. Lynne paused for a moment; her eyes moistened.

"Well first, I have the perfect husband for me," she said eventually. "He is like a rock. He believes in everything I stand for. I know he would say it has been his privilege and honor to give me to the world. The love we share means he doesn't own me, he loves me, which includes giving me the space to honor my destiny. But I didn't make the Halloween costumes for my children, I missed the championship soccer games, I didn't drive them to the orthodontist. I grieve over that sometimes, but I also know they are fine. They are all in their twenties now, and all involved in global work; three happy, contributing human beings."

"When my kids were six-, eight-, and ten-years-old, I had a meeting with them because I realized this hunger thing had taken me over. I am the end of hunger; I'm living it, surrendered to it in a way that means I can't just manage it, I have to be it. I met with the family and asked their permission to do this work instead of being a carpool mom so I could help create a world free from hunger that they could inherit. They gave me their blessing, and raised themselves. Now they are so proud of their mom."

She just met with Mme. Aviola, she tells me, the daughter of the elected president of Nigeria who was ousted in a coup by the present leader, imprisoned, and tortured. Then recently they assassinated her mother, so this young daughter is now head of the family.

"She said to me, as the daughter of parents who died for their principles, 'Go ahead and risk your life, your children will be fine. I must have reverence for Abacho's human life (the man responsible for her mother's death) at the same time as not standing for the behavior of his leadership. He too has a heart and soul.' That was so affirming for me, you know." She was looking directly at me now with burning brown eyes. "I have risked my life for what I do, and I shall continue to do so. I know my kids are fine. It's untidy, it's upsetting, but it is what it is and it's our life together. My husband and I are as close and devoted to each other as ever, after thirty-one years."

In making a leap of faith for what she believes in, Lynne Twiste has bridged the postmodern woman's dilemma, I thought, as I embraced her before leaving. She has dived into her work, yet in doing so she has not lost but found her family, and they have found her. This woman, I realized, as I turned to go, is all courage and vision; a true feminine spirit of our time.

Two days later, in Calistoga, Dale and I were to hear of another such woman, doing what she does for the love of it, living life as the main event; except in an entirely different, and improbable context. It was Susan who would meet her. Calistoga is a spa town up in the Sonoma wine country, an hour north of San Francisco. It is famous for its mud baths. Dale and I had appointments at the men's bath, Susan at the women's. Mine was predictable. The Mexicans, who piled the mud on me, hearing I was English wanted to know which soccer team I supported, Manchester United or Liverpool. Was I here with my girlfriend? Were my wife and kids at home? A few snickers and winks and they were on to the next client. Dale's experience was as inconsequential as mine was, though pleasant, for all that.

Susan's experience was different. She had to wait a few moments while the attendant, an elderly Mexican woman, helped someone else out of the bath. Immediately aware of the attendant's graceful movement, she was touched by the respect and attentiveness she showed to her young client. Her silent gestures seemed to have the effect of making the young woman feel like a princess, drawing her up to her full height and encouraging a sense of dignity. The Mexican lady took the woman's hand, and led her to the shower. Then she returned to Susan, sat her on the side of the bath, and, like a mother, showed her without words how to put one hand in position for balance, and how to ease herself into the tub.

Susan sank into the mud, and with surprising energy and power the old woman shoveled more mud over her body. Susan was instantly aware of how gathered the woman's attention was, how simple her movements; how she was doing nothing yet communicating everything. She was in the presence, she realized, of someone who was in total service to whomever she was with. It was a long while that she lay there, Susan told us; and when she eventually climbed out of the tub the woman flashed her a smile and continued hosing down the floor. As Susan was about to go through the door to the steam room, she turned to thank the woman and saw that she was facing her with two fingers raised in a blessing like the annunciation.

"Who is that woman in there?" Susan asked the receptionist. "There's something very special about her."

"That is Evelia," came the reply. " She has just said a prayer for you—she prays for every client she meets. She is wedded to God. With her tips she goes to the local bakery and gives bread to the poor. The rest of us secretly change our names to hers on some of our gratuity envelopes, because we know where it's going."

Susan had met the angel of the mud baths there in Indian Springs, and it struck me as she told the story how the words *madre, mud, matter,* the French *mer,* the words *magic, make, imagine,* all sound like they stem from a common root. Evelia was a timeless expression of the deep feminine spirit that, being of the earth, is the mother of all things; which with its magic of compassion makes everything matter. And Evelia—surely connected to the French *eveiller,* to wake up, the Awakened One. There is magic in words, I thought, as we drove back to Marin County; which is why mantras, prayers, incantations, all cast their spell, and why names matter: they call us to become the quality of the name, and Evelia seems to have responded.

Chapter Twenty-Three

Larger Than Life in the East Bay

A name that I had heard of for years without ever coming across the person himself was Wavy Gravy. I did know that he lived in the Bay area. I also knew that for some thirty years he had been a walking public-service announcement for positive and compassionate social change, a master of the one-liner who had put humor to the service of the sixties idealism that he had lived and breathed all his life. It so happened that Susan Shannon was a veteran volunteer at Winnarainbow, Wavy's summer camp for kids in Northern California, and she arranged for me to visit with Wavy one day at his home, just off Shattuck in downtown Berkeley. The day after I arrived in San Francisco from Whidbey Island I went there to see him.

"Come on up," he hollers from a room upstairs, and I do, finding Mr. Gravy (as *The New York Times* used to call him) sprawled on a bed in a room literally crammed with the most unlikely assortment of objects I had ever seen in one place. Shelves and tables were stacked with pairs of false teeth, plastic pigs, dozens of furry toys, a rubber squeak Buddha with a cellphone, a tin of pork brains, a small head of Abbie Hoffman, a Christ, a Buddha, the archangel Michael, and a voodoo doll someone had given him for his birthday.

"See all those pigs," he says when I ask about his collection, "they represent Pig for President, from the days when we supported LBJ against Goldwater because Goldwater was gonna loose atomic weaponry all over the place. Then LBJ got into Vietnam, so we ran Pig for President in 1968. She was the first female black and white candidate. She went on the road with us in the Magic Bus."

Out of context Wavy's explanation sounds like the ramblings of an inmate in the film *One Flew Over the Cuckoo's Nest*. But I knew what he was talking about, being from the same era. That film was based on the book by Ken Kesey, the leader of the Pranksters who careered around the country in their Magic Bus stoned on acid in the sixties. When the Pranksters were in Los Angeles, someone had offered them a farm on a mountain rent-free if they would feed the pigs. That was the birth of the Hog Farm Community, and they ran one of their pigs for the presidency.

Of course they were mad. You had to be mad to attempt to offer free breakfast, granola served in Dixie cups, to the crowds at Woodstock One—one of the Hog Farm's early feats. Wavy's most famous one-liner dates from that time, when he went on stage and said, "Good morning. What we have is breakfast in bed for four hundred thousand."

The wind-up clicking teeth, he continues, represent Nobody for President, their candidate in 1976. The perfect candidate: Nobody keeps all campaign promises; Nobody's perfect; Nobody should have that much power; if Nobody wins, Nobody loses. Wavy Gravy became Nobody's fool, and they called their bus Nobody One, as a spoof on Airforce One. They even staged assassination attempts to show that Nobody would live forever. At the New Hampshire Primary, Ram Dass wanted to be Nobody's guru. "What should I do?" he asked. "Sit at this table. The bumper stickers are one dollar and the buttons fifty cents," Wavy told him.

"I got a press pass to the Kansas City Republican Convention in seventy-six," says Wavy, arms behind his head, sprawled full length on his bed. "I put on a three-piece suit and handed out press releases about Nobody to the world press. A Secret Service agent searched me, and felt a bulge in my pocket. He reached in, took out what he thought was a gun and found it was Nobody's teeth. They started clicking in his hand. I said, 'Quiet, our leader is speaking.' He rolled his eyes, gave the teeth back to me and said, 'Get out of here, you're too weird to arrest.' "

Wavy—B. B. King gave him his name at a Texas pop festival—has a thousand stories like that. His life reads like a who's who of the hip and cool in the sixties and seventies, but more impressive is that the man is as active at the turn of the millennium in the cause of a more compassionate world than he ever was. In the seventies the Hog Farm took its bus on the overland trail to India, and in Nepal they became aware that 90 percent of the blind people there simply needed a cataract operation to see again. Wavy Gravy, Ram Dass, and friends founded Seva Foundation in 1978 and started A Solution in Sight, which twenty years later had almost eradicated blindness from Nepal. Seva's current project addresses the prevalence of diabetes on the Indian reservations, encouraging the people there to return to their traditional food, green vegetables and buffalo.

In the last fifteen years Wavy has organized ten major rock benefits for Seva and other charitable causes, including recently, the Wavy Gravy Sixtieth Birthday Benefit for Just About Everything. The Grateful Dead, not surprisingly, have always been his staunch supporters. Wavy's success as a rock concert impresario owes no small debt to his own integrity and ability to form a personal connection with the artists. They know the money is going exactly where he says it is.

For twenty five years he and his wife, Jahanara, have run Winnarainbow, a performing arts summer youth camp where volunteers teach juggling, unicycling, tight rope, trapeze, art, and of course, music to 150 young people from every kind of background. They hold four two-week sessions and one for kids who have never been away from home before. When I ask him what the kids have given him, he says a nostalgia for the future: they are so inspiring he would love to see the world they create. The whole show is supported by the royalties from the ice cream flavor that Ben and Jerry's dedicated to Wavy's name.

"It's totally changed my life being a frozen dessert," says Wavy. "It's very rain-forest friendly, with a brazil nut cashew base, then for decadence, chocolate hazelnut swirl with toasted almonds. Because of the ice cream *The New York Times* doesn't call me Mr. Wavy any more."

Everything he does, he does with a smile. No ordinary campaigner, fund-raiser, he's more of a clown than anything else, a clown with a style that would touch anyone's heart. What he's trying to do, he says, is to make doing good look hip and fashionable, to get across the message that it's a cool thing to do, helping others.

"I do think it's a kinder culture now than in the sixties," he muses. "I mean, interconnectedness is no longer just an abstract concept. Kids today really get it. And there's a new enthusiasm for volunteerism at the end of the nineties because affluent people realize that the second BMW just doesn't fill the gap. Look at the new wave of concerts for Tibet, with the Beastie Boys and others. They didn't have a clue about the issue before they started doing these gigs. Now they're getting their tongues pierced for Tibet, if you see what I mean."

When I ask him why he does what he does he roars with laughter, big frame shaking. "Because it gets me high, of course—higher than anything you could find in the pharmaceutical cabinet. It's nice to be nice. It gets me off. It's pure selfishness."

"So how did you get to be a clown? Is it what you always wanted to be when you grew up?"

"No, when we first moved to Berkeley someone wrote me up as being this hippie social worker. Some doctors from Oakland Children's Hospital came by and asked me to come and cheer up their kids. I was on the mend from my third spinal fusion—I got beat up a lot by the police during the Vietnam protests—and was very enamored by the Fool of the Tarot. So I said okay, it was something to do rather than sitting around all day feeling sorry for myself. Someone handed me a red rubber nose, then a retiring clown gave me his giant shoes, someone else gave me a clown suit."

Wavy is moving on, telling me now about a political demonstration he went to in his clown suit. It was at the People's Park here in Berkeley, and he discovered that the police didn't hit him when he had his clown suit on. It didn't stop him getting arrested, though.

"Some people like collecting stamps, I like to get arrested for acts of civil disobedience for stuff I believe in. I've been arrested as a clown, as Santa Claus, even the Easter Bunny. Santa Claus was at Diablo Canyon, on an antinuclear rally. 'Don't mess with me,' I cried, 'you'll get nothing in your sock.' In jail I emceed a talent show called The Tornado of Talent. When you go in with a whole lot of people it becomes a truly sacred space, and they had arrested so many of us they had to put us in the gym of Cuesta College. Jackson Browne was one of the arrested, and I got the captain to smuggle in a guitar. It was such a great talent show the officers all brought their wives. It was the hottest ticket in California."

It's a truism to say there are tears behind every clown's smile, though Wavy's tears are for the world, not in the least sentimental. When I mention the sadness of the clown, he turns even that into a joke. "Yeah," he says, "Joseph Grimaldi went to a psychiatrist in Vienna he was so down. 'Go to the circus,' said the psychiatrist. 'Go see Grimaldi.' 'But I am Grimaldi.' See, what Wavy says is that if you don't have a sense of humor it just isn't funny any more."

I come at it another way, and ask him when he has found it difficult to laugh. After his third spinal fusion, he says. It never seemed to be getting better; it was so painful then to wake up in the morning. When I wonder if there is anything left for him to do, his answer is at least half-serious.

"I'd like to put on a rock concert with one great single band at Ayer's Rock. Then I could say I'd held the world's largest rock concert. I did try to get the Dead to perform in a hotel by Everest once, but it didn't come off."

Does this man ever stop, I find myself thinking. Ever stop laughing, but also ever stop working?

"Oh, I schedule an hour's meditation three times a week, and then two days a month I'll chill. I've been doing retreats with Thich Nhat Hanh. You probably know his meditation, breathing in the supreme moment, breathing out wonderful moment, just smile. Tailor made for Wavy

Gravy. You know, I like it all. I just use what lights me up most. Religion for me is how you live your life and how much you are willing to contribute. All I try and do is make my life like a sail and trust the wind will blow me in the right direction."

He's caught the westerlies all right, the wind at his back, the Irish would say. Just then a lady with a presence almost as large as Wavy's walks in, a friend of his from down the street, and he introduces me to Pat Sullivan, whose current passion is photographing all the ways that people make a sacred space in their workplace. It's a shift of direction, a whole ninety degrees, but then why not, Wavy and me, we're following the wind, so instead of leaving right away I let her tell me about her project, Altars in the Workplace, she calls it.

Pat used to work as a temp some twenty years ago and she would notice that almost every desk she took over had a Bible in the drawer, or some poetry, the *Bhagavad Gita,* something the person got inspiration from. She herself would always take a poetry book of her own wherever she went. The staff would ask her what she was reading, and would tell her about their own spiritual experiences. Once the chief executive of an accounting firm called her into his office and told her about his dreams.

"Because I was a temp," Pat explained, "and because he was aware of my interests, he could feel safe telling me about a side of his life that he had not shared with people. I was a listening ear for that dimension which normally doesn't have a place at work—the dimension of meaning, visions, dreams, aspirations. That was twenty years ago. Today, that realm is more acceptable, even encouraged, at work. Now when I go into offices I see that the inspirational books are on the desk, not in a drawer. People have all manner of ways of personalizing their workspace, with photographs of saints, teachers, inspiring figures, scenes from nature, and so on."

When you nurture a thought, it starts to manifest everywhere. Pat would notice the way people had made little sacred spaces in her local law firm; in the local surgery there was a whole wall of sayings and pictures under a banner saying Hold On To Your Dreams. She discovered that even the local meter maid carried a Bible and a book of inspirational sayings in her van. She began seeing the reflection so often she decided to research it and record different examples around the country with her camera. *Altars in the Workplace* is a photographic celebration of what she has found. Now she acts as a consultant to help firms give more public credence to that part of people's lives.

I left Pat and Wavy to their own conversation finally and went to Oakland, where I was due to meet a man named Levandis Butler outside the McArthur BART. Levandis had agreed through a mutual friend to let me come to his "street" yoga class that he gives every week for girls in a halfway house. He was no ordinary yoga teacher, my friend had told me. Yoga is his calling card. What he does is pour undiluted love and being into some of the most neglected corners of the culture. If anything is sacred in America, she had said, it is the invisible work of thousands of unsung individuals like Levandis who do what they do not out of obligation, not as a job, not to get a message across, not as an effort to do good even. They do it out of joy, pure and simple, because they have so much love for the world they don't know what to do with it.

He is standing in the rain leaping up and down and waving his arms about like a teenager, this wiry African American approaching fifty with a pack on his back. "Hey Rog, we made it!" he cries, leaping into the car. We are on our way to the halfway house, which is for girls between the ages of twelve and seventeen who have been taken away from their families and made into wards of court to protect them from abuse. They stay for six months or so before being moved on to a foster home.

"They're suspicious, guarded, they act up easy, but I just beam unconditional regard at them," Levandis says. "I love to work with the elderly and the disabled, too, the whole point of the work being to give away love, that's the bottom line, Rog."

I agree, and ask him how he came to that conclusion. Levandis tells me he started out lucky, grew up in an integrated block in Berkeley, with a scholarship to UCLA, thank the Lord. He started training in martial arts, then a black guy turned him on to yoga. He went into the air force to join the band (that's another story) and instead got a prolonged strain of flu. Languishing in the hospital, he remembered something his teacher had said, that health comes from yoga, meditation, and the Bible.

"I picked up the Bible and there was Job. I tell you, that book blew me away. It was so perfect for my condition. I come from a long line of preachers, though I was never involved in the church myself. Job really hit me. I saw that the breath of yoga was the Holy Spirit, that if you turn your attention that way then yoga is infused with spirit and nothing less. So yoga is a vehicle for the sharing of that."

We draw up outside a low square building in the drizzling rain. Levandis pulls a shopping bag out of the trunk, saying it is full of little gifts for the girls. We are barely in the door when a dozen girls, all black, are clustering round him. "What ya got, Yoga Man, what ya got?"

"Later, later, girls, you know the staff hands these things out. Now, come on, push back the sofa, let's get started. Straight spines is what we want, because slouching don't let the spirit through and you all wanna feel good, don't you? Quit lying down and sprawling and let the life pour through your veins. Hey, hold hands, get in a circle, who wants to say the prayer?"

He tells us to bend our heads to the floor and a couple of girls snort and say they ain't doin' that, the carpet stinks. Then a fifteen-year-old says she wants to offer the prayer, and in a staccato voice she shouts out loud, "Dear God, bless all the people in this house, bless the staff (everyone snickers), bless our families, and keep them safe."

"Thank you and praise the Lord, praise Jesus, he's right here with us. Now, take your toes and kiss them, go on, one by one, they like that, your right leg up like this, oh, what a beautiful foot."

"That's disgustin' yoga man, I ain't gonna put my foot in my mouth."

"Yeah, well, your beautiful foot was made by God and it has the perfume of the Holy Spirit on it if only you treat it the right way."

Yoga Man wheels his body round on its axis, making every posture a turn in a dance and I can see that if he gets half of them to do three or four movements in the hour he is doing well. Even the ones lying down, though, feigning disinterest, are moved by his spirit, his warmth for them all that they cannot ignore. At one point he is showing them some hand exercises.

"You mean like this, Yoga Man?" laugh a couple of girls, breaking into gang hand code language.

"No, I don't wanna learn gang language," Yoga Man replies. "My movements free up the spirit as well as the wrists."

For an hour he keeps up an incessant stream of positive messages without any expectation for them to do more than they do. In a moment the end is here and they rush over to the staff to collect their gifts: a few bottles of scent, some soap bars, posters of rock stars, lipsticks, sweets.

"When you comin' again, Yoga Man?" they cry.

Celine, one of the staff members, tells me he helps them as much as the kids. Everyone looks forward to him coming, he gives their morale such a boost. Levandis is standing by, and when he hears Celine he almost sings.

"You got the power, sister, you got the power, and you know you can use it. Now don't forget, girls, you are all a bundle of energy and stiffness is your enemy. Stiffness is energy blocked up and locked up. Remember what I say, sit like a bell, stand like a tree, run like the wind, don't lean. And smile, everything is vibration. When you smile your organs smile and the universe smiles too. One last thing girls, you know what I say every week. Don't compete with your neighbor, grow your own garden."

Yoga Man is out of the door now and on to his next class, in an old people's home, his actions and energy speak for themselves. So many invisible bees in this world making sweet honey out of what seems to be failure. Death, sickness, old age, loss, betrayal: they all have their hidden door into another life, and people like Levandis are pointing the way.

Chapter Twenty-Four

The Techno Mass

The next evening I discover that others in Oakland are making their own honey by means of ritual, coming together at Mayor Jerry Brown's We The People Auditorium for a postmodern Christian celebration called the Techno Mass. The Techno Mass was brought to the Bay Area from England by Mathew Fox, the controversial priest who was sacked by the pope a few years ago for his radical views and has since found safe haven among the Presbyterians. Fox had witnessed a rave dance celebration in a church in Sheffield, a city in the north of England, and immediately decided to extend the idea and bring it to an American public.

I head down to the auditorium and find a couple of hundred others already there. The people, mostly white, though there are many African Americans and a few Hispanics, seem to be in their twenties to forties. In the middle of the hall someone has erected an Ark of the Covenant decked with colored streamers and paper. A projectionist is sitting on its roof in the middle of four projectors, which are beaming slides on the walls of nebulae, snow crystals, waterfalls, angels, African gods, icons from all cultures.

A rave beat is thumping around the room and people are milling around. A couple of rappers, one black, one white, prowl around the ark telling us in surly staccato tones how all the great traditions point to the one ineffable truth.

There's not a Baptist moon
And a Methodist tree
There's not a Buddhist river
that flows to a Jewish sea
There's not a Hindu sun

on a Catholic plain
A fundamentalist cloud
with agnostic rain

Enough of the human centered
its time we entered
the indivisible whole that can't be splintered
One life one breath one Earth one revelation
We all have creation in common.

Every creature's a preacher—a voice of the Creator
the divinity within is the common denominator
The Buddha Nature the unified field
the diverse universe where the One is revealed
Split a piece of wood break open a stone
and there you'll find the Divine on Her throne

Drew Dellinger, the white rapper, wrote the words. Strange to hear such a potent message delivered like this, no holy, no bullshit, straight from the hip. And it works. It works because it bypasses the mind and sentimentality and goes straight to the belly, to the embodied place. Then a gloriously large African woman in traditional dress lumbers up to the ark, takes a microphone, and moving round the four sides of the structure, wails out a prayer to each of the directions, honoring all the peoples who live there. When she finishes, she looks out over the assembly, and growls into the microphone, "Now dance your asses off!"

So we do, images of beauty and delight pouring over us and cascading onto the walls, colored lights beaming down on us from above, the beat getting louder, everyone sweating now. Yet this is no ordinary dance, drug free but high on the beauty of the universe projected all around us. Then eventually the music fades, we fall into silence, the room goes dark, and we sink to the floor as images of another kind begin to fill the walls: images of suffering, destitution, the rape of the earth, abuse, violence, and death. The music is slow now and lilting, drawing me down to the earth and the taste of my own sadness.

This is the Via Negativa, the valley of the shadows, which Mathew Fox had said at the beginning would follow on from the first stage, the Via Positiva—the traditional stages of Christian mysticism, there in Dante as well as Pilgrim's Progress and John of the Cross. What Fox is attempting here, I realize, is to take the universal mystical journey of descent and rebirth and to recast them in terms familiar to young people; the very sector of the population you no longer, or rarely, see in churches.

The images of wrath and destruction fade away at last, the music picks up, the strobe lights return, and the art of the world tumbles over the walls, celebrating the Via Creativa, the creative spirit that can spring from the valley of tears. Our dancing feet slow finally, and the last, transformative stage is upon us. The communion with bread and goblets of red wine is being brought from the ark and offered in each of the four directions to Jewish prayers as well as Christian ones, and even a Hindu chant, Fox dedicating the whole event to the Great Spirit of All.

I seek Fox out afterward and find him in a small back room talking to one of the rappers. When I say how much I liked the postdenominational lyrics Fox says they are not just that, they are postnational, postethnic, just like the Internet, an international youth Esperanto that people in Thailand and Japan dance to as well as in Oakland. I did enjoy the Techno Mass, I tell him; I can see he is recontextualizing Christianity within the contemporary pluralist culture. Yet at the same time I wonder about the dangers of syncretism, of mixing bits of different traditions together for effect. Ritual grows out of a cultural context as an organic community bond; it isn't something that can be put together as a good idea, a construct of the mind.

"Well, the Techno Mass isn't syncretism," Fox responds. "It takes place within the tradition of Christianity. It's a version of the Mass, after all. There is a pluralist dimension to it, and of course that is intentional. The rabbi was chanting the words of Jesus in Hebrew, which after all is the language and the tradition out of which he spoke. That belongs. Pluralism is essential today, though it is vital to have a form that holds the different elements. I believe we have that, though I agree it is a fine line between syncretism and pluralism."

Fox may be postdenominational, but he is still a Christian rather than a Universalist. There's one stream, and we acknowledge that, he says. But there are many wells, and we in the West inherit the genetic and cultural code of our ancestors: that is our starting point. Chartres is a universal temple, but one inspired and created out of the gospel vision. Yet we have to simplify our religion as we move into the twenty-first century because the young just aren't buying the whole package and we have to decide what is worth keeping and what's not. We need, Fox says with a certain urgency, to create something new from what we have; we have new questions today, ones that previous generations have never had to face before.

"One of the reasons I'm so passionate about the Techno Mass is because it is bringing the power of worship back to our tradition," Fox explains. "Worship has to be a bodily experience, which is why dance is so important and the rave culture is on to something. When the body gets involved the body politic can change, and that is when we will be able to reinvent politics, health care, and the like. We'll have the energy to do it then because our vital centers will be working. We won't change the West by becoming Buddhist. We must deconstruct our own tradition and reconstruct it for these times, demanding more of it."

That's a provocative comment, I thought, the one about Buddhism; the Dalai Lama has said the same thing. Jung always maintained that we could not be pirates thieving wisdom from foreign shores that took thousands of years to develop, as if our own culture was an era outlived. Toynbee once said that one of the greatest events in the twentieth century would be the meeting of Buddhism and Christianity. We need both, the fiery Jewish prophetic voice and the contemplative, long-suffering peace of the Buddha. It is significant, perhaps, that Jesus died at the age of thirty-three for causing trouble and Buddha died peacefully in his seventies. When we lack either one—the experience of the universal or its incarnation in sociohistorical reality—we lose our balance, limping without a crutch.

"Christ was life-affirming," said Fox, passionate now. "He didn't believe, as Calvin and Freud did, in the helplessness of humanity. For Freud the unconscious is always deciding things for you, and for Calvin it's all predestined. I was reading something in Calvin yesterday where he says if we had a different cosmology—if we knew we were related to the stars— he would rewrite his books. But we're not, we're related to mud, inside and out, body and soul. He was wrong. We now know—indigenous peoples have always known, and even science now admits—that we are indeed related to the stars. I tell you, this puts the Presbyterian Church out of business. I can hardly wait to lecture on this in a Presbyterian Church."

This man Fox, he thrives on controversy, I thought. That's part of his role, to kick the embers. He returns to the subject of the Techno Mass, and tells me that of the people who came up to him at the end, one was a Jewish cantor who told him she had never been so moved in her life, and that she wants to join the volunteer staff. A couple of young men, one black, one white, came up and said that they go to raves all the time, and what was missing was there tonight, the spiritual focus. They also told him how they loved dancing with people of other generations.

"What we need," Fox concluded, as we got up to leave, "is an intergenerational wisdom. You know, I really don't think that, without spirituality, humanity will survive. We know the government, science, or technology won't save us. Only an attitude of experiencing life as sacred gives us our common ethic and trust in the future. We're not going to save the environment without seeing it as sacred. That's why, as far as I can see, spirituality is fundamental to our survival."

Chapter Twenty-Five

San Francisco and the Frontiers of Faith

> Everything will turn out alright unless something unfore-
> seen turns up.
>
> Samuel Beckett

San Francisco, surely the most beautiful city in America, continues to match its reputation for pushing the envelope, as people say here; experimenting with new products, lifestyles, attitudes, philosophies, spiritual techniques, therapy for your dog. The rest of the country laughs, and a year or two later they are following the Bay Area trend.

Yet it's not heaven for everyone in this sparkling city. Hundreds sleep out in the Golden Gate Park nightly, and are hassled daily by the police. Only 14 percent of the population is black, yet 85 percent of those in jail are from that small percentage of the city's people. California has a bigger budget for prisons than it does for schools. Even so, this being San Francisco, there are those working for change in unusual ways. In the early eighties Katherine Sneed had a revelation while ill in hospital reading *The Grapes of Wrath*. Steinbeck showed her that if you can connect people with the land you can help them find hope and strength. Katherine, an African American, had worked for years as a prison counselor, but saw that her clients kept ending up back in jail, so what good was she doing? The prisoners had given up, she had given up.

When the sheriff came to visit her in hospital she jumped out of bed and told him she wanted to start a garden project with the prisoners. "Okay, okay, but you need to get better first." "I am better!" she exclaimed. "I'm going home!"

The Garden Project began in 1991, and for three years a study followed three hundred ex-cons. It found that within four months of release

29 percent of general release prisoners were rearrested, while only 6 percent of those who had worked on the project came back. After two years the figures were 55 percent and 29 percent respectively. More than ten thousand inmates have now gone through the program.

Sneed showed me round the city garden one morning, out in the Bayview district, and told me the garden hires ex-cons to work there for $6 an hour on the understanding they enroll in college classes and seek substance abuse counseling. A dozen men and women were working there when we arrived.

"The reason this works is because organic gardening is an affirmation of life," Sneed explains as we stroll around. "Can you believe it, kids who were selling crack are now growing leeks. The point is, farming nurtures people, gives them a sense of their own creativity and usefulness. I take these big crack dealers and show them the roses we have cut back. They say, 'These ain't no roses, these are dead sticks.' So I say, 'You watch those dead sticks. They're just like you. Get rid of the dead stuff and the new stuff will grow. Weed out the obstacles in your life like you might do to this bed.' See, the eventual aim is to empower the disenfranchised to become job ready. If you have a criminal record you can't get a job, and I guess I identify with these people through the color of my skin."

We stopped for a moment to talk to Roy, in for drug offenses like most people here. He picked up a beet. "See this," he said proudly. "This is a golden beet. It grows long, not like the other beets. I bake 'em, put 'em in the fridge and sprinkle them with vinegar. Then this is arugula. You heard of arugula? Can you say that name? Man, I never heard it till I came here. That's rocket, the wild one—shoots you right up. The arugula is more subtle, takes you by surprise."

The city garden and the one at the county jail sell their produce to smart restaurants like Chez Panisse in Berkeley, and donate what is left over to San Francisco's soup kitchens. These people were in prison because they did harm to others, Sneed reflects; yet now they are part of the healing, the fruits of their work going to feed the hungry. The program has a half million-dollar budget, nearly half of which the sheriff's department covers, the rest coming from produce sales and donations.

Sometimes, if you hit lucky (or maybe it is written on your forehead from the day you were born), I thought, as I left Katherine Sneed to her work in the garden, you don't even need a garden project. Sometimes the lightning of grace can lift you clean out of your world and set you down in a whole new way of living a life. The next day was a Sunday and I had the good fortune then to meet such a man. Franzo King grew up in a tough world, but he was different; he had a saving grace, and that was music. Not just any music, but the sound of John Coltrane.

I went that Sunday morning in San Francisco to a church the likes of which you will find nowhere else in the world; another testimony to this city's generous embrace of anyone's dream, as long as he can show it will hold its own along with all the others here. Up there on Divisadero is the African Orthodox Church, whose entrance is a converted storefront. Inside, perhaps forty people, black and white, were standing gazing at the altar, in the center of which was a large figure of Christ looking like Bob Marley, and a loaf of sweet bread.

On the walls were icons painted in the traditional Eastern Orthodox style, except several of them were of the patron saint of this church, John Coltrane. There he was before me on high, seated in the posture of a saint, with flames pouring out of his trumpet. To one side of the altar sits a man at a drum kit, and a woman with Ethiopian features, tall, lithe, astonishingly beautiful, with an electric guitar. We are all in silence.

From behind a thin curtain the long figure of the Most Reverend F. W. King, bishop of this church, appears and walks in high solemnity toward the altar, a crimson cap on his head, wearing a long white robe with fine lace embroidery at the hem, tenor sax in hand. The Reverend Father Roberto de Haven follows him out in solemn black, tenor sax also in hand. The drum kit starts up, the Ethiopian beauty picks at her guitar, and the two very reverends bring their horns to their lips, and as one, begin to sway, bend at the hip. Thus begins one of the most ecstatic jazz improvisation sessions I have ever heard, more or less continuous for three and a half hours; broken now and then by a prayer, a reading, the communion, and supplemented at times by the voices of three soul sisters up at the front.

In his sermon the Most Reverend King told us we live under a mountain of fear and we don't even know it; that love is the only way out. Love the Lord, he implores us, and all things shall come to us. "He don't like ugly, he ain't too concerned about pretty either. He only know love. Only love, then you can cease to be afraid."

The show, the service, the dancing, the prayers, the wailing of the saxophones over finally, I follow Franzo King behind that thin curtain to find a line of street people waiting to be served lunch, as they are every day in the church of Coltrane. Franzo beckons me into a tiny office, sits me down in a battered leather chair, and tells me that the African Orthodox Church of America, under whose aegis his own church is recognized, was founded in 1920 by Alex Mcguire as a blow for ecclesiastical freedom for African Americans. In an unusual, even odd, cooperation between East and West, the North American Metropolitan of the Orthodox

Church gave Mcguire a license to found an independent Episcopal place of worship, whose cathedral today is in Chicago. Franzo King did two years training at their divinity school, and was a dean at the Chicago cathedral.

He took the formal training to protect his own young church, which was being called a cult by the press because of its perceived mission to have John Coltrane recognized as a messenger of God. The bishop in Chicago sent a message offering his protection, and King accepted in 1981. "We Orthodox, man, I say to the press from then on. Don't put us in no cult bag."

It all started in 1965, Franzo explains. His elder brother, Landers Charles King Jr., used to play jazz records in rebellion against their strict upbringing, in which jazz and blues were considered to be the devil's music. One night he put on John Coltrane; Franzo, who was seventeen, was transfixed. Coltrane, Billie Holliday, and Martin Luther King's speech—for Franzo they all carried the same sound. It was the sound, rather than the message, that penetrated him. Then he went to hear Coltrane in concert, and that evening changed his life forever. He has no idea which melodies were played, all he knows is that he underwent a transformation of the spirit through the music. As soon as Coltrane walked onto the bandstand Franzo was overwhelmed by his presence, and the whole evening he was in a state of arrested, undivided attention. "See, I got the Holy Ghost through John," Franzo grinned.

Franzo, whose mother still runs the Brighter Day Academy of Bible Studies, felt a lot of anger toward the church in his younger days. People said much and did little. "Those preachers are howling preachers," he says, not without bitterness. "Me, I started a speakeasy, the Yardbird Temple, in a double garage. I had a mentor then, Billie Ross, he helped me build my record collection and grow up in music. We sold liquor after hours, and we aimed to provide work for musicians. I started out on the sax. Then my brother became a vegetarian, and I followed. We did a lot of religious reading, but the man who really helped me articulate my intuitions about sound and spirit was a Sufi from India, Hazrat Inayat Khan. Then my mother gradually brought us round to Christianity, which ended up fitting in fine, because John's message is love. John became like Krishna for me; you know, Coltrane Consciousness. I see music to be a means of creating vibrations that can change the thinking of people, connect them to God. That's what John was about."

When I asked him what was happening inside while he was playing the sax, he said that for him it was the deepest form of prayer, an unconscious praying in spirit, beyond the mind. I wondered what kind of relationship he felt he had with Coltrane. His church has been celebrating now for almost twenty years, so the inspiration must be coming from somewhere. He replied that he dreamt often of Coltrane.

"Like when I dreamt of him by the piano, man. He held out his hand, and I knelt and kissed it. You won't believe the joy I felt. He had a big Afro haircut. I tell you, he still alive, man. Just before then some guy tried to mess up my mind, telling me you had to have a living teacher. Then John came in the dream. He alive alright. That's how he speaks to me."

I knew that John Coltrane had once said he would like to have been a saint, and here was Franzo King doing him the honor by having the courage to stand by a vision that was uniquely his own. As I left by the back door, weaving my way through the lunch line, he called out, "Make sure you mention my brother!"

"You mean Landers? Where is he?"

"He been in jail twenty years now. He got life for murder. But it weren't his fault. Man, you grow up in the kind of world we did, it's almost impossible to stay outa jail. I was just lucky."

Maybe Landers works on the garden project, I thought. I hope so. What a rare constellation of family destiny, one brother a lifer, the other a bishop, both connected forever through John Coltrane.

Franzo's church has to be the most unusual in a city where the unusual is almost run of the mill. Yet what these idiosyncratic forms of praise all have in common is that they each in their own way celebrate the vision of some individual or group who has had the courage to follow their own calling. Lauren Artress brought the labyrinth to San Francisco's Grace Cathedral, and inadvertently started the labyrinth craze, which is finding its way across America now. A copy of the labyrinth at Chartres has been set into the nave at Grace, and is used for rituals in which people find their way back to their own center. At Glide Memorial Church, the Reverend Cecil Williams has established a multiracial community of some ten thousand members who run social and care projects all over the city. In a 1998 reader's ballot by the *San Francisco Examiner,* Williams was voted the person who had done more than anyone else in the city for social change.

I first visited Glide in 1971, and was practically the only white person in the building. Cecil was there then, too, and his rousing choir, already famous, was entirely African American. Twenty-seven years later, the choir is a reflection both of the congregation and of the city in general— white, black, Asian, gay, straight, Buddhist, lapsed Christian, firm believers, the whole world is there at Glide, every color, creed, and stripe.

I arrived late, and as I came in the door an usher literally jived up to me and led me to the back of the church, which was full to overflowing, everyone on his feet, swaying and clapping. On stage a young black man was doing sign language with a rhythm and energy that made him a star performer all on his own. Behind him the choir was singing "Amazing Grace" with a passion I had never heard in my life before. The soloist, an African American woman whose own posture drew me up tall, stepped forward and began unfurling every word from the depths of her heart. Then the trumpeter—just listen to that trumpeter—she, the soloist, being in ecstasy with his plaintive, oh so gentle notes that literally sparkled from the mouth of his horn.

Then up came Cecil Williams, a broad, beaming presence, joining the soloist in a final "How Sweet You Are," and straight into his sermon, on forgiveness, it turns out. He had recently been to see a church member who was in hospital with AIDS, just a few days away from death. The young man told him that he had finally forgiven his family for making him an outcast because of his homosexuality. And that it was Glide, all the love of the people, their acceptance of him for just who he was, that enabled him to accept his own family.

"So we're all in training," Cecil cried, "here every week singing and praising, helping each other to feel whole enough, good enough just as we are, so that we too can accept and praise others just as they are."

He had told the AIDS story the previous week, and taped it. Some members of the community had gone to the hospital and played it to the patient, telling him, "You did the sermon this week, you are the inspiration for us all!"

Cecil went on to say that he had heard the same message of forgiveness recently at the White House, where Nelson Mandela had addressed an audience of black ministers. He told them that his greatest insight had happened as he was being led out of the Robben Island prison where he had spent twenty-seven years of his life. Mandela suddenly realized that if he walked into freedom with hate in his heart for the politicians who had imprisoned him, he would be carrying his prison along with him. His freedom, he saw, depended on his own state of mind.

People often ask, Cecil concluded, why everyone is accepted at Glide, atheists, agnostics, Methodists, transsexuals, everybody. "And I tell them, this is an open church, this is a San Francisco church, and it is open because the spirit of God is present here. This ain't no cemetery church! The spirit of God is here and I don't want to do anything to chase him out. If anyone is excluded, so too will the spirit be."

The entire assembly is on its feet again, clapping, cheering, the choir pouring out a final ode to joy. Where can you go from here, I wondered, stumbling out onto the street finally, my head reeling. Only one place: to the silent source of all joy, beyond life and death, beyond all notion of good and bad, right and wrong. And who better to lead me to such a place than those teetering on the brink of life and death, whose health has been broken in such a way that everything they thought they were has been scattered by the winds of fate?

Death and illness have always been seen as a curse; even more so in the age of modern medicine, which prides itself on its cures and is terrified of failure. It is unbecoming in this age of the image to look less than one's best, to seem out of control, in the hands of something greater than one's own will or that of one's physician—a free radical, an unfortunate gene, a minuscule clot of blood. Death in America has for decades been hidden behind cosmetics. It has been sanitized, dealt with by professional parlors, not talked about, the last taboo.

Yet in the last decade there has been a quiet revolution taking place. Increasing numbers of people are revisioning their notion of death and illness. These facts of life are coming to be seen in America as events that, far from being catastrophes, can lead an individual to the deepest sense of meaning and purpose they have ever known. Today, leaving Glide and on my way down Eddy in search of a taxi, I have a date with some individuals of just that kind.

My first visit is with a man who has suffered a serious stroke. His name is Ram Dass. Since the seventies he has been perhaps the most seminal influence in America in the propagation of Eastern teachings in a vernacular Western form; an inspiration to people all over the world, a lover of God, and a man dedicated to the service of others. Much of the profit from his lecture circuit was channeled into Seva, the charitable organization he set up in the seventies with Wavy Gravy and other friends to respond to a variety of needs around the globe.

In 1997 Ram Dass suffered a huge stroke that has left him paralyzed and with impaired speech. He always used to refer to himself jokingly as Mr. Rent-a-Mouth. His speech was his life, and what he often used to talk about was how suffering can be grace, the fastest way to God. Now it takes him some time to string a sentence together. He can't read. Gone are the tennis, the golf, the cello practice, the strolls on the beach. Gone are the filled lecture halls around the world. Ram Dass now lives in a wheelchair with twenty-four-hour care.

He is tired when we meet, and we spend just a short while together. The same grin, the same mellow eyes, the same repartee in slow motion that I had known years before when I had invited him to give lectures in Europe. In his last life, he reminds me, he played golf and talked a lot.

Poststroke, he sits mostly in silence. He has embraced that as his new life now, no longer identifying himself as the Ram Dass he was. The trigger that causes suffering is comparison between the two, and he finds he rarely goes there. Ram Dass sees the whole drama to be the play and the grace of his guru, Neem Karoli Baba, the Indian sage who turned his life around when he met him in the seventies. He perceives his stroke to be the deepest grace his guru has given him, obliging him to drop the public persona of Ram Dass and be the silence he has always talked about.

"I don't know why it turned out this way," Ram Dass murmurs, "but I can guess. He wanted to rub my nose in a little suffering to hone me down, temper my rough edges. I have quite a lot of pain, and that is always a fair match for any spiritual practice. The situation calls for spiritually conscious behavior, and in that sense it is a wake-up call, getting me ready for the passage through death. The doctors at one of the hospitals I went to couldn't understand why I was so content when I had just had a stroke. I told them I saw myself as a soul not as a body, and that the soul has its own mysterious wisdom. I don't believe, like you," I said, "that I'm a brain which merely responds to stimuli."

"As for my role in the world, it has changed form but I still seem to be doing the work of my guru, despite myself. It seems like my new incarnation has made me some kind of collective symbol for people who need to learn about suffering. I get bundles of letters every day from people who have dreamt about me or who get inspiration from what they think I must be going through. And I just sit here, not doing anything. I guess it must be good karma, being a collective symbol of compassion, so I can't complain." Ram Dass laughs, that laugh that I have joined so often, laughing both at himself and at the world.

For Ram Dass it is his guru who is the larger intelligence at work in his life. For others, it may be Christ, or simply, as with Byron Katie—or indeed Susan Shannon—life itself, the What Is as it reveals itself. However we term it, it casts a whole different light on life when we see it as an intelligence beyond our own, with its own inscrutable designs that we can participate in with our awareness but not control with our will. Every religious tradition calls us to this, yet in contemporary America there is the opportunity for perhaps the first time in history to respond to life in this way without having it circumscribed or confined by a dogma. It is just what it is, just how it is; faith by any other name.

Not only a spiritual leader like Ram Dass, but people in all kinds of circumstance are beginning to wake up to a deeper reality through the challenge of a life-changing illness. This is an unconventional perspective on healing: healing, not so much as cure—that may or may not happen—but as a deeper freedom from the contingencies of one's own conditioning. From this perspective, death may come, and even turn out to be the greatest healer of all.

Maureen Redl is a psychologist who started Healing Voices in 1989 following her own recovery from metastatic cancer. The idea was simple. People faced with a life-threatening illness come together to share their stories and support each other in their healing toward freedom. Groups meet regularly all over the Bay Area, and with Ram Dass's eyes following me softly to the door, I head off to another part of the city to join one of these healing circles. A dozen people are sitting quietly in the round, and I take my place between a young woman in her thirties and a lean, bright woman in her eighties. One by one they share their stories, without intervention, advice, or questioning. Together, they generate a "listening field"—a nonjudgmental, empathic atmosphere that serves to draw out in one speaker after another a voice that comes from the authentic heart.

One man, John Hake, is a doctor with an undiagnosed crippling pain in his hip. He tells us how great a patient he had been, doing everything he was told, on top of strenuous physical therapy and swimming. He had been sure that he could cure himself just by being a good patient and using his will to vanquish the problem. After all, that is what he had always told his own patients. And he was a marathon runner, mountain climber; an outdoors man. He had always had the athlete's attitude of, If it hurts, just run through the pain. But the pain just kept getting worse, and after five months he realized he had tried everything he could.

"The pain wasn't the real problem," he told us quietly. "No, the real problem was the loss of everything I thought I was. I couldn't imagine who I'd be if I wasn't running marathons or climbing mountains. Those activities are what gave me a sense of myself, and that part of me was dying. Who was dying was the one who thought my power and control were the most important things about me. Without them I was surely nobody. And it's only recently that I realized how much I had to grieve the death of that part of me before I could move on."

"Seeing it wasn't enough," he went on, looking up at the faces around the circle. "I really had to feel the loss of that person who had carried me through some really tough times in my life; a ship that had sailed through many storms, and had served me well. But in this storm it sprang so many leaks it just had to sink. I had to let it go, and what I was left with were the perennial questions: Why am I here? Who am I, in truth? Illness has been the path that has brought me to those questions, and the answers I have received have been a source of joy and peace of mind the like of which I have never known before in my life. This is what my journey has shown me, that the most important part of healing is to find that sense of who we are and why we are here."

He fell into silence, and no one spoke for a few minutes. Then a woman called Marianne Pomeroy told us she had been living with cancer for almost twenty years, beginning with breast cancer in 1981, a skin tumor in 1984, and metastatic breast cancer in the chest wall in 1991. Now she was on the edge of death, yet she had discovered over the years that preparing to die meant discovering how to live.

"I'm in this," she says, in a voice that trembles on the edge of laughter, "and a lot of the time it is really painful. Awful, literally shitty. But, and I know I am not romanticizing, even that can turn into beauty. What cancer has shown me is that healing means to be fully awake and alive to whatever moment I'm in. And especially recently, when I have been having a really hard time with the chemo. I actually had a day of suffering this week, and I joked with myself about it, because all the while I'm suffering I'm going through this dialogue—'You thought you were going to go through this without suffering? You're dying, for God's sake, you're supposed to suffer!' Then this other voice kept whining, 'No, I don't want to suffer, I can do this without suffering.' "

"The healing came the next day. I suddenly felt like the back part of my heart, the part no one had ever seen, had softened suddenly; that a great ice floe of holding on had fallen away. And from that moment I could sense that I was being with people in a different way, more with them, present to who they were. I really believe that this happened because I allowed myself to experience the full weight of the suffering I was in. I think I am healthier now than ever in my whole life. Everything seems different. It's all shot through with something that connects us beyond our personal identities. It has to do with finally being responsible for this life and taking it on fully. And it has to do with worship—worship of everything, of life itself—and gratitude, gratitude for everything. Cancer has opened my heart to a love of the world. I am so thankful."

Marianne and her companions have filled me with gratitude, too, for the courage and joy that they stand for in the midst of their suffering. On leaving the building, I pause for a moment at the corner of California and Powell and watch the light of day turn to blue and rose and then to violet as if to say the time has come. The time has come to see through the clear crystal to the other side of darkness. The tapering tower down in the Financial District stands sharp and silent against a sliver of piercing blue, though the rolling pink is descending now and brings with it the finality of the coming night. And there on that corner, I feel myself joining the chorus of faith that lifts its song on the air of this beautiful city and over the whole country. To find words for that chorus is my challenge now; to write the book that first entered my mind in another world, on the banks of the Ganges in Benares.

Epilogue

I left San Francisco on a plane bound for London. My love and I put our house on the market and it sold in two weeks. I sold my library, and was ready to start a new life with two suitcases and a laptop. On the last night of our twelve years together we invited our closest friends to the house and, sitting in their midst, told them how much we loved each other yet how we both knew we were each being called to different lives, though we didn't know what they were.

I felt like the goat in the picture on our calendar, in midair between two crags. I booked a room in a retreat house in a remote corner of Michigan. There I would stay until the writing was over. After that, my life itself was an open book. With no foreseeable reason to return to Europe, I was freer than I had ever been of plans, responsibilities, or preconceptions, entirely open to the new and unknown. Just before I left England, the center phoned to say that they were overbooked for the first ten days of my stay, but had arranged for me to stay at a Christian Mennonite Retreat Center that was adjacent to their land. After those ten days, I could walk over the fields and stay with them.

So it was that, after a couple of weeks in Manhattan, I found myself opening the door of a converted barn in Michigan one evening in the fall. Two elderly Mennonites ran the center, and they had given me the apartment on the top floor. It was late, and they had left a note; I saw no one. In my journal that night I wrote about how relieved I was to be in one place at last: alone with a book to write, the rest of my life before me. I could spend a year in a Buddhist or Christian monastery, I wrote; I could go to Bali for six months, or start a project in Africa. Anything was possible.

I went down to lunch the next day—all meals were in silence—to find a long refectory table with the two Mennonites at one end and someone at the other end, with my place laid opposite her. I sat down, looked up, and was met by—what else can I say?—the smiling eyes of unselfconscious love from a tall, erect woman, with blond hair falling around fine chiselled bones and wide-open eyes. Her gaze remained on me, showering me with a direct, uncomplicated warmth, as if she were welcoming a dear friend. My own soul fell present suddenly in the looking. I tried not to laugh; the Mennonites were eating their dessert, oblivious. I was filled with disbelief, incomprehension, and inexpressible joy.

Maria had arrived the day before me, and would be there for ten days. We were the only guests. Two days after our meeting, I was looking at her out of the corner of my eye, thinking, Who *are* you? Instantly she turned and said, laughing, "Haven't you recognized me yet?" After three days the elderly couple said they had to go away for a week. Would it be alright if we were on our own for that time? They would have someone come and cook meals for us.

It *was* alright that we were on our own for that time; though it took me a day or two to let Maria past my preoccupation with writing and to acknowledge that—even though the last thing I had in mind was an encounter such as this, the embers of my previous relationship still being warm—life had delivered me into a situation that I simply could not ignore.

When I was wasn't writing—I did try keeping to some sort of schedule—we spent the week walking the fields and the woods, hearing something of each other's stories—though with ample intervals of silence, Maria content to listen to the presence of the season among the trees. It began to dawn on me that I was in the company of a rare individual; one deeply trusting of the moment, who genuinely seemed to respond to everything and everyone—the cat, the housekeeper, the ants across her path, as well as to me—with an unfettered warmth and embrace. She is the sun, I thought one day, glancing at her as we strolled up and over the meadow. She is the sun, and she comes on strong. Sometimes I needed to shade my eyes. She liked candy bars, too, and came from a suburban world in New Jersey, the like of which my own prejudices had kept me well away from all of my life. Yet a spring had broken out in Maria somehow; or perhaps it had been flowing from the time she was born. She had her own native wisdom, undeniable at every turn.

When the time came for her to leave, we both acknowledged that our meeting had taken place entirely outside of the framework of ordinary time and space, and that it may have no connotations for our everyday lives. So we exchanged no details. Maria's life in the world was not, anyway, without its complications. If the blessing of our encounter was meant to continue in time, then surely the intelligence that had brought us together would arrange for it to continue, without our having to manipulate circumstance.

Just as she was leaving, Maria gave me a card. It was a picture of *The Birth of Venus* by Botticelli. Later that afternoon, I suddenly remembered: the scallop shell! The face in the scallop shell that had woken me in England—of course—it was Venus. Not only that, it was Maria who, of all people, was Venus personified. I knew in that moment beyond any doubt that my life was not my own; that its unfolding was not in the hands of my daylight mind. There is a greater life that lives its way through us. We can open the door onto that deeper well or languish for decades in a prison of preconceptions.

Perhaps even that—the languishing we all do at one time or another—is part of the same wisdom: is there any blade of grass that can lie beyond its pale?

Maria and I did meet again, and have continued to do so when time has allowed. What I still do not know, and do not expect to, is what it means. Time alone will tell. Of itself, our meeting in Michigan was a gift from life, even if we had never met again. Interpretation, I have come to realize, kills the living mystery. It veils the ongoing revelation of life even as it serves to reassure us that we know who we are and what is happening. Life will weave its own exquisite, if not always painless, symmetry— and all the more gracefully as I embrace it.

I tell this story to point again to the pattern of intelligence within which we all live and breathe. To keep faith with this larger picture we need not to abrogate responsibility to some higher power, but to live from the wellspring of authentic, individual being. Such faith connects the particular with the universal through resonance. It is a far cry from belief: belief is a conceptualization of the truth as one would *lief* or wish it to be. There is a place for belief, yet belief is not faith. Faith, as lived by Marianne Pomeroy, by Byron Katie in Barstow, by Toni Packer up near Rochester, by Janell Hanson in Wyoming, is an unreserved opening of the mind to truth; to the dynamic force of reality, however it may turn out to be.

It is a readiness to hear and live by that intelligence that I have found emerging all this country. It is there in Michael Beckwith's words, when he said in Agape Church that our purpose is to be present for the embodiment of something greater than ourselves, rather than trying to hoist ourselves into greatness. Jim Wallis, in D.C., avoids burnout on his punishing schedule by knowing that there is a grander design than his own at work; that, while doing all he can for what he believes in, he is not in control of how life turns out.

From *salaam,* the peace passing understanding at the heart of us all, declared Sayed Nasr in Georgetown, ensues a trust in the emerging process of life, at the same time as action for the greater good. It is the source of action because compassion naturally arises from wisdom, and wisdom is the nature of that peace, since our eye becomes clear and single when the mind quiets down. That peace is at the heart of Susan the letter carrier's work in San Anselmo; of Evelia's job in the mud baths of Calistoga; of Kristen Ragusen's work as a financial consultant in Boston, and of countless others besides.

This larger life doesn't need dreams, visions, or spectacular events to make itself known. It happens anyway, anywhere, all the time; some of us just need a knock over the head to wake up to its voice. Life happens anyway, and it is inherently wise, however painful or joyful it happens to be.

Not only our personal lives, but also the life of a culture, of the planet, happens with an intelligence inscrutable to our logical, even moral, minds. We all have a story—we can't not have a story and be in a physical body—and the story will have its way; our smaller, individual ones, and the bigger one we all share in. We are like the sandpipers on the beach, moving this way and that as a single wave, said David Abram on Whidbey Island; we are immersed in the depths of a conscious, living world. Our peace of mind is commensurate with our faith in the inherent purpose and wisdom of life as it emerges. Yet that wisdom is not located anywhere outside of us; no one is doing something to us; we are embedded in it, and serve to shape it through our conscious and willing participation.

In some paradoxical way, it seems to me—from both my own experience and that of the people I have encountered—the more we live in that faith, the more we are free to be who we can be; and the more life opens into a greater fullness, ever surprising. As we exercise that freedom—so different to the imagined freedom of the ego—we begin to embody the essence of democracy, and in so doing, we contribute to the fulfillment of our culture's promise. Sacred America, I would suggest, is that increasing communion of souls who are living their lives, not by some external dictate of creed or culture, but by the prompting of the knowing, intelligent heart—the original meaning of conscience. This, rather than yet more experts and priests, is the fertile ground for a leaderless spiritual emergence; for a truly democratic postmodernism of belonging and wonder. And in America, once you start looking, it is everywhere, including suburban New Jersey, and in abundance.

Finally, I am reminded that the first true democrat was none other than a man called Jesus. Jesus lived that faith and freedom. He upheld the equality of women, but also of the poor and the criminal in the sight of God. He taught not from the book but from the universal wisdom of the broken heart, and his life and death were exemplars of the mystery of the spirit. The Western spiritual tradition may yet find its full flowering beyond the confines of church and creed, in the hearts and minds of people of conscious faith. Which is what you might expect in the most practical, the most secular, and also, I have come to realize, one of the most spiritually vibrant cultures on earth.

Index